OECD
Economic Surveys

United States

2007

OECD

ORGANISATION FOR ECONOMIC CO-OPERATION AND DEVELOPMENT

ORGANISATION FOR ECONOMIC CO-OPERATION AND DEVELOPMENT

The OECD is a unique forum where the governments of 30 democracies work together to address the economic, social and environmental challenges of globalisation. The OECD is also at the forefront of efforts to understand and to help governments respond to new developments and concerns, such as corporate governance, the information economy and the challenges of an ageing population. The Organisation provides a setting where governments can compare policy experiences, seek answers to common problems, identify good practice and work to co-ordinate domestic and international policies.

The OECD member countries are: Australia, Austria, Belgium, Canada, the Czech Republic, Denmark, Finland, France, Germany, Greece, Hungary, Iceland, Ireland, Italy, Japan, Korea, Luxembourg, Mexico, the Netherlands, New Zealand, Norway, Poland, Portugal, the Slovak Republic, Spain, Sweden, Switzerland, Turkey, the United Kingdom and the United States. The Commission of the European Communities takes part in the work of the OECD.

OECD Publishing disseminates widely the results of the Organisation's statistics gathering and research on economic, social and environmental issues, as well as the conventions, guidelines and standards agreed by its members.

> *This survey is published on the responsibility of the Economic and Development Review Committee of the OECD, which is charged with the examination of the economic situation of member countries.*

Also available in French

Table of contents

This Survey is published on the responsibility of the Economic and Development Review Committee of the OECD, which is charged with the examination of the economic situation of Member countries.

The economic situation and policies of the United States were reviewed by the Committee on 4 April 2007. The draft report was then revised in the light of the discussions and given final approval as the agreed report of the whole Committee on 27 April 2007.

The Secretariat's draft report was prepared for the Committee by Hannes Suppanz, Peter Tulip and Gregory Wurzburg under the supervision of Patrick Lenain.

The previous Survey of the United States was issued in December 2005.

This book has...

StatLinks

A service that delivers Excel® files from the printed page!

Look for the *StatLinks* at the bottom right-hand corner of the tables or graphs in this book. To download the matching Excel® spreadsheet, just type the link into your Internet browser, starting with the ***http://dx.doi.org*** prefix.
If you're reading the PDF e-book edition, and your PC is connected to the Internet, simply click on the link. You'll find *StatLinks* appearing in more OECD books.

BASIC STATISTICS OF THE UNITED STATES

THE LAND

Area (1 000 sq. km):	9 826	Population of major cities, including their metropolitan areas, 1st July 2005 (thousands):	
		New York-Northern New Jersey-Long Island	18 747
		Los Angeles-Long Beach-Santa Ana	12 924
		Chicago-Napperville-Joliet	9 443

THE PEOPLE

Resident population, 1st July 2006 (P)[1] (thousands)	298 400	Civilian labour force, 2006 (thousands) *Of which:*	151 413
Number of inhabitants per sq. km	30.4	Unemployed	6 993 000
Annual net natural increase (average 2001-05)	2 843 400	Net immigration (annual average 2001-05)	1 198 600
Natural increase rate per 1 000 inhabitants (average 2001-05)	4.1		

PRODUCTION

Gross domestic product in 2006 (billions of USD)	13 247	Origin of national income in 2006 (per cent of national income[2]):	
GDP per head in 2006 (USD)	44 197	Manufacturing	12.6
Gross fixed capital formation		Finance, Insurance and real estate	17.1
Per cent of GDP in 2006	19.6	Services	28.5
Per head in 2006	8 696	Government and government enterprises	11.7
		Other	30.2

THE GOVERNMENT

Government consumption in 2006 (per cent of GDP)	15.8	Composition of the 110th Congress as of 2007:		
Government current receipts in 2006 (per cent of GDP)	33.9		House of representatives	Senate
Federal government debt held by the public (per cent of GDP), FY 2006	37.0	Democrats	233	49
		Republicans	202	49
		Independents	0	1
		Vacancies	0	1
		Total	435	100

FOREIGN TRADE

Exports:		Imports:	
Exports of goods and services as per cent of GDP in 2006	11.1	Imports of goods and services as per cent of GDP in 2006	16.8
Main exports, 2006 (per cent of merchandise exports):		Main imports, 2006 (per cent of merchandise imports):	
Foods, feeds, beverages	6.5	Foods, feeds, beverages	4.0
Industrial supplies	25.8	Industrial supplies	15.5
Capital goods	40.1	Petroleum	12.1
Automotive vehicles, parts	10.4	Capital goods	22.3
Consumer goods	12.5	Automotive vehicles, parts	13.7
		Consumer goods	23.6

1. Projection.
2. Without capital consumption adjustment.

Executive summary

Despite a sharp housing market correction, overall growth has been holding up fairly well. Strong foreign demand and a decline in import growth have slowed the rise in the external deficit. With activity near capacity limits, some inflationary pressures have emerged. Reining them in without stifling growth is the main challenge for monetary policy. Looking further ahead, the key challenges are to sustain healthy growth and ensure fiscal sustainability in the face of population ageing. Against this backdrop, the Survey focuses on the following issues:

- **Enhancing the economy's growth potential.** Trend growth is slowing because labour productivity gains, though remaining high, no longer suffice to compensate for the deceleration in potential employment due mainly to demographic factors. Prospects for productivity growth appear favourable, but further efficiency gains could be achieved by tackling unfinished business in the area of structural reform. Labour supply could be boosted by increasing work incentives for the disabled, raising the earned income tax credit and delaying retirement eligibility.

- **Ensuring fiscal sustainability and reforming taxation.** The federal budget deficit has narrowed, but eliminating it requires increased spending discipline. In this context, reinstating expired statutory budget enforcement rules would be helpful. The reform of entitlement programmes, which will come under increasing pressure from population ageing and medical cost increases, is essential to ensure fiscal sustainability in the longer run. On the revenue side, priority should be given to reforms that would broaden the tax base by reducing tax preferences, but consideration should also be given to consumption-based indirect taxes.

- **Reconsidering housing support.** Direct and indirect support to homeownership may have led to higher house prices, and thus to increased borrowing by housholds. Tax preferences are costly and may create distortions, mostly benefiting high-income households that have easy access to homeownership anyway, and should be reformed over time. The regulation of government-sponsored enterprises needs to be tightened, as their activities have developed beyond their original mandate and pose a risk to financial stability, and their role should be refocused on their initial objective of promoting home ownership.

- **Improving primary and secondary education.** US school students are outperformed in international tests by their peers in many other countries. Although the causes of this are unclear, a partial explanation is that decentralised standards, curriculum and examinations are undemanding. Federal legislation that aims at addressing such system weaknesses is in general well conceived. However, it could be strengthened, for instance by extending the legislated framework of standards, assessment and accountability through high school. Responsibility for education lies primarily with the states and local authorities, which have to adopt and implement more challenging standards.

- **Facilitating access to higher education.** Despite shortcomings through the secondary level, the higher education system is generally performing well. However, one problem is that many potential students cannot afford to enrol. Policymakers have proposed addressing this by increasing student grants. Arguably, a more cost-effective, efficient and equitable means of reducing barriers to access would be to promote income-contingent student loans. Raising student loan limits would help students and promote access at little cost to the taxpayer.

ISBN 978-92-64-03271-2
OECD Economic Surveys: United States
© OECD 2007

Assessment and recommendations

More than five years into the recovery, the economy continues to perform impressively

The economic expansion that followed the 2001 recession continues at a healthy pace. This is all the more remarkable since economic growth in 2006 – 3¼ per cent as in the year before – was achieved in the face of strong headwinds, such as surging energy prices until the summer and a sharp decline in home construction through the year. The resilience and continued good performance of the economy can in part be traced to past regulatory reforms that created a very competitive environment by international comparison and contributed to impressive efficiency gains over the past decade. With robust growth, labour markets have tightened and some capacity pressures have emerged. Still, given the energy price shock, core inflation has remained relatively well contained, as price and wage setters have expected the monetary authorities to keep inflation low. Although the fiscal stance has been broadly neutral, government finances have continued to improve thanks to an ongoing buoyancy of revenues that has outweighed additional spending. At the same time, the current account deficit has broadly stabilised relative to GDP – albeit at a high level, reflecting the strength of export growth and lower energy prices.

With the expansion less dependent on household spending, the near-term outlook looks favourable

While household demand used to be the mainstay of activity in the first few years of the recovery, last year saw a shift of demand toward business investment and exports. This bodes well for a continuation of the economic expansion. Some spill-over effects from the housing market correction are likely to damp activity in the near term, but growth should pick up again when the housing market adjustment has run its course. Easing capacity pressures and the fading impact of last year's energy price increases would bring core inflation down to more comfortable levels, while strong exports, supported by increasing activity abroad and a favourable competitive position, would prevent the external deficit from widening. There are significant risks to such a benign scenario, however. On the one hand, the housing market correction and spill-over effects onto consumption could be more pronounced than generally expected. On the other hand, consumer spending may hold up better than projected, despite the negative household saving ratio, and cause price pressures to increase rather than ease.

*The challenge for monetary authorities is to rein
in inflation without imperilling growth prospects*

The Federal Reserve faces the difficult task of carrying out its dual mandate in an environment where inflation remains uncomfortably high and real economic growth, while still apparently solid, faces downside risks. In the first few years of the recovery, it has successfully balanced the need for supporting activity and preserving price stability. With increasing signs that the upswing had become self-sustained, monetary stimulus was appropriately withdrawn over the two years to mid-2006, when the monetary stance turned slightly restrictive. Since then, the monetary authorities have refrained from further monetary tightening, although core inflation has remained above their comfort zone. This reflects their view that some of the factors that had pushed up core inflation are transitory, that inflation expectations apparently remain well anchored, and that the cooling housing market should, over time, ease resource and price pressures. There may be scope for reductions in interest rates once core inflation is on a clear downward trajectory. For the moment, however, *it seems appropriate to keep policy on hold until a clearer picture of output and inflation trends emerges. Should core inflation fail to ease, a further policy firming might be needed to keep inflation expectations in check.*

*The key challenges in the long run are to boost
growth potential and ensure fiscal sustainability*

The Administration has emphasised economic growth as a top priority. Ensuring such an outcome will be a challenging task, however, despite recent accomplishments. The growth in the labour force is slowing as the population ages and participation among certain groups is levelling off. Thus, the economy will increasingly depend on productivity gains to achieve GDP growth that can maintain the rise in standards of living for both the working age and the dependent population. Policies and global trends that have made the economy more open, flexible and dynamic – thereby boosting productivity and overall prosperity – may have increased inequality. If unaddressed, concerns about inequality have the potential for eroding support for such policies. There is a crucial need to improve education outcomes, which are central both to reducing inequality and boosting efficiency. Population ageing, along with medical cost pressures, will also put enormous pressures on government finances that need to be addressed early on to avoid an excessive burden on future generations and eventually a fiscal crisis. While economic growth is unlikely to solve the country's long-term fiscal problems, it can help mitigate budgetary pressures in both the short and long run. In view of these various long-term challenges, this *Survey* focuses on the following important policy areas:

● How to respond to slowing labour-force growth?

● What reforms to entitlement programmes could restore fiscal sustainability?

● Should public support to housing be reduced?

● What are the appropriate policies to raise educational achievements and facilitate access to higher education?

While productivity performance has been
impressive, slowing labour force growth
is limiting economic growth

Trend GDP growth is slowing because labour productivity gains, albeit remaining high, no longer suffice to compensate for the deceleration in potential employment. The latter reflects a levelling off of labour force participation of women and the fact that the baby boom generation is entering low-participation years. Productivity growth has weakened recently, but this is attributable, to a large extent, to cyclical factors. Over the past decade or so, productivity performance has been above the OECD average by a wide margin. The initiating force behind the productivity resurgence in the mid-1990s was the information technology revolution, together with the fact that, given the favourable economic environment, the United States has been better placed to benefit from the opportunities provided by technological advances than most other countries. In recent years, strong productivity growth has spread from the high-tech sector to other sectors, in particular service-producing industries, where it has outpaced that in (non-high-tech) goods-producing industries. The diffusion of new technologies and their application to more firms and sectors should continue to underpin productivity gains, although their pace is likely to fall short somewhat of the brisk growth recorded in the first half of this decade.

Structural reform can help sustain productivity
gains and boost employment

Even if productivity growth can be sustained at a reasonably good rate, this is unlikely to prevent potential output growth from slowing, given the trend decline in labour-force participation. This suggests that it would be prudent to deal with unfinished business in structural reform. For instance, *further efficiency gains could be achieved by reducing trade-distorting support to agriculture, and continuing trade liberalisation.* As to labour market trends, many of them reflect changes in preferences and demography that governments cannot influence. Nevertheless, there are some policy measures to boost employment that should be helpful. For instance, the disability insurance system appears to be discouraging a rising share of the population from staying in the workforce, probably to an unnecessary degree. This partly reflects replacement rates that have risen to unusually high levels, partly as a result of trends in health costs. To combat adverse incentive effects, these *high replacement rates should be reduced and screening requirements tightened.* Moreover, *raising the age at which workers become eligible for full Social Security benefits would discourage premature retirement* and also make the Social Security system financially more secure. Finally, with some evidence that increases in tax rates tend to reduce labour supply, *efforts to restrain taxes and government spending may also be beneficial* in this regard.

Growing inequality is undermining the support
for successful free-market policies

As noted earlier, the very factors that have contributed to economic success and rising overall standards of living – market liberalisation and globalisation – have had some side effects that risk undermining the support for such policies. Workers and households experience variability in their earnings and income from year to year and, over the past

25 years or so, income inequality has increased considerably. To a large extent, the rise in inequality reflects an increase in returns to investing in skills. This, in turn, is associated with technological advances, such as improvements in information technologies, which tend to raise the productivity and hence the wages of high-skilled workers relative to those of low-skilled workers. In addition to technological change, globalisation has been a factor behind rising inequality, though probably a less important one. There is some evidence to suggest that immigration has depressed somewhat the wages of domestic low-skilled workers, and outsourcing appears to have had a similar effect. As to international trade more generally, any effect on the rise in income inequality appears to be small. Nonetheless, with a view to attenuating the adverse side effects of skill-biased technological change and globalisation, consideration should be given to *expanding trade adjustment assistance programmes (including wage insurance and health-care support) to include additional, if not all, dislocated workers, regardless of the cause of dislocation.* With skill differentials a major source of inequality, focusing on improvements in education is of key importance (see below). Raising the minimum wage is a poor means to address inequality and poverty. Even though the effects of recent legislation are likely to be limited, such a measure helps many workers who are not poor, fails to help many who are poor, and risks job losses. *The Earned Income Tax Credit should be raised, because it reduces poverty more effectively than the minimum wage and delivers more favourable employment outcomes.*

The Administration's medium-term fiscal target has been achieved ahead of time

The federal unified budget deficit declined further in fiscal year 2006, to just below 2% of GDP. This met the Administration's objective of halving the deficit (relative to a 2004 baseline) three years ahead of schedule. As in the previous year, it was not the result of discretionary measures but reflected an unexpected boom in tax receipts, which expanded at almost twice the rate of GDP. *The narrowing of the deficit is welcome, not least in light of the low level of national saving.* But it has to be put into perspective. With the economy operating close to capacity, the deficit is largely structural, and the structural budget balance is still worse than at the beginning of the decade (to the extent of 3 percentage points of GDP, although there are significant uncertainties attached to such estimates). The Administration has set a new fiscal target, which calls for the elimination of the federal budget deficit by 2012. *This would seem to be the minimum, given the demographic and other pressures that threaten both fiscal sustainability and the country's future prosperity.*

Strong revenue growth should continue to be devoted to deficit reduction, not spending growth

While accelerating budget consolidation might be desirable, even attaining it over the medium term involves considerable efforts. Indeed, with a substantial structural deficit remaining, more radical fiscal tightening than in recent years will be necessary to achieve budget balance. The temptation to spend any revenue windfalls should be resisted (the buoyancy of revenues has persisted in the first few months of fiscal year 2007). And discretionary spending, which has grown faster than GDP in the first half of this decade, will have to be tightly controlled. Changes to the budget process could be helpful in this regard. The budget enforcement rules that expired in 2002 – including expenditure caps and pay-as-you-go rules requiring new measures to be budget neutral – contributed to fiscal consolidation in the 1990s, although they were undermined by loopholes (such as "emergency spending"). *Statutory caps on discretionary spending and pay-as-you-go requirements for increases in mandatory spending and tax cuts should be reinstated, and loopholes in the previous system eliminated.*

Reforming entitlement programmes is essential to ensure long-term sustainability

The major entitlement programmes – Social Security, Medicare and Medicaid – are the main reason that government finances are on an unsustainable course. Under current law, public spending on retirement and health programmes is expected to rise toward 20% of GDP by the middle of the century; resulting soaring budget deficits would entail a government debt twice the size of GDP at that time. Raising tax rates to finance such spending would be an expensive and inefficient solution. Entitlement reform is therefore essential to address this longer-term fiscal challenge. The problem facing Social Security is population ageing. As the post-World War II baby boomers retire while increases in life expectancy continue, the ratio of people receiving retirement benefits to the working-age population will rise steadily. Relatively limited changes to programme parameters would suffice to put the scheme on a solid financial footing, but it has been difficult to reach an agreement on the appropriate measures. A compromise package for *Social Security reform could include: an acceleration of the already legislated increase in the normal retirement age and indexing benefits for rising longevity; a reduction in replacement rates for higher earners; and an increase in the taxable maximum amount of earnings subject to Social Security tax.* The situation is more challenging for health-care programmes, where medical cost pressures compound the effect of population ageing. The growth in costs per beneficiary has exceeded that of per capita GDP by a large margin. To address this problem, *ways should be sought to improve efficiency in Medicare-related health delivery, so as to be able to limit payments to providers without affecting access to and quality of care.* At the same time, *premiums for higher-income beneficiaries could be raised further. Cost-conscious decisions would be encouraged by expanding individual health savings accounts and eliminating the tax bias towards high-cost insurance.* The Administration has proposed to achieve the latter by replacing the unlimited tax exclusion of employer-furnished health insurance plan premiums by a tax deduction available to everyone. Arguably, a tax credit would have a greater effect on health insurance coverage.

Tax reform would enhance efficiency

On the revenue side, it may be difficult to sustain the recent reductions in marginal tax rates, while meeting the fiscal burden from entitlement programmes, although this would be clearly desirable. *To the extent that revenues have to be raised, the tax base should be broadened, rather than reversing reductions in marginal tax rates.* Since the comprehensive tax reform in 1986, which broadened tax bases and reduced marginal rates, most of the resulting gains in simplicity and efficiency have been lost through a renewed expansion in tax expenditures. To be sure, not all of them are undesirable. However, *tax expenditures, which are distorting, ill-targeted and ineffective, should be reduced or abolished.* The President's Advisory Panel for Federal Tax Reform has recommended, *inter alia*, that tax preferences for mortgage interest payments, employers' contributions to health insurance plan premiums, and state and local tax payments should be reduced. But, in addition to the Panel's proposals, *consideration should also be given to shifting the tax burden from direct taxes to consumption-based indirect taxes – such as a national sales tax or a value-added tax.* This would produce efficiency gains, including reducing disincentives to saving. *Furthermore, higher taxation of carbon-based energy consumption would help reduce greenhouse gas emissions.*

Housing support needs to be reconsidered

The housing market is an example of the adverse effects of certain tax concessions. In principle aimed at promoting homeownership to lower and middle income households, tax preferences have mostly benefited high-income households with easy access to homeownership. Furthermore, tax preferences have encouraged investment in residential property at the expense of other household assets, possibly affecting capital formation elsewhere in the economy and, thereby, productivity growth. *The mortgage interest tax deduction should be replaced with a tax credit available to all homeowners, with a maximum amount reflecting the average cost of housing,* so as to promote homeownership without unduly subsidising housing consumption. *The interest deductibility on home equity loans and second homes should be eliminated* to avoid encouraging overinvestment in housing. Other distortions arise from the activities of government-sponsored enterprises. Their large portfolio of mortgage-based securities poses a risk to financial stability and results in a large contingent liability for the federal government. *The regulation of government-sponsored enterprises (GSE) needs to be tightened and their role refocused, and eventually restricted, as their activities have developed far beyond their original mandate of promoting homeownership. As well, it would be useful to review the legislation considering GSE debt as government securities, as this suggests that such debt is guaranteed by the government.*

Primary and secondary education outcomes are unsatisfactory

A country's ability to compete in an ever more integrated world economy crucially depends on a highly educated workforce. It is thus a matter of concern that US students are outperformed in international tests by their peers in many other countries. It is also a concern that many students seem underprepared for work and higher education. Although large achievement gaps persist between population groups, performance is broadly unsatisfactory, including among affluent and academically successful students, and hence appears to reflect above all system-level weaknesses. Available evidence does not unambiguously establish the reasons for this. This Survey focuses on one partial explanation, the role played by academic standards, curriculum and examinations, which are undemanding by international comparison. These weaknesses appear to be linked to the combination of the highly decentralised character of education delivery and the lack of central steering related to learning objectives and assessment. Other factors thought to be related to student achievement, including teaching quality and school choice, are not discussed in this Survey.

*Academic standards need to become
more challenging*

While responsibility for education lies primarily with states and local authorities, the federal government can play a role by making financial support conditional on the achievement of certain objectives. Federal legislation – the No Child Left Behind Act of 2002 – calls for annual testing and greater accountability. In particular, it requires states to establish clear contents standards and thresholds for adequate yearly progress against which performance can be assessed. Preliminary indications, including test results, assessments of educational observers and international experience, are consistent with it raising school performance and narrowing achievement gaps. *The No Child Left Behind Act is in general well conceived and should be re-authorised.* But it could be strengthened. For instance, it would be desirable to *extend the legislative framework of standards, assessment and accountability through high school.* Although the federal government cannot set standards, it could *strengthen incentives for states to adopt more challenging standards.* Indeed, standards by which performance and yearly progress is evaluated are very low in some states. *States and school districts need to implement more challenging curricula and levels of performance. Advanced Placement and the International Baccalaureate provide models of standards that could be adopted more widely.* As tests are often focusing on the wrong things, *states need to align tests more closely with curriculum and expected levels of performance.* Moreover, *No Child Left Behind should require the states to implement curriculum-based external exit exams.*

*Enhanced student loans would improve access
to college*

The US higher education system is one of the best in the world. However, one problem it faces is that many potential students cannot complete college because of inadequate preparation or financial resources. Despite the expenditure of considerable government funds through direct provision, grants, tax concessions and loans, significant financial barriers to access still exist. Student loans provide the most efficient and equitable means of overcoming these barriers. The loan programme in the United States compares favourably with those in other countries, although there is room for improvement. Most important, *student loan limits should be raised substantially,* especially for unsubsidised direct loans, so as to cover the full cost of study, including living costs. Doing so would benefit students and promote access at little cost to the government. While it might encourage further increases in tuition fees, this is a likely effect of any measure to ease access barriers. To assist risk-averse students, repayments should vary with income. Such an option already exists but is little used, partly because of a lack of information. Accordingly, *the default repayment plan should be income-contingent, and borrowers who are risk-averse should be advised that they will be better off with that option.*

*Less cost-effective forms of government assistance
should be reduced*

Were a good student loan system in place, with high limits and income-contingent repayments, the rationale for means-tested "Pell" grants, which are favoured by the Administration and many policymakers, would be greatly weakened. In contrast to loans, grants involve large fiscal costs, redistribute money to those with high lifetime incomes, and appear to be of doubtful effectiveness. There remains *some scope for grants in dealing with informational problems and externalities, but this would probably involve fewer payments.* The Administration is to be commended for planning to simplify the application process for financial aid. This should include *removal of unimportant means-testing criteria and abolition of the asset test.* Tax concessions for higher education benefit middle-and upper-income families, rather than those on lower incomes where the main barriers to access are. Accordingly, they are an inequitable and cost-ineffective means of promoting access. They interact badly with the financial aid system. Most important, they are complicated – so much so that many eligible tax filers do not claim them. These problems outweigh the theoretical advantages of the concessions. Accordingly, *these tax concessions should be simplified, or even abolished.* Finally, with a good system of student loans, state government subsidies would no longer be necessary to promote access. However, perceived social benefits from higher education would justify retaining some level of government support.

ISBN 978-92-64-03271-2
OECD Economic Surveys: United States
© OECD 2007

Chapter 1

Challenges facing the US economy

Economic performance has improved considerably in the past decade or so. This is most manifest in the marked acceleration in productivity, the major determinant of standards of living. More recently, economic growth has remained fairly solid despite a sharp housing market correction, and prospects are good for continued expansion, although capacity pressures pose some inflationary risks. Nonetheless, there are a number of longer-term challenges facing the economy. Potential growth is slowing as demographic changes weigh on labour supply while there are considerable public spending pressures as the population ages. It is therefore all the more important to pursue policies that are conducive to further efficiency gains. Together with entitlement reform, this would facilitate putting government finances on a sustainable footing. Tax reform is also essential, both for efficiency reasons and better targeting those in need. In particular, it would be desirable to reduce the distorting and poorly targeted tax concessions in the housing market. Finally, improvements in the education system, which produces mixed results, are important to long-run productivity growth and competitiveness.

Longer-term economic performance

Since the mid-1990s, economic growth in the United States has been considerably faster than in the other OECD countries as a whole (Table 1.1). While in the preceding decade growth performance was similar, it has subsequently improved in the United States and deteriorated on average elsewhere. The picture is the same for GDP per capita, although the positive growth differential is smaller given stronger population growth in the United States. This is especially impressive, since per capita GDP in the United States is already among the highest, and other countries might be expected to catch up to the best performers. The United States owes its good performance in terms of per capita GDP in large part to stronger labour productivity growth. Labour utilisation peaked at a high level by international comparison and has trended downward in recent years. Labour productivity growth, in turn, has been primarily driven by efficiency gains (reflected in total factor productivity) and, to a lesser extent, by capital deepening, in particular in the form of investment in information technology capital.

Table 1.1. **Relative long-term performance**

	United States		OECD less USA	
	1985-1995	1995-2005	1985-1995	1995-2005
Real GDP[1]	2.9	3.2	2.9	2.4
Real GDP per capita[1]	1.9	2.1	2.4	1.8
Labour productivity[1, 2]	1.3	1.9	1.5	1.5
Total factor productivity[1]	0.5	0.9	1.2	0.9
Labour force participation rate[3]	76.1	76.6	68.9	69.9

1. Average per cent change.
2. Per person.
3. Percentage of population aged 15 or 16 to 64.
Source: OECD, *Labour Force Statistics* and Economic Outlook database.

Given that other countries have similar access to technological improvement and financial markets, the question arises why most of them have not been able to benefit to the same extent from opportunities that developed from the rapid advance of information technology. The answer probably lies at least in part in the comparatively favourable economic environment in the United States that is characterised by competitive product markets, flexible labour markets and deep financial markets. Regulatory reform efforts that began in the 1970s have meant that competitive forces became stronger in the United States than in other OECD countries by the mid-1980s. As shown in Figure 1.1, since then the United States has been able to maintain its status as the country with the lowest degree of policy intervention in product and labour markets, although most other countries have also liberalised markets considerably. Administrative hurdles and costs of business entry are low by international comparison. Flexible and lightly regulated markets have created an environment that fosters entrepreneurship and innovation. International openness has also

Figure 1.1. **Extent of intervention in product and labour markets**

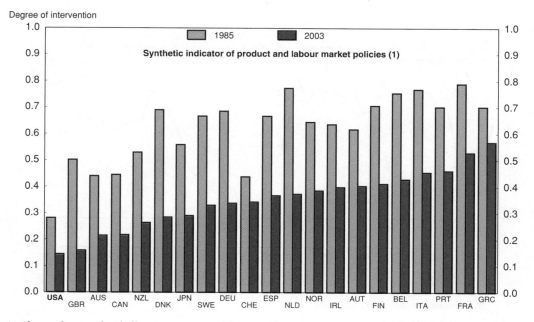

1. The product market indicator covers regulations in energy, transport and communication sectors. The labour market indicator covers employment protection, benefit systems, implicit tax rates on old-age work and labour tax wedges. All indicators are normalised ranging from 0 to 1, where 1 indicates the highest degree of intervention.
Source: OECD Economics Department Working Paper No. 501, 2006.

StatLink *http://dx.doi.org/10.1787/008401144445*

contributed to efficiency gains by increasing competition. Barriers to trade and – to a lesser extent – foreign direct investment are below the OECD average.

Despite a generally propitious environment, sustaining good performance over the longer run poses a number of challenges, and recent economic success has had some unfortunate side effects or created vulnerabilities that need to be addressed. As the population ages, growth in the labour force will slow and the country will have to depend increasingly on productivity gains to achieve increases in GDP that can maintain the standards of living for both the working age and the dependent population. Population ageing will also put enormous pressures on government finances that need to be addressed early to avoid a fiscal crisis. While globalisation has improved overall living standards, it has also involved painful dislocations and seems to have contributed both to a decline in the wage share in national income and an increase in income inequalities. Strong economic growth has been accompanied by rising domestic and external indebtedness that poses financial stability risks. There is a need for improving educational attainments since human capital development will be important for long-run productivity growth. These longer-term challenges and others are reviewed below, against the backdrop of recent economic developments and the near-term outlook, which is favourable.

The economic situation

The economic expansion, which began in late 2001, has continued at a solid pace, with real GDP growth in 2006 slightly exceeding that in the preceding year (Figure 1.2, Panel A and Table 1.2). This is all the more remarkable since it was achieved in the face of a sharp housing market correction and record-high energy prices for most of the year. Residential construction, which had made a substantial contribution to growth in previous years,

Figure 1.2. **Aggregate economic indicators**

Per cent

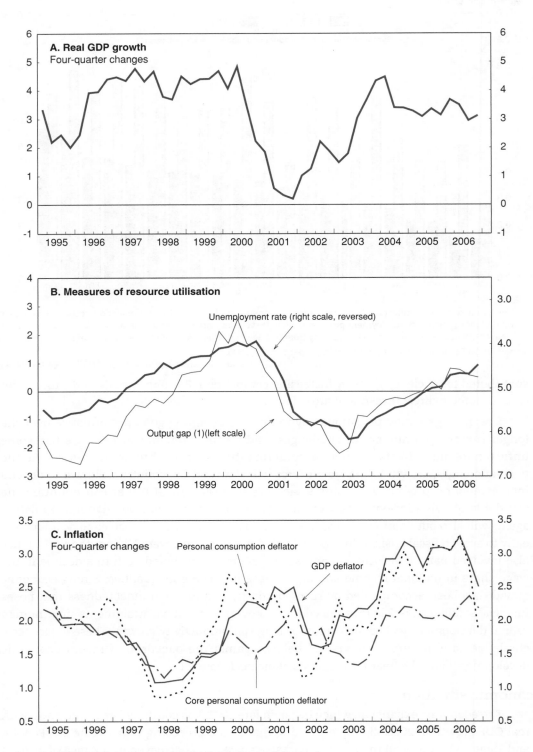

1. Per cent difference between actual and estimated potential output.

Source: Bureau of Economic Analysis, Bureau of Labor Statistics and OECD Analytical database.

StatLink 🔗 *http://dx.doi.org/10.1787/008404374625*

Table 1.2. **Contributions to GDP growth**

Percentage points, volume terms, chained 2000 prices

	2000	2001	2002	2003	2004	2005	2006
Private consumption	3.2	1.7	1.9	2.0	2.7	2.4	2.2
Private residential investment	0.0	0.0	0.2	0.4	0.5	0.5	−0.3
Private non-residential investment	1.1	−0.5	−1.1	0.1	0.6	0.7	0.7
Government consumption and investment	0.4	0.6	0.8	0.5	0.4	0.2	0.4
Final domestic demand	4.5	1.8	1.8	2.8	4.0	3.6	2.9
Stockbuilding	−0.1	−0.9	0.4	0.1	0.4	−0.3	0.2
Total domestic demand	4.4	0.9	2.2	2.8	4.4	3.3	3.1
Net exports	−0.9	0.2	−0.7	−0.4	−0.7	−0.3	0.0
GDP	3.7	0.8	1.6	2.5	3.9	3.2	3.3
Memorandum items:							
Growth rate of:							
Private consumption	4.7	2.5	2.7	2.8	3.9	3.5	3.2
Private non-residential investment	8.7	−4.2	−9.2	1.0	5.9	6.8	7.3
Core PCE inflation	1.7	1.9	1.8	1.4	2.0	2.1	2.2
Output gap	1.9	−0.2	−1.3	−1.5	−0.4	0.1	0.7

Source: Bureau of Economic Analysis and OECD Analytical database.

contracted in 2006. However, the weakness in housing market activity and associated slower appreciation of house prices do not seem to have spilled over to any significant degree to other sectors of the economy. Consumer spending continued to expand at a solid rate, remaining the mainstay of economic growth. It was supported by rising employment, gains in real income and increases in household wealth. Despite sharply higher energy prices, real disposable income accelerated as wage growth picked up. The rise in disposable income was again outpaced by that in spending, so that the personal saving ratio moved further into negative territory. The household financial obligation ratio continued its upward trend to reach a record high. Despite the negative saving ratio, household wealth kept growing because of capital gains and, relative to income, is still well above the historical average. The growth contribution of corporate fixed investment changed little, as accelerating business construction outweighed decelerating outlays on equipment and software. The fundamentals supporting business investment remained favourable: profits continued to grow strongly, user cost for equipment declined further, and interest rates and credit spreads remained relatively low. With export growth picking up and well exceeding import growth, the real foreign balance ceased to be a drag on economic expansion (as it had been in the first few years of the recent recovery).

Ongoing economic growth above its estimated potential rate probably led to the emergence of a positive output gap in 2006 (Table 1.2 and Figure 1.2, Panel B). At the same time, unemployment fell below its estimated structural rate, despite some pick-up in labour-force participation. Resource pressures along with surging housing rents and the indirect effects of higher energy prices contributed to a modest rise in core consumer inflation (that is, excluding food and energy). Overall inflation remained at the higher levels already recorded in 2005, reflecting the continuing upward trend in energy prices (Figure 1.2, Panel C). With the recent sharp decline in energy prices, overall and core inflation have converged. Despite some deterioration in the terms of trade, the widening of the current account deficit has slowed markedly, given the improved export performance stemming in part from exchange rate depreciation in recent years (Figure 1.3, third Panel).

Figure 1.3. **Financial indicators and current account**

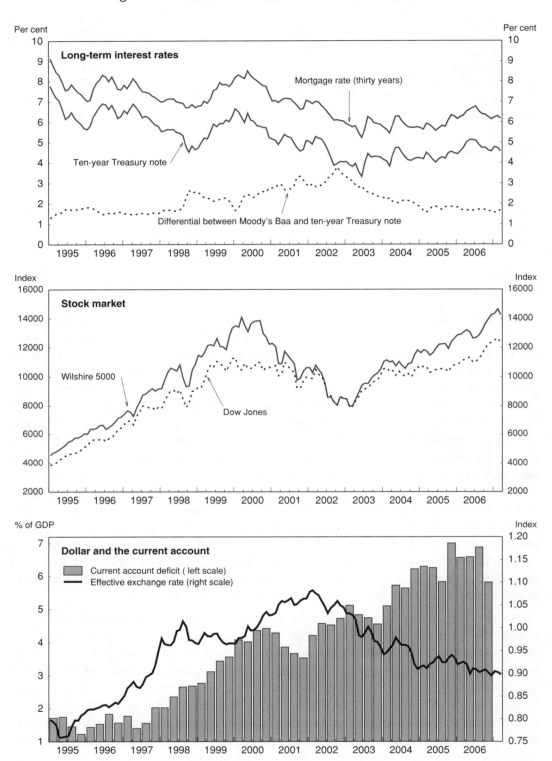

Source: Board of Governors of the Federal Reserve System, Bureau of Economic Analysis, Thomson Financial; OECD Analytical database.

StatLink *http://dx.doi.org/10.1787/008465663486*

The macroeconomic policy stance

Monetary policy

The Federal Reserve began to withdraw monetary stimulus in mid-2004 when the recovery had attained considerable momentum. After rising steadily for two years, the federal funds rate has levelled out at 5¼ per cent, although the economy is probably operating above potential and core inflation is higher than desirable. This only mildly restrictive policy stance reflects the authorities' dual mandate – to achieve both high employment and low inflation – and the forward looking nature of policy decisions. The cooling in the housing market is a substantial drag on the economy and, despite the resilience of consumer spending so far, is likely to moderate economic activity and employment. This, in turn, would help reduce inflationary pressures over time. Moreover, inflation expectations have been well contained, fluctuating in a narrow range, which should limit secondary effects of transitory factors (such as surging energy costs). That said, the authorities have reiterated that some inflation risks persist and the direction of further changes in monetary policy will depend on incoming data.

The response of long-term interest rates to the substantial rise in the federal funds rate (by 425 basis points) has been limited (Figure 1.3, first Panel). They have remained low by historical standards and, together with substantial gains in equity prices, this has made for financial market conditions that continue to be supportive of economic growth (Figure 1.3, second Panel). Changes in long-term interest rates have been largely tied to changes in the perceived outlook for economic growth and inflation. Interest rates across the maturity spectrum increased in the first half of 2006 as incoming data exceeded market expectations and market participants projected further increases in the federal funds rate target. However, the increase in market rates was reversed in the second half of the year as expectations for economic growth and inflation shifted radically and market participants began to project a fall in the federal funds rate rather than a further rise. Current market expectations appear to be consistent with an easing in monetary policy starting later this year. Although financial markets have undergone significant fluctuations in recent weeks, forward looking measures of uncertainty about monetary policy inferred from interest-rate options suggest that such uncertainty is low by historical standards. The Federal Reserve, which has worked to enhance the transparency of its decision-making process, has appointed a committee to examine whether further changes – for instance, the publication of more frequent and detailed forecasts – might improve communications with the public.

Fiscal policy

The federal unified budget deficit narrowed further in the fiscal year 2006 (ending in September), to just under 2% of GDP. This was significantly below what had been anticipated at the start of the year. While some of the improvement may be due to transitory factors, some of it should persist. The decline, like that of the previous year, does not reflect policy measures so much as an unexpected boom in tax receipts, which grew at almost twice the rate of GDP. While corporate tax payments roughly matched the robust growth in profits, income tax receipts from individuals considerably outpaced the rise in taxable personal income. Although the increase in revenue cannot yet be adequately explained, contributing factors probably include increased capital gains realisations, a further shift in the income distribution, and the effect of taxpayers moving into higher tax brackets as their real incomes increased. Federal receipts amounted to almost 18½ per cent

Figure 1.4. **Federal budget developments**
Per cent of GDP

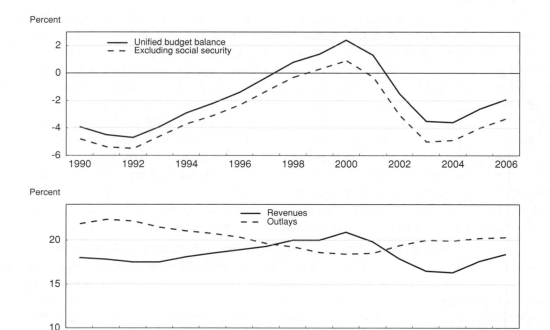

Source: Congressional Budget Office, Office of Management and Budget.

StatLink ⟨ms⟩ *http://dx.doi.org/10.1787/008475435643*

of GDP, close to the long-term average and up by about 2 percentage points from their recent fiscal year low in 2004. At more than 20% of GDP, federal outlays were well above their recent fiscal year low in 2000 (Figure 1.4, second Panel). In cyclically-adjusted terms, they are estimated to have risen by 1½ percentage points since then. The structural budget balance is estimated to have deteriorated by almost 3 percentage points over the same period (with the economy operating close to capacity, the structural deficit in 2006 was practically the same as the unadjusted one). With the Social Security surplus remaining broadly unchanged at 1½ per cent of GDP, the on-budget deficit has developed broadly in line with the unified deficit (Figure 1.4, first Panel).

The 2008 Budget expects the federal unified deficit to narrow only marginally as a share of GDP in the fiscal year 2007. This is based on the assumption that the Administration's request for supplementary spending for the war in Iraq and Afghanistan is approved by Congress. With continued strong revenue growth in the first few months of fiscal 2007, the outcome might be better than the Budget estimate. Further out, the decline in the deficit is projected by the Administration to accelerate and budget balance to be achieved by 2012, despite the extension of the tax cuts of 2001 and 2003 beyond their expiration date at the end of 2010. On the other hand, the Budget does not provide for spending on the war in Iraq beyond 2009 (when it is assumed to drop sharply) and for indexation of the Alternative Minimum Tax beyond 2008. This would mean that some 25 million Americans would be affected by AMT after 2008 as compared with about 4 million in 2006. Moreover, the Budget assumes that the rate of growth of non-security discretionary spending can be held to 1% per year, well below the rate of inflation, which is quite ambitious given that it has not only exceeded inflation but also nominal GDP growth in recent years.

The general government financial deficit (national accounts definition) narrowed to 2¼ per cent in 2006. Although the fiscal positions of state and local governments have tended to improve further, they are less favourable than usal at this point of the business cycle. The sustained strength in revenues, along with efforts to restrain spending for health care, has enabled these jurisdictions to step up spending on other programmes. The outlook is less favourable. In the near term, more subdued house prices are slowing the rise in property tax revenues and, in the longer term, most governments will have to face the budget pressures of providing pension and health benefits to an expanding number of retired employees, while states' costs for Medicaid are expected to rise substantially as the baby-boom generation ages.

Near-term prospects and risks

Real GDP growth is projected to be below its potential rate this year before picking up next year as the housing correction runs its course (Table 1.3). Growth is supported by buoyant overseas demand, lower oil prices and momentum in non-residential construction. On the other hand, slowing house prices, a likely rise in the saving ratio and government spending restraint provide dampening influences. The labour market is likely to respond to the weakness in activity with a lag, and the unemployment rate is expected to rise somewhat. Together with reduced capacity pressures and the fading effects of higher energy prices, this should take core inflation back to more desirable levels. Strong demand abroad coupled with slower growth at home, as well as a more competitive exchange rate, should stabilise the current account deficit as a share of GDP.

As is often the case, the risks to this benign outlook are significant. On the downside, the duration and ultimate extent of the housing market correction is difficult to foresee and may prove to be greater than projected. Spill-over effects from developments in the housing market onto consumer spending and employment in housing-related industries may be more pronounced than expected. The recent weakness in capital spending could be a possible harbinger of such effects. On the upside, consumer spending may continue to expand at a pace that would ultimately lead to an escalation of pressures on resources and prices. Such inflationary pressures could be compounded by a renewed rise in energy prices. Inflation expectations, which so far have remained contained in the face of energy shocks, could rise and monetary policy would need to tighten (rather than ease at the turn of this year, as assumed in the projections above).

Longer-term challenges

Slowing potential growth

Trend GDP growth is slowing because labour productivity gains no longer suffice to compensate for the deceleration in potential employment (Figure 1.5). The reasons for decelerating labour inputs, and some policies to address this issue, are discussed in more detail in Chapter 2. In brief, after a steep rise since the 1970s, labour-force participation of women has levelled off; with the ageing of baby boomers, a large share of the population is entering low-participation years, pulling down the aggregate labour-force participation rate; although work participation of older workers has increased, perhaps owing to better health and increased longevity, this has not offset falling labour-force participation of

Table 1.3. **Near-term projections**
Percentage change, volume terms (chained 2000 dollars)

	2006	2007	2008
Private consumption	3.2	3.1	2.4
Government consumption	1.6	2.5	2.5
Gross fixed investment	3.1	−2.9	1.8
Private residential	−4.2	−16.0	−3.4
Private non-residential	7.2	2.6	4.0
Government	4.1	2.4	2.5
Final domestic demand	2.9	1.9	2.3
Stockbuilding[1]	0.2	−0.2	0.0
Total domestic demand	3.2	1.7	2.4
Exports of goods and services	8.9	5.6	7.1
Imports of goods and services	5.8	2.0	4.7
Foreign balance[1]	0.0	0.3	0.0
GDP at market prices	3.3	2.1	2.5
GDP price deflator	2.9	2.6	2.2
Private consumption deflator	2.7	2.4	2.2
Output gap	0.7	0.1	−0.1
Potential output	2.7	2.7	2.7
Unemployment rate	4.6	4.7	4.8
Federal funds rate	5.0	5.3	5.0
Ten-year Treasury note rate	4.8	4.6	4.8
Net lending of general government			
$ billion	−301.6	−374.7	−416.1
Per cent of GDP	−2.3	−2.7	−2.9
Current account balance			
$ billion	−856.7	−841.9	−904.8
Per cent of GDP	−6.5	−6.1	−6.2
Household saving rate[2]	−1.1	−1.2	−0.8

1. Contributions to GDP.
2. OECD definitions.
Source: Bureau of Economic Analysis and OECD estimates.

youth, which is a general phenomenon and not just due to longer school attendance. Policies that could limit the decline in work participation include: increasing the retirement age (which would also improve the financial situation of the Social Security system), and reforming disability insurance that is increasingly locking a large share of the population out of the workforce. Nonetheless, economic expansion will be increasingly dependent on productivity growth, which could also benefit from policy measures, although most experts believe that the recent productivity resurgence has not yet run its course (see below).

The major sources of the resurgence in labour productivity growth are shown in Figure 1.6. The estimated contribution of skill increases (as a result of rising rates of college attendance and increased experience of the workforce) has remained broadly constant over time. Instead, capital deepening and efficiency gains have been the key productivity-raising factors. The contribution of increases in the quality and quantity of the capital stock doubled in the second half of the 1990s and has remained unchanged thereafter. By contrast, the contribution of efficiency gains, which had also doubled in the second half of the 1990s, further increased by half in the first half of the current decade. The likely

Figure 1.5. **Decomposition of economic growth**

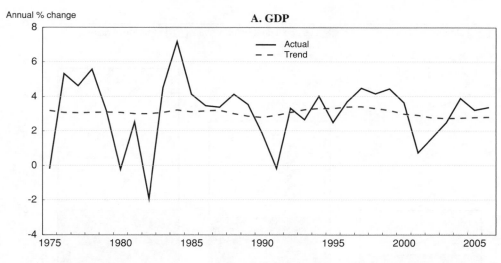

Annual % change
A. GDP

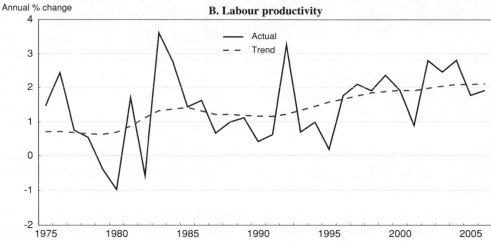

Annual % change
B. Labour productivity

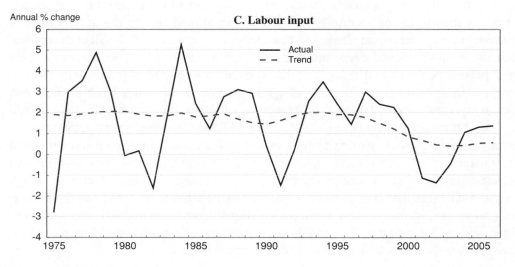

Annual % change
C. Labour input

Source: OECD, Analytical database.

StatLink http://dx.doi.org/10.1787/008520832607

Figure 1.6. **Sources of labour productivity growth**[1]

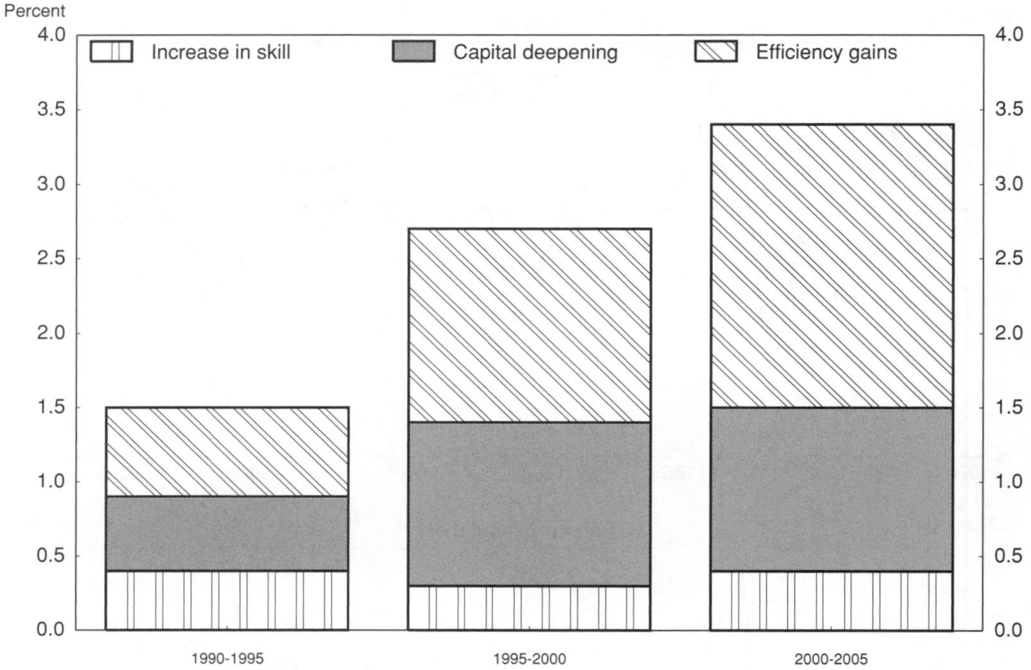

1. Private business sector.

Source: Department of Labor, Bureau of Labor Statistics.

StatLink ⌐ᵢₗ⅗ *http://dx.doi.org/10.1787/008558527187*

explanation of this pattern is that firms needed time to develop processes that best used the new capital, but as they gradually succeeded in doing so productivity growth received another boost.

It is now commonly accepted that the initiating force behind the productivity acceleration was the information technology (IT) revolution. IT, both in the form of capital deepening and efficiency gains, is estimated to have contributed nearly 60% to labour productivity growth in the second half of 1990s, and almost 80% to the acceleration in productivity during that period (Table 1.4). The picture changes in the first half of the current decade, when non-IT-capital deepening and efficiency gains outside IT production become more important again. Nonetheless, IT still accounted for one-third of productivity growth, although IT investment is less than 5% of aggregate output. Efficiency gains in high-tech industries still greatly exceed those in other sectors, although some are catching up (Corrado *et al.* 2006). Efficiency growth since 2000 has been highest in sectors that made large IT investments in the 1990s, in particular the distribution sector (including retail and wholesale trade, transportation and warehousing). Finance and business services have also showed strong efficiency gains and hence productivity gains. Non-high-tech manufacturing, which has made small investments in IT capital compared to the other sectors, has had the slowest recent growth in efficiency. Indeed, the most striking difference between the pre- and post-1995 periods is that productivity growth in service-producing industries has picked up noticeably, exceeding growth in goods-producing industries.

Although some observers have focused on the recent cyclical deceleration in productivity growth, there is little evidence to suggest that the economy will revert to the

Table 1.4. **The contribution of information technology to labour productivity growth**[1]

Per cent

	1973-1995	1995-2000	2000-2005
Capital deepening	27	37	20
Total factor productivity	16	22	13
Total contribution	43	59	33

1. Private business sector.
Source: Jorgenson, D.W., M.S. Ho and K.J. Stiroh. "A Retrospective Look at the US Productivity Resurgence", February 2007.

slower pace of productivity growth of the 1970s and 1980s. Instead, there is cautious optimism that the strong productivity performance of the post-1995 era will continue for some time (see, for instance, Federal Reserve Board, 2006a and 2006b, and Jorgenson *et al.* 2007). The rate of technological progress appears to be proceeding apace. But, whatever the pace of future technological progress, the predominant view is that further diffusion of existing commercially relevant technologies (made possible by increased cheap computing power) and applications to more firms and sectors (notably health care and other services) should continue to underpin productivity gains. Leading economists expect labour productivity growth in the business sector over the next ten years to be in the vicinity of 2½ per cent per annum, which is below the average since 2000 and close to the rate recorded in the second half of the 1990s, implying economy-wide annual growth of around 2%.

To be sure, there are downside risks to such projections. The factors behind the recent favourable performance are still not completely understood, and the fact that IT spending remains less buoyant than before the 2001 recession may reflect the absence of major new business applications. Moreover, even if productivity growth is sustained at a reasonably good rate, this would probably not prevent potential output from slowing, since policy action is unlikely to be able to arrest the deceleration in the labour force. All this warrants tackling unfinished business in the area of structural reform (see Annex 1.A1). Further efficiency gains could be achieved, for instance, by reducing trade-distorting support to agriculture, continuing trade liberalisation, removing remaining barriers to foreign direct investment and implementing tax and education reforms (see below).

Inequalities

The distribution of economic well-being has become more prominent in the public debate (see, for instance, Federal Reserve Board, 2007). In part this reflects concerns that rising inequality of economic outcomes could undermine support for market liberalisation and globalisation that have been crucial to favourable productivity performance and overall standards of living. While a more "flexible" economy has helped reduce macroeconomic volatility, workers (in particular those with less education) and households experience substantial variability in their earnings and income from year to year (Congressional Budget Office, 2007). Moreover, over the last quarter century, real earnings of those near the bottom of the income distribution have risen only little and the median wage only modestly, with most of average real earnings growth coming from those near the top of the distribution. Broader measures of financial well-being, such as real disposable household income, give a similar picture. The share of income received by households in the top fifth of the income distribution has increased from 42% to 50%, while the share of those in the bottom fifth has declined from 7% to 5%; at the same time, the share of those in the top 1% of the income

Figure 1.7. **Labour share**[1]

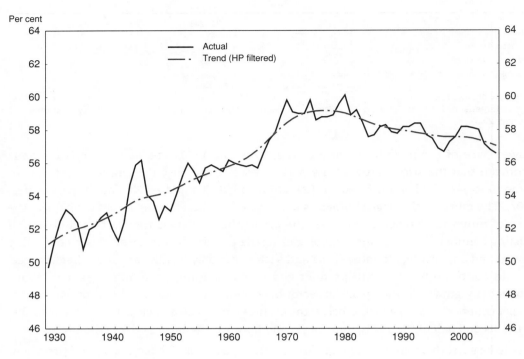

Per cent

1. Compensation of employees as a percentage of Gross Domestic Income.
Source: Bureau of Economic Analysis.

StatLink ᴍ᠍ᴤ᠍ᴘ *http://dx.doi.org/10.1787/008585751857*

distribution has grown from 8% to 14% (Congressional Budget Office, 2006). It has been argued that these data are distorted by changes in taxation (Reynolds, 2007). However, the general picture of growing income inequality over the last quarter century cannot be disputed (Council of Economic Advisers, 2006). Over the same period, labour's share in national income has been on a slight downward trend, after trending upward in the preceding half century (Figure 1.7).

Understanding the sources of the long-term tendency toward greater inequality remains a major challenge for economists and policymakers. Earnings inequality has increased in a large majority of OECD countries, although this tendency is less clear for disposable income, reflecting the effect of taxes and transfers (Forster and Mira d'Ercole, 2005, and Saez, 2006). To a considerable extent, the rise in inequality reflects an increase in returns to investing in skills (Council of Economic Advisers, 2006). In the United States wages of workers with more years of formal education have increased much more than those of workers with fewer years of formal education. For instance, over the last quarter century, the hourly earnings of college-educated workers have grown by more than a fifth, while those of high school drop-outs have actually declined somewhat. Most economists believe that fundamentally this is traceable to technological change. Technological advances, such as improvements in information technologies, tend to raise the productivity and hence the wages of high-skilled workers more than that of low-skilled workers. However, skill-biased technical change cannot explain completely recent trends. For instance, the sharp rise in IT investment in the 1990s was not accompanied by a higher rate of increase in wage inequality; more recently, although workers in the middle of the income distribution are typically better educated, their wages have grown more slowly than those of workers at the lower end of the distribution (Autor *et al.* 2006), one possible partial explanation being a deceleration in educational attainments in the past two decades; and, most importantly, the link between skill-biased technical change and the especially large wage gains at the top of the distribution is not obvious.

In addition to technological change, globalisation is also widely seen as a factor in the rise in inequality. Most immigrants arriving in the country have relatively low levels of skills, which, by itself, increases measured inequality. As to the effect of low-skilled immigration on the wages of less-skilled domestic workers, studies of local markets suggest that they have been small, but studies that examine national data tend to find somewhat larger wage-dampening effects (Borjas, 2006). Similarly, outsourcing abroad tends to slow the wage growth of domestic low-skilled workers since it has so far mainly concerned low-skill activities. As to international trade more generally, there is little evidence that it has had a significant effect on inequality. This is confirmed by a recent study, which finds, however, that openness to trade and increasing trade with developing countries have had a negative effect on the labour share in national income, along with capital-augmenting technological progress (Guscina, 2006). Although available evidence suggests that the effect of globalisation is less important than that of skill-biased technological change (Feenstra, 2007), there is some interaction, since international integration through trade, capital and labour flows is accelerating the pace of technological diffusion.

Whatever the reasons, growing economic inequality, along with the increased risk of job loss, weakens the support for globalisation, as attested by opinion polls. This presents a challenge of how to best assist people affected without giving up the economic gains that openness makes possible. The appropriate policy response is two-fold. *First*, with skill differentials a major source of inequality, focusing on improvements in education is the most promising direction to look at (Chapter 5). People with more education not only earn more but are also better positioned to adapt to changing demands in the workplace. *Second*, as recommended in the previous *Survey*, consideration should be given to an expansion of trade adjustment assistance programmes (including wage insurance and health-care support) to include younger and service-sector workers, if not all dislocated workers, regardless of the cause of dislocation. Indeed, the number of job losses due to trade-related adjustments is small compared with the overall rate of job destruction in the economy (Mankiw and Swagel, 2006). Moreover, although it may serve a purpose in as much as it alleviates political opposition to globalisation, targeted assistance has not proved to be very effective in terms of labour-market outcomes. Expanding adjustment assistance would be costly, but it would ensure that income security is provided without hampering structural change. Finally, while minimum wage increases are popular and may reduce some measures of inequality to a small extent, they are only a second-best solution, since they may also lead to reduced employment of low-skilled workers (Chapter 2).

Fiscal sustainability

While the current federal deficit, at around 2% of GDP, is low enough to keep the debt-to-GDP ratio stable, it is hardly satisfactory in the light of the longer-term fiscal outlook. The same is true for the Budget proposal to eliminate the deficit by 2012. As discussed in Chapter 3, under current law, population ageing and medical cost pressures mean that federal spending on Social Security, Medicare and Medicaid will double relative to GDP to reach 15% by 2030 (the current overall federal spending ratio is about 20%). In addition, lower potential output growth will slow the rise in tax revenues (while it will not do much, in itself, to lower spending growth). Given this longer-term fiscal challenge, the fact that virtually no progress has been made in reforming entitlement programmes and the tax system is a matter of concern (tax measures have been limited to *ad hoc* adjustments, *e.g.* reducing the impact of the Alternative Minimum Tax in the near term). Reform of the entitlement programmes is a policy priority. Strengthening budget enforcement rules can be helpful to achieve deficit targets in the short run, but they are no solution to the longer-term fiscal problem. Among the entitlement programmes, Social Security seems to be comparatively easy to put on a sound footing, requiring relatively limited adjustments to programme parameters. Medicare and Medicaid pose greater challenges. Those programmes face the same demographic pressures as does Social Security, but also the pressures of rapidly rising health-care costs, with costs per beneficiary growing considerably faster than per capita GDP. Whether higher tax rates will eventually be necessary depends on success in curbing spending and political decisions regarding the appropriate size of government. But tax reform is desirable in any case to enhance economic efficiency. The President's Advisory Panel on Federal Tax reform has offered a number of options for gradually reducing various ill-targeted and distorting tax expenditures.

Household indebtedness

The problematic effect of some of the tax concessions is illustrated by current housing policies; these are, in principle, aimed at promoting homeownership but, in practice, have encouraged overinvestment in housing at the expense of more productive uses, thereby depressing productivity in the longer run (Chapter 4). An increase in household borrowing is not unusual during a period of economic expansion and, in recent years, it has made consumer demand more resilient in the face of repeated negative shocks. However, in a longer term perspective, it has been unprecedented and, although similar run-ups occurred in other OECD countries, the increase has been particularly pronounced in the United States. While these trends result in part from market forces, there is ample evidence that government policies play a role. The favourable tax treatment of housing investment has encouraged the accumulation of home-secured debt. In addition, government-sponsored enterprises have accumulated large mortgage loan portfolios, which pose a risk to financial stability and represent a significant contingent liability for the taxpayer. The challenge for policymakers is to tighten the regulation of these enterprises and refocus their activities on their original mandate of promoting homeownership. As to housing taxation, the challenge is to reform it in a way that reduces distortions to investment decisions and better targets support, which currently mostly benefits high-income households with easy access to homeownership.

Education

A country's ability to compete in an ever more integrated world economy depends crucially on a highly educated workforce. However, with many countries making more progress in this respect, the United States has lost its leading position (Chapter 5). Test scores at the compulsory level are at or below the OECD average and lag those in many other major economies (Figure 1.8). Large achievement gaps persist, but performance is broadly unsatisfactory, with many students apparently underprepared for work and higher education. This is a pre-occupying outcome, especially so considering the high level of spending. Available evidence does not clearly establish the reasons for this, but one factor

Figure 1.8. **Education performance at the compulsory level**
Average of mean PISA scores in mathematics, science and reading, 2003

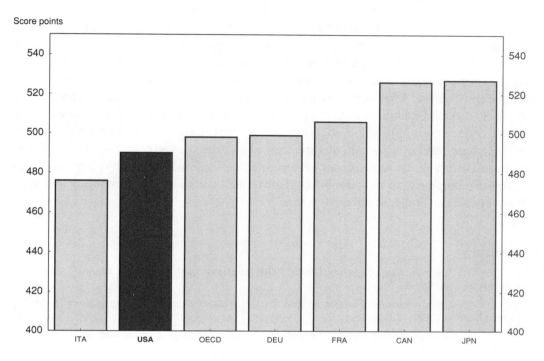

Source: OECD, PISA 2003 database and OECD, *Education at a Glance*, 2006.

StatLink ᴍᴙ *http://dx.doi.org/10.1787/008608572373*

seems to be that standards, curriculum and examinations are undemanding, in part because they are set at a de-centralised level. While responsibility for education lies primarily with states and local authorities, the federal government can play a role by making financial support conditional on the achievement of certain objectives. Federal legislation that requires annual testing and greater accountability – the No Child Left Behind Act of 2002 – is in general well conceived, but could be strengthened. Standards by which performance and yearly progress are evaluated are very low in at least some states. Though the federal government cannot set standards, it could reinforce incentives for states to adopt more demanding ones. Moreover, it would seem desirable to extend the legislative framework of standards, assessment and accountability through upper secondary education. The challenge for Congress when it reauthorises No Child Left Behind this year will be to amend it in a way that increases the chances that the legislation's medium-term objectives of raising school performance and closing achievement gaps will be attained.

Despite shortcomings through the secondary level, the higher education system is generally performing well. But there are increasing concerns that many potential students cannot afford to enrol despite considerable government support (Chapter 6). Policy makers have proposed to address financial barriers to higher education by increasing student grants, and Congress is likely to move in this direction. Arguably, a more cost-effective, efficient and equitable means of reducing these barriers would be to increase student loans. The limits on these mean that they are insufficient to finance tuition and living expenses. If access to higher education is to be subsidised, this should be through reducing

– and not just deferring – loan repayments on an income-contingent basis. Indeed, fears of low post-college income appear a more serious barrier to enrolment (and, in conjunction with lack of insurance, a more obvious market failure) than previous year's parental income, and hence a better basis for means-tested subsidies. Although income-contingent loans appear to promise an efficient and equitable means of financing higher education, they are not very popular. Lack of awareness may be an important factor, and making income contingency the default repayment option would help to address that. Were a good loan system in place, with high limits and income-contingent repayments, other costly and poorly directed means of educational assistance could be reduced, including grants and tax concessions, although social benefits from higher education would justify retaining some level of government support. In sum, the challenge in the area of higher education is to reassess the current system of government support that involves large fiscal costs but appears to be of doubtful effectiveness, with a view to promoting access by the most equitable and cost-effective means.

Bibliography

Autor, D.H., L.F. Katz and M.S. Kearney (2006), "The Polarisation of the Labor Market", *American Economic Review*, Vol. 96, May.

Borjas, G.J. (2006), "Native Internal Migration and the Labor Market Impact of Immigration", *Journal of Human Resources*, Vol. 41 (Spring).

Council of Economic Advisers (2006), *The State of the US Economy and Labor Market*, Remarks by Chairman Edward P. Lazear, Washington DC, 2 May.

Congressional Budget Office (2006), *Historical Effective Federal Tax Rates: 1979 to 2004*, Washington DC, December.

Congressional Budget Office (2007), *Economic Volatility*, Statement of Director Peter R. Orszag before the Committee on Ways and Means, US House of Representatives, Washington DC, 31 January.

Corrado, C., P. Lengermann, E. Bartelsman and J.J. Beaulieu (2006), *Modeling Aggregate Productivity at a Disaggregate Level: New Results for US Sectors and Industries,* Federal Reserve Board, July.

Federal Reserve Board (2006a), *Productivity*, Remarks by Chairman Ben S. Bernanke, 31 August.

Federal Reserve Board (2006b), *What Drives Productivity Growth? Implications for the Economy and Prospects for the Future*, Remarks by Governor Randall S. Kroszner, 27 September.

Federal Reserve Board (2007), *The Level and Distribution of Economic Well-Being*, Remarks by Chairman Ben S. Bernanke, 6 February.

Feenstra, R. (2007), "Globalisation and its Impact on Labor", *Global Economic Lecture 2007, Vienna Institute for International Economic Studies*, Vienna, 8 February.

Forster, M. and M. Mira d'Ercole (2005), "Income Distribution and Poverty in OECD Countries in the Second Half of the 1990s", *OECD Social, Employment and Migration Working Papers*, No. 22, OECD, Paris.

Guscina, A. (2006), "*Effect of Globalisation on Labor's Share in National Income*", IMF Working Paper WP/06/294, Washington DC, December.

Jorgenson, D.W., M.S. Ho and K.J. Stiroh (2007), *A Retrospective Look at the US Productivity Growth Resurgence*, Federal Reserve Bank of New York Staff, Report No. 277, February.

Mankiw, G. and P. Swagel (2006), "The Politics and Economics of Offshore Outsourcing", *Journal of Monetary Economics*, Vol. 53, Issue 5, July.

Reynolds, A. (2007), *Has US Income Inequality Really Increased?*, Policy Analysis No. 586, Cato Institute, Washington DC, 8 January.

Saez, E. (2006), "Income and Wealth Concentration in a Historical and International Perspective", in A. Auerbach, D. Card and J. Quigley (Eds.), *Public Policy and the Income Distribution*, Russel Sage Foundation, New York.

ANNEX 1.A1

Progress in structural reform

This annex summarises recommendations made in previous *Surveys* and action taken since the last *Survey* was finalised in September 2005.

Recommendations	Action taken since the previous *Survey* (September 2005)
A. LABOUR MARKETS	
Avoid increasing the federal minimum wage.	The federal minimum wage is being raised.
Identify strategies to increase employment of the disabled.	No action.
Tighten work requirements for welfare recipients.	TANF work requirements have been tightened.
Monitor whether guidelines for labour market programmes are being followed	The 2008 Budget proposed legislation to reduce UI overpayments.
Expand trade adjustment assistance.	No action.
B. EDUCATION	
Bring more schools up to standards now in place.	The No Child Left Behind (NCLB) Act of 2002 that aims at improving school performance is being implemented.
Expand competition in primary and secondary education.	NCLB provides for parental choice if schools fail.
C. AGEING AND HEALTHCARE	
Raise the early and normal retirement age.	No action beyond the already legislated increases.
Reduce the replacement rate for higher earners and raise the Social Security tax cap.	The Administration has proposed "progressive indexation" of initial benefits.
Introduce savings accounts to complement Social Security.	Under the Administration's proposal, such accounts would be financed out of existing payroll taxes.
Ensure that prescription drug benefits do not jeopardise Medicare's long-run solvency.	The 2008 Budget proposes premium increases for high-income earners.
Roll back the unlimited tax exclusion of employer-furnished health insurance.	The Administration has proposed a standard tax deduction for health insurance.
D. PRODUCT MARKETS	
Improve energy infrastructure, in particular electricity transmission.	The 2005 Energy Policy Act requirements aimed atimproving electricity transmission and emergency response capabilities are being implemented.
Roll back extra support given to farmers in recent years.	The Administration has proposed to reduce support over the next five years by cutting off payments to wealthy farmers and overhauling subsidy schemes.

Recommendations	Action taken since the previous *Survey* (September 2005)
E. FINANCIAL MARKETS	
Break links of government-sponsored enterprises with the federal government	No action.
Continue corporate governance and accounting reforms.	The 2002 Sarbanes-Oxley Act is not yet fully implemented as some deadlines have been extended.
F. TAXATION	
Increase the limits for contributions to tax-free savings accounts.	Congress recently lifted contribution limits for tax-free health savings accounts.
Reduce deductions for mortgage interest and state and local income tax.	The President's Advisory Panel on Federal Tax Reform recommended the elimination of these deductions.
Increase reliance on consumption taxation and consider the introduction of a value added tax.	No action.
G. ENVIRONMENT	
Consider introducing a domestic cap-and-trade system for CO_2 emissions.	The Administration has set a target of cutting GHG intensity by 18% over 10 years but is opposed to a cap-and-trade system for CO_2.
Increase fuel taxes in lieu of tightening CAFE (fuel economy) standards	Following a tightening of standards for light trucks and SUVs, tighter emission standards for heavy-duty trucks took effect in January.
Consider a carbon tax on all carbon-based energy products.	No action.

ISBN 978-92-64-03271-2
OECD Economic Surveys: United States
© OECD 2007

Chapter 2

Potential employment

The trend growth rate of GDP has slowed, mainly because of tighter limits on how quickly employment can grow. In particular, the labour force participation rate, which used to be rising quickly, is now trending down. Against this background, this chapter considers three policies that bear on long-term employment trends. Raising the age at which workers become eligible for full social security benefits would discourage premature retirement and make the social security system more financially secure. The disability insurance system is discouraging a rising share of the population from staying in the workforce and should be made less generous and more selective. Substantial increases in the federal minimum wage are planned; however, increases in the Earned Income Tax Credit would achieve the same objectives more effectively and with less risk of job losses.

Employment limits are slowing economic growth

The growth of the US economy is slowing. Whereas GDP rose at an annual average rate of 3¼ per cent in the 1970s, 80s and 90s, it has risen at a rate of only 2½ per cent so far in the 2000's. OECD projections are that this slower rate of growth will continue, more or less, over the next few years. A major reason for this slowdown is a reduction in the sustainable rate of growth of employment (or, more broadly, labour input).

This can be seen if GDP is decomposed into its "potential" or normal level, and cyclical deviations about this level. Potential GDP can then be further decomposed into labour input (aggregate hours), services from the capital stock, and productivity. Growth in labour input can be expressed as the sum of growth in the working age population, the labour force participation rate, the full-employment rate (one minus the NAIRU), average hours worked, and a discrepancy that reflects data differences and (negligible) aggregation errors.[1] Table 2.1 and Figures 2.1 and 2.2 show how these components have grown over time. Accounting identities that link these variables are set out in Annex 2.A1. Data measurement is discussed in OECD (2006a). For further details, see Beffy, Ollivaud, Richardson and Sédillot (2006).

Table 2.1. **Growth rate of potential output and its components**

Average annual percentage change

	1964-69	1970-79	1980-89	1990-99	2000-06	2007
Potential GDP	3.9	3.3	3.1	3.2	2.8	2.7
Of which:						
Labour productivity	2.5	1.4	1.2	1.5	2.2	2.1
Labour input	1.4	1.9	1.8	1.7	0.6	0.6
Of which:						
Hours	−0.5	−0.5	0.0	0.0	−0.2	−0.1
Employment	1.9	2.4	1.9	1.7	0.8	0.7
Of which:						
Population	1.6	2.0	1.3	1.2	1.2	1.2
Participation	0.3	0.5	0.4	0.1	−0.2	−0.3
Full employment rate	−0.1	−0.1	0.1	0.1	0.1	0.0
Discrepancy	0.1	0.0	0.1	0.3	−0.3	−0.2
Memorandum items:						
Total factor productivity	1.6	0.6	0.5	0.6	1.0	1.0
Capital services	4.3	4.4	4.3	4.6	4.4	3.9
Actual GDP	4.4	3.4	3.1	3.3	2.5	

Note: All series except actual GDP are smoothed.
Source: OECD Analytical database.

Not surprisingly, the slowdown in GDP from the stronger growth rates of previous decades to the more moderate growth in recent years is matched by a similar slowdown in the growth rate of potential GDP. The slowdown in potential reflects a large slowdown in the sustainable growth rate of labour input. Whereas potential labour input grew, fairly

Figure 2.1. **Potential GDP and its components**

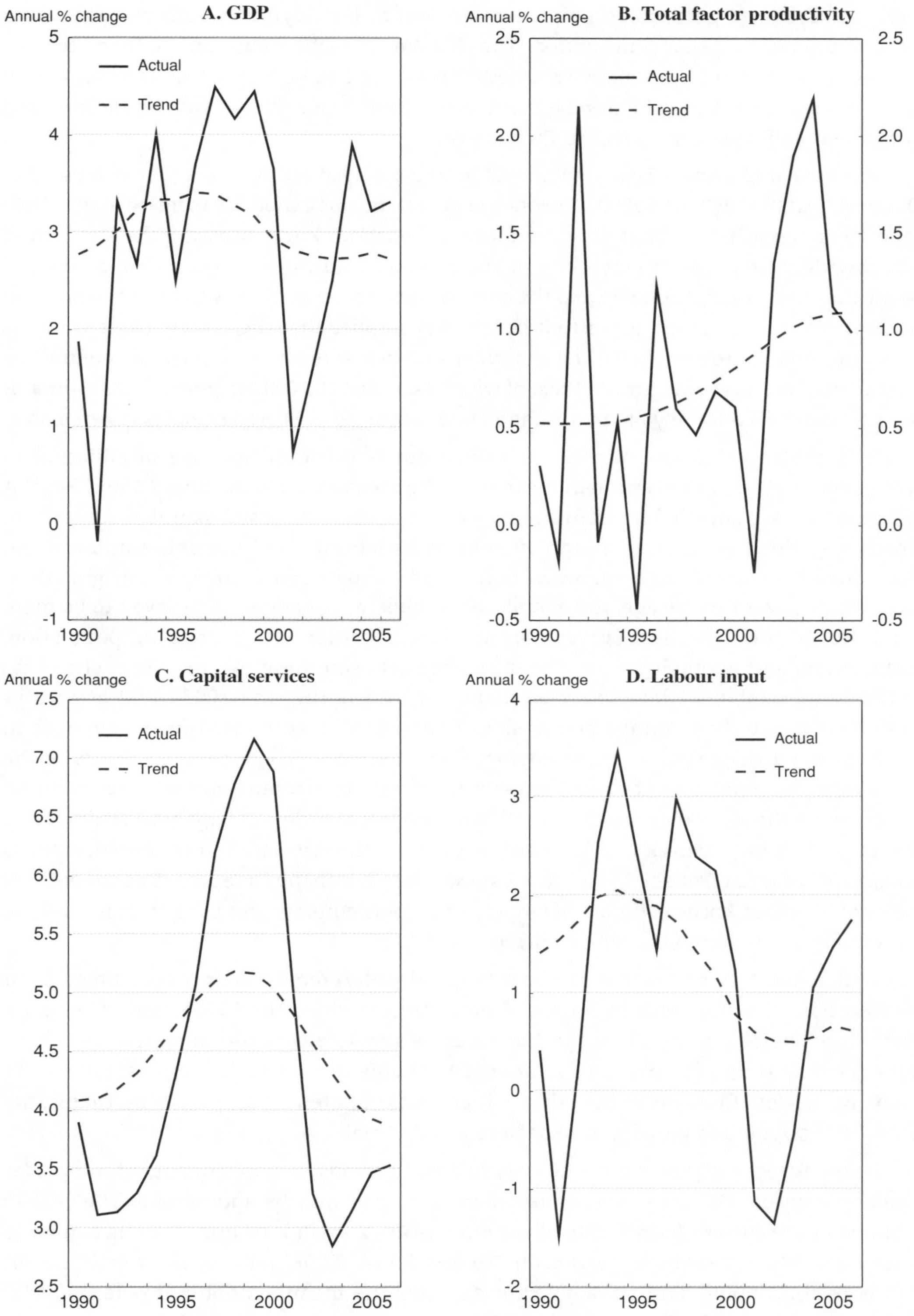

A. GDP
Annual % change

B. Total factor productivity
Annual % change

C. Capital services
Annual % change

D. Labour input
Annual % change

Source: Bureau of Labour Statistics; Bureau of Economic Analysis; OECD, Analytical database.

StatLink 🔗 http://dx.doi.org/10.1787/008618474621

steadily, at an annual average rate of about 1¾ per cent over the previous several decades, it has been growing at a much more modest rate of 0.6% since 2000. That slowdown in turn largely reflects a 1 percentage point deceleration in employment, with average hours worked making a smaller contribution. The slowdown in labour input more than offsets a marked acceleration in productivity, whether measured as output per hour or on a total factor basis. For example, the trend growth rate of total factor productivity has accelerated from about half a per cent a year to 1% more recently.

Potential employment is now estimated to be growing at about 0.7% a year, compared to 1¾ per cent in the 1980s and 1990s. This slower growth means a monthly increase in non-farm payrolls of about 80 000. That provides a useful benchmark for assessing the strength of monthly data on employment – one of the primary indicators of economic activity. If population, the participation rate and the employment discrepancy are growing at trend, then employment growth in excess of that benchmark implies that the unemployment rate is declining. Payroll growth of 80 000 a month is well below recent estimates of "neutral" or "break-even" employment growth, most of which exceeded 100 000. However, those estimates seem to assume a relatively flat participation rate, which, as discussed below, is questionable.

Interpreting changes in trend employment is difficult because of substantial divergences between the two main measures. The measure used in Table 2.1 and Panel A of Figure 2.2 uses payroll data from a survey of employers (the "establishment survey"), to which are added estimates of employment in agriculture and the self-employed. An alternative measure, from a survey of households, shows considerably faster growth in employment over this decade. In general, the establishment survey is believed to be more accurate, but the household survey permits decomposition into changes in population, participation and unemployment. The difference between these two measures shows up as the line in Table 2.1 labelled discrepancy. It means that the 2007 trend growth in employment is 0.2 percentage points slower than can be accounted for by changes in population, participation or unemployment. Furthermore, 0.5 percentage points of the deceleration in employment since the 1990s is difficult to attribute among these factors.[2] Hence, while the slowdown in GDP growth over the last decade can largely be attributed to slower growth in potential employment, explaining the deceleration in employment is considerably harder. Panel F of Figure 2.2 shows the discrepancy, measured as the ratio of the establishment-based estimate of employment (plus employment in agriculture and the self-employed) to that of the household survey.

With respect to factors that can be more easily interpreted, about ¼ percentage point deceleration in the growth in potential employment since the 1990s, and over half a percentage point since the 1970s and 1980s, can be attributed to a turnaround in the labour force participation rate (Figure 2.2, panel D). This is discussed in more detail in the following section. Changes in the other components of potential employment, that is, the NAIRU and population growth, have been relatively small.

Before turning to issues more directly related to trends in employment, a few broader comments on the OECD's estimates of potential output may be appropriate. The OECD's estimate of the current growth rate of potential GDP – 2.7% in 2007 and 2008 – is similar to other forecasts. For example, Jorgenson, Ho and Stiroh (2007, Table 4) show eight recent estimates from public and private sector experts. The mean estimate of potential GDP growth is 2.7% (standard deviation, 0.2). OECD estimates for productivity and aggregate hours growth also lie well within the range of recent estimates.

Figure 2.2. **Components of labour input**

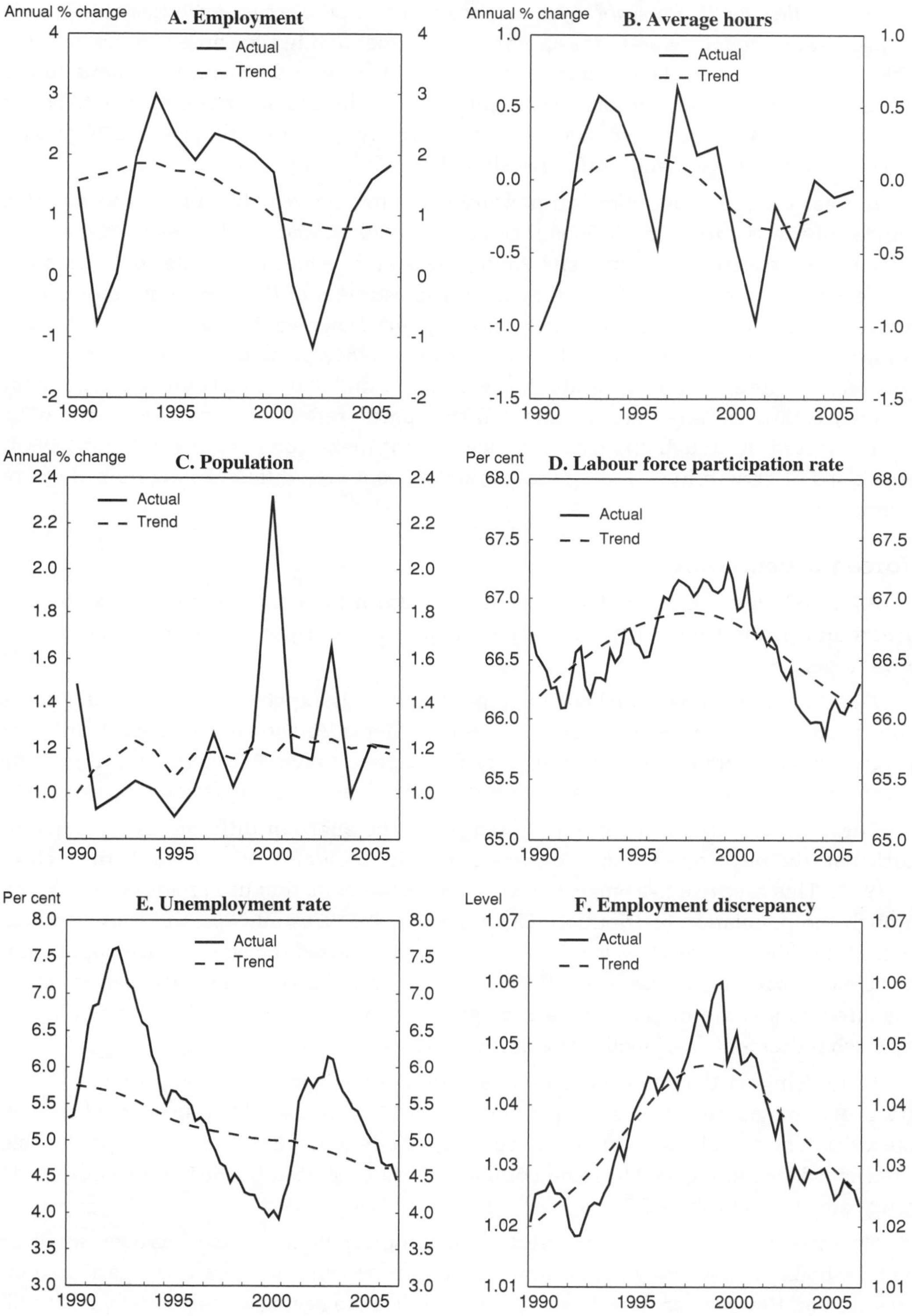

A. Employment
Annual % change
Actual
Trend
B. Average hours
Annual % change
C. Population
Annual % change
D. Labour force participation rate
Per cent
E. Unemployment rate
Per cent
F. Employment discrepancy
Level
1990
1995
2000
2005

Source: Bureau of Labour Statistics; OECD, Analytical database.

StatLink http://dx.doi.org/10.1787/008643160807

OECD estimates have been revised down substantially over the last year, as have those of other forecasters. Projections of current and expected growth in potential GDP had hovered a little over 3% for several years, rising to 3.4% in the *Economic Outlook* of late 2005. Changes in methodology and measurement make identifying the causes of this revision difficult. However, one clear and important factor has been downward revisions to the estimated trend in the labour force participation rate. Whereas this was projected to be flat a few years ago, it is now projected to detract 0.3 percentage points from trend GDP growth. Other forecasters have made similar revisions.[3]

A great deal of economic commentary over the last year has discussed possible changes in the growth of trend labour productivity (discussed in Chapter 1). The annual revisions to the National Income and Product Accounts reduced estimates of investment over recent years, leading to a markdown in the estimate of the contribution of capital services of one to two tenths of a percentage point. Downward revisions to GDP had a similar effect on estimates of total factor productivity growth. But offsetting these revisions, incoming data on productivity through mid 2006 had been strong. Recent quarterly estimates have been weaker, but that partly reflects cyclical lags and may be heavily revised. Although changes in measurement make comparisons difficult,[4] OECD projections of growth in GDP per hour worked are not very different now from those of several years ago.

Labour force participation

As noted above, a major factor in the slowdown in economic growth has been a turnaround in the trend labour force participation rate. Figure 2.3 shows longer term movements.

The downward trend in labour force participation is expected to continue for some time, in large part because of demographic developments. As shown in Figure 2.4, different age groups have very different labour force participation rates. Workers tend to join the labour force in their late teens or early twenties, then leave in their sixties.

These movements interact with changes in the share of different age groups. In particular, the birth rate in America was unusually high after World War II through to the 1960s. This gave rise to a bulge, known as the baby boom, that has progressively moved through the population distribution (Figure 2.5). In the 1970s and 80s, the baby boomers entered the labour force. However, this movement also raised the working age population, so the participation rate was little affected. (In the United States, the participation rate is measured as a share of the population aged 16 and over.) Now, as the baby boomers approach retirement age, labour force participation will decline.

Multiplying participation rates by population shares gives a simple estimate of the effects of demographic changes. Aaronson *et al.* (2006) do this for 28 disaggregated age-sex categories. Their analysis includes Census projections out to 2015. Given the predictable patterns evident in Figure 2.5, some confidence can be placed in these projections. The results are shown in Table 2.2.

Over the last two decades, the effect of changing population shares has been small, as the baby boomers have progressed through their prime working years when participation rates are flat. However, as they move into their sixties the aggregate participation rate will decline substantially. This aging of the population, by itself, will reduce the participation rate by 2 percentage points over the next decade, or 0.2 percentage points a year.

Figure 2.3. **Labour force participation rate**

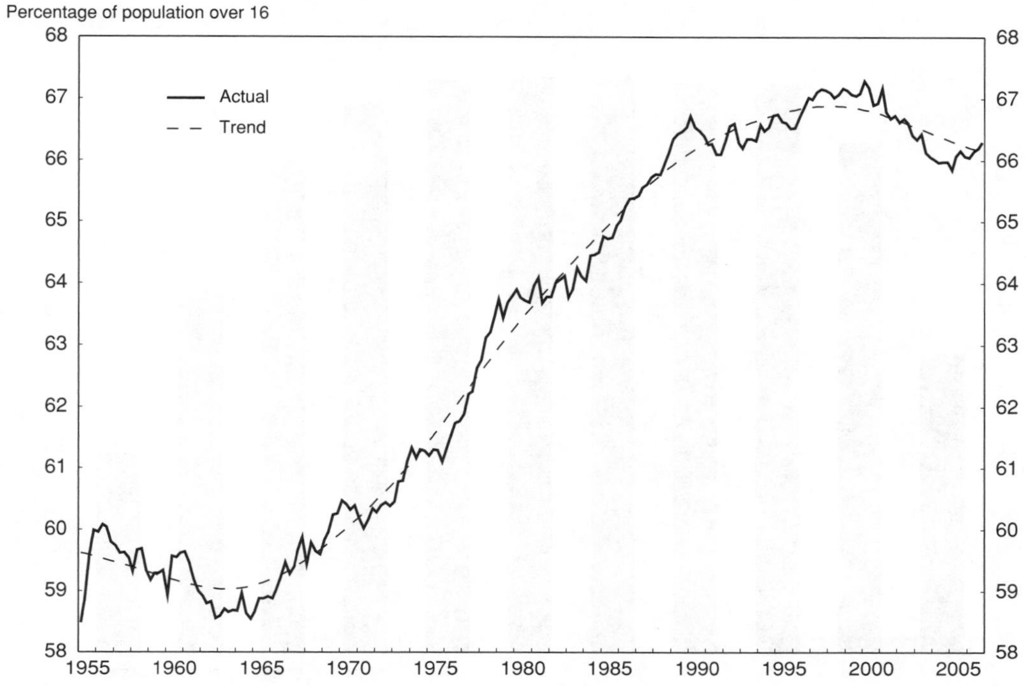

Percentage of population over 16

Source: OECD Analytical database.

StatLink ⬛ http://dx.doi.org/10.1787/008704653143

That estimate assumes that the participation rate of each age-sex demographic category will be constant. However, there are reasons for expecting participation rates within age-sex categories to decline, so the aggregate participation rate will decline by more than the above shift-share analysis indicates. In particular, the participation rate of prime-age males has been declining steadily by a percentage point or two each decade since the 1950s. This is partly due to increased resort to disability benefits, discussed in a following section, and to earlier retirement. There are doubtless many other factors at work, but the steadiness of the decline makes disentangling these difficult. However, that steadiness also makes forecasting simple: previous trends might be expected to continue. For a long time, the downward drift in male participation was offset by a much larger increase in female participation. The increase in female participation is often attributed to changing social and legal views. Goldin and Katz (2002) emphasise the role of oral contraceptives. These factors seem to have stabilised and the trend in female participation has levelled out over the last decade.

Taking these and other factors into account, Aaronson et al. project the aggregate participation rate to decline by about 0.3 percentage points (of the working-age population) a year over the next decade. This represents a significant reversal of previous trends. For example, the participation rate rose at an annual average rate of 0.23 percentage points from 1970 to 2000. Holding other factors (such as productivity per worker) constant, this turnaround takes three-quarters of a percentage point away from the annual growth rate of potential GDP.

Figure 2.4. **Labour force participation rate by age**

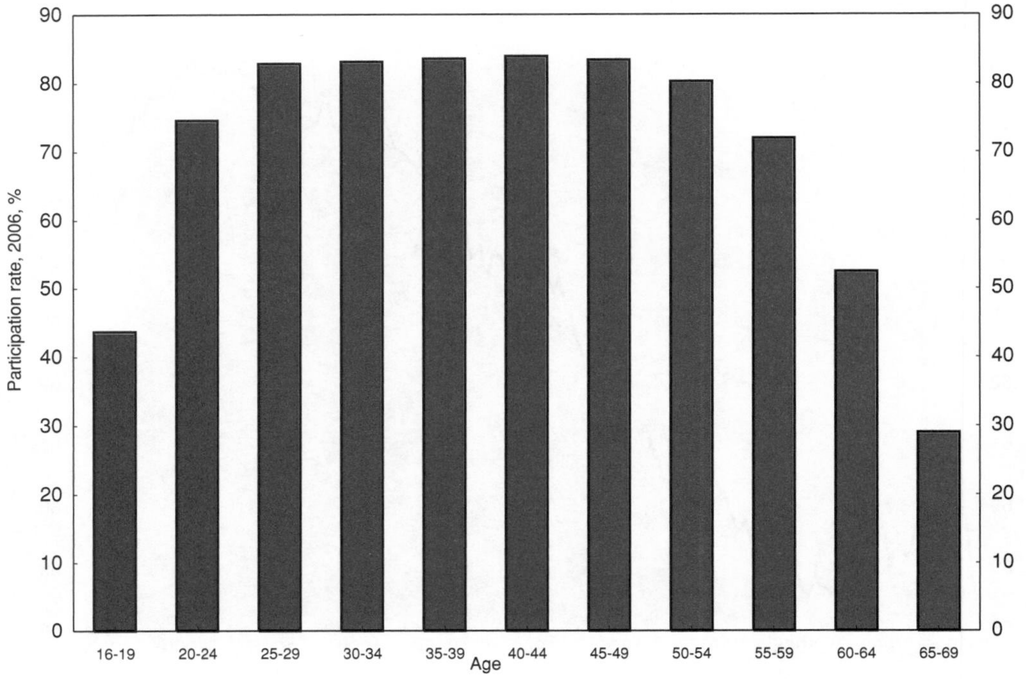

Source: Bureau of Labour Statistics, *Employment and Earnings*, February 2007, Table 2.

StatLink ᴍˢᴸ http://dx.doi.org/10.1787/008705837450

Aaronson *et al.*'s projections are also substantially lower than those for other forecasters, including the Congressional Budget Office (CBO), the Bureau of Labor Statistics, and the Social Security Administration. With regard to the estimates of the CBO (2006), which rival Aaronson *et al.* in terms of thoroughness, a small part of the difference reflects projections of population shares – the CBO assumes higher immigration inflows than census projections, and hence a less dramatic aging of the population. The main difference seems to lie in the within-group projections, though the reasons are not entirely clear. Since Aaronson *et al.*'s estimates were published, the participation rate has *risen* markedly. Taking these and other factors into account, OECD projections assume a trend decline in the labour force participation rate of 0.2 percentage points a year.

Policies to increase the participation rate

A declining participation rate is not, in itself, an obvious cause for concern. If individuals choose to retire, or withdraw from the workforce for some other reason, then that decision presumably reflects a balancing of the costs and benefits and they are better off for it. However, taxes, social insurance benefits, and retirement income programmes can distort these decisions. It is important that such distortions be no larger than necessary, given the various objectives facing governments.

The most obvious of these distortions is the disincentive to work caused by taxation. In theory, the effect of taxes is ambiguous, with the effect of lower incomes boosting effort, while substitution effects lower it. In practice, substitution effects appear to be more important, particularly for temporary changes in taxes. Interesting evidence on this comes

Figure 2.5. **Distribution of US population by age**

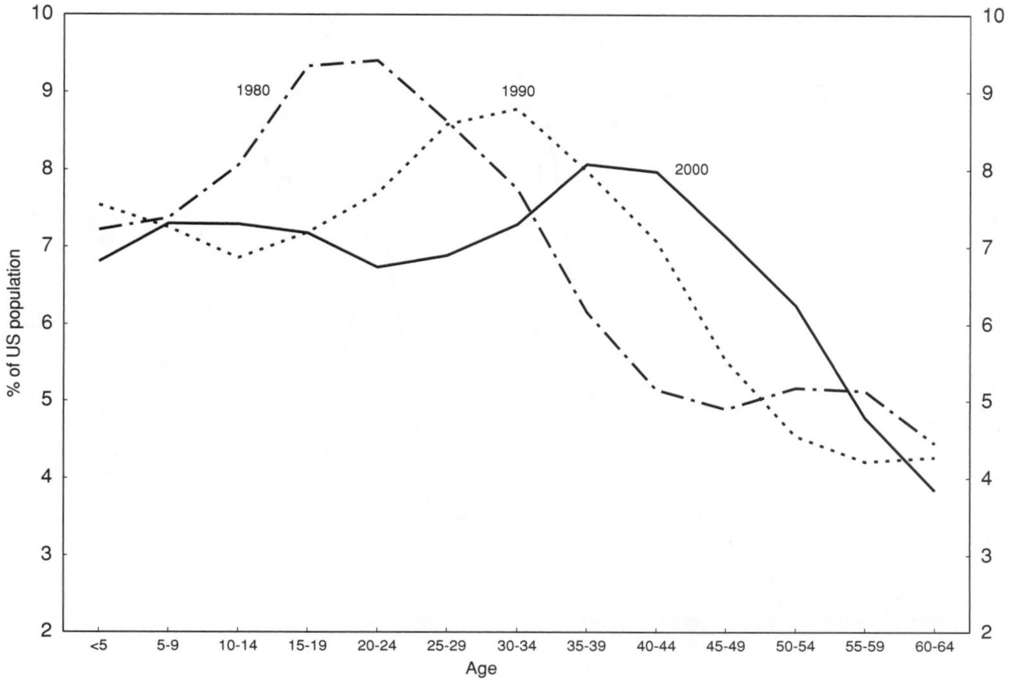

Source: Statistical Abstract of the United States, 2007, Table 11. Resident Population by Age and Sex.

StatLink ᔈᔈᔈ *http://dx.doi.org/10.1787/008734502330*

Table 2.2. **Contribution of changing population shares to change in the aggregate labour force participation rate, 1980-2015**

	Total change accounted for by changing population shares	Total change in aggregate labour force participation rate
1980-1995	0.6	2.4
1995-2005	−0.4	−0.4
2005-2015	−2.1	

Source: Aaronson *et al.* (2006, Table 2, Figure 3).

from Iceland's one-year "tax-holiday". As a result of a change from taxing previous year's income to current-year income, income earned in Iceland in 1987 was untaxed. Bianchi, Gudmundsson and Zoega (2001) found that this led to a one-year spike in the employment rate from 78% of potential weeks worked to 81%. On average, they found that each 1% rise in after-tax wages led workers to work 0.4% more weeks.

For many purposes, the more interesting issue is the response to long-term changes in tax rates, which is likely to be lower than the response to temporary changes (because income effects are larger and substitution effects are smaller). There is a very large literature devoted to this. For recent surveys, see Blundell and Macurdy (1999) or Gruber (2005). This finds that work decisions of "primary earners" (the main source of income for a household) respond fairly weakly to changes in after-tax wages, with an elasticity of labour supply with respect to after-tax wages of about 0.1. However, other workers in the family are much more responsive, with elasticities of between 0.5 and 1. Most of the

Figure 2.6. **Retirement hazard rate, males**

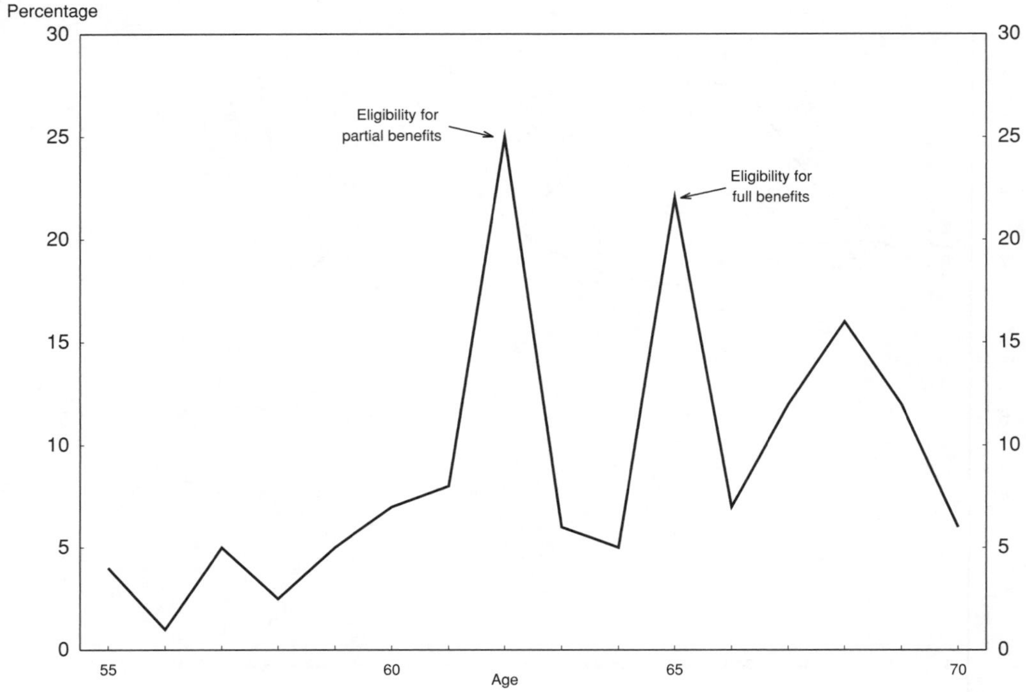

Source: Gruber and Wise (1999).

StatLink ᴍᴵˢᴸ http://dx.doi.org/10.1787/008760462334

response of these "secondary earners" comes from the decision to work at all, with a smaller part coming from the decision over how many hours to work.

These findings provide some (arguably modest) support for policies aimed at lowering taxes over the long term and restraining the growth in government spending. Specifically, government subsidies for public goods need to not only be justified by the benefits of those goods but also by enough to cover the deadweight efficiency losses arising from lower labour supply.

One policy intervention aimed at changing labour force participation rates is the Earned Income Tax Credit (EITC). The primary aim of this policy however is distributional: that is, to assist those on low incomes. The EITC is discussed at the end of this chapter, in the context of the minimum wage, a policy with much the same objectives, but much higher on the current policy agenda.

Another policy with important implications for labour supply is social security. Figure 2.6 shows retirement hazard rates for men at different ages. (The hazard rate, also called the exit rate, is the number of retirements as a proportion of the number of workers). There are dramatic spikes in retirement rates at age 62, when workers are first eligible for partial social security benefits and at age 65, when full benefits are paid. Interestingly, there was no spike at age 62 before the introduction of early retirement in 1961. Furthermore, countries that start paying benefits at age 60, such as France, Germany or the Netherlands, have large spikes in retirement rates at age 60 instead (Gruber and Wise, 1999). The clear implication is that the age at which social security benefits are paid provides a very powerful lever for influencing retirement decisions. Gruber and Wise (1999) provide further evidence.

Increasing the age at which benefits can first be claimed raises difficulties. Gruber and Wise find that the social security system is neutral with respect to retirement decisions at this age. A retiring worker gets an extra year of benefits and pays one year less of payroll taxes. However, benefits for early retirees are reduced to reflect their likely longer duration. This, together with the tendency of wages and hence benefits to increase, exactly offset the benefits of early retirement. Hence, although raising the early retirement age would increase labour supply and income, it would do so by creating a distortion (penalising early retirement). Furthermore, because the reduction in benefits for early retirees is actuarially fair, it would not improve the financing of Social Security.

A stronger case exists for delaying the age at which workers receive full benefits, which is gradually phasing up from 65 to 67. Beyond this age, the social security system provides strong disincentives to continue working. Workers who postpone retirement receive a Delayed Retirement Credit but this is insufficient to compensate for the loss of benefits. In contrast to raising the early retirement age, raising the Full Benefits Age reduces distortions. Perhaps more important, increasing the Full Benefits Age would represent a reduction in the generosity of the Social Security system and hence move it toward actuarial balance. The previous *Economic Survey* of the United States considered issues relating to social security in some detail and recommended speeding up the transition from 65 to 67 for the age at which full benefits are paid and indexing it thereafter to changes in average life expectancy. The passing of time has raised the priority of this recommendation.

Disability benefits

One of the under-appreciated features of the US labour market has been the dramatic increase in the number of people receiving disability benefits. As shown in Figure 2.7, the share of the population aged 16 and over receiving benefits (specifically, disabled workers, excluding dependents) has grown from zero, when the programme was introduced in 1956, to 3% in 2005, representing an average rate of increase of 0.06 percentage points a year. The current rate of admissions to the programme exceeds the rate of exit by a substantial margin, suggesting that this growth will continue for some time. This cumulative diminution of labour supply is large relative to many other factors that influence potential output. Furthermore, whereas other large influences often reflect shifts in preferences or technology, which governments do not control, the increase in disability rolls has been heavily influenced by government policy.

Why have the disability rolls grown so much? It does not seem to be because of increasing physical impairment: the annual mortality rates of men and women aged 50 to 64 fell by 29% and 17% respectively between 1981 and 2001. Other measures of health show similar improvement over time. Nor does the aging of the population account for any but a small part of the increase, which has doubled over the last two decades.

According to Bound and Waidman (2001) and Autor and Duggan (2006), much of the recent increase reflects a relaxation of eligibility restrictions in 1984. For example, the new provisions made it easier for sufferers from back pain, arthritis and mental impairments to get benefits. Musculoskeletal and mental disorders (the corresponding data categories) have subsequently grown from afflicting a small share of disability recipients in 1983, to

Figure 2.7. **Disability recipients as share of over-16 population**

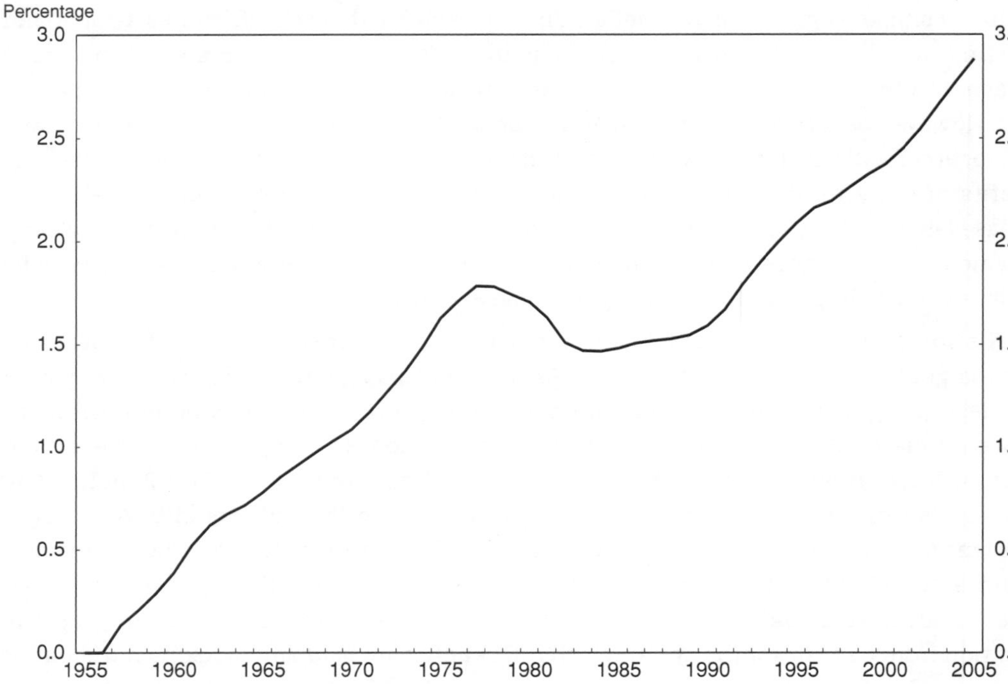

Percentage

Source: Social Security Bulletin, Annual Statistical Supplement, table 5.D3; OECD Analytical database.
StatLink ⟨⟨⟨ http://dx.doi.org/10.1787/008806033123

accounting for most new awards in 2003. Furthermore, because these conditions have early onset and low mortality, the expected duration of benefits has lengthened from 6 years in 1983 to 14 years in 2004.

A second important factor has been the increasing generosity of the programme. Disability beneficiaries receive heavily subsidised medical care, the relative value of which has increased substantially. Furthermore, key parameters in the formula determining benefits are indexed to average wages, which have increased faster than the wages of unskilled workers. These factors have increased replacement rates, particularly at the bottom of the wage distribution and for workers without health insurance. As shown in Table 2.3, the replacement rate for a male worker in his 50s at the 10th percentile of the wage distribution has risen from 68% in 1984 to 86% in 2002. That seems high. This increase did not reflect any direct legislative action and appears to have been unintended. Indexing the bottom bracket to the Consumer Price Index would help restore original replacement rates.

Table 2.3. **Replacement rates for men aged 50-61**

Per cent

	1984	2002
10th percentile	68	86
Median	34	46
90th percentile	18	22

Source: Autor and Duggan (2006).

As might be expected following this, a large part of the growth in beneficiaries has been among low-skilled workers. The enrolment rate of male high-school dropouts aged 55-64 rose from 15% in 1984 to 20% in 2004. Meanwhile, the enrolment rate of similar workers with a college degree rose from 3% to 4%.

Originally, disability insurance was conceived as providing benefits for the "totally and permanently disabled". If that intention had been put into effect then the incentive effects of high replacement rates would not be a problem. However, as the programme has been reinterpreted and administered, benefits are often paid to those who are capable of work. The clearest evidence of this is that factors unrelated to physical impairment, such as education (see previous paragraph) or the business cycle have large effects on the number of beneficiaries. In both of the last two recessions applications rose by about a quarter, before falling back as the economy recovered (Autor and Duggan, 2006, Figure 4). Although there are good reasons for expecting education and unemployment to be strongly correlated with *partial* disability, it is less clear that they should affect total or permanent disability.

Precise measurement of the effect of disability benefits on labour supply is difficult. However, Bound (1991), Bound, Burkhauser and Nichols (2001), and Chen and Van Der Klauuw (2005) find that the labour supply of men aged over 45 applying for disability benefits would have been about a third higher were it not for the availability of the programme. Gruber (2000) analysed changes in Quebec's insurance system; this was quite similar to that of the United States, but permitted unusually clear tests. He found a 36% increase in benefits lead to a 12% increase in non-participation by older men.

Disability benefits in the United States are not unusual by international standards (OECD, 2003). Recipiency rates in the United States are near the OECD average (Figure 2.8)[5] though growing relatively quickly. Replacement rates seem to be similar (though standardised measurement is difficult); however, reflecting lower unskilled wages, overall benefit levels tend to be somewhat lower in the United States. As this suggests, the fundamental goals of the programme are widely shared.

Consistent with this, appropriate policy with regard to disability insurance can involve some difficult tradeoffs among competing objectives. However, there does seem to be a case for change. Current legislation was last reviewed substantially in the early 1980s and, as discussed above, the programme has evolved in unintended ways since then. In particular, replacement rates at the bottom of the wage distribution and for workers without health insurance have risen to punitive levels, encouraging capable workers to leave the workforce.

Proposals to make disability benefits less generous have obvious political and economic difficulties. An alternative means of reducing replacement rates would be to provide medical insurance to partially disabled workers. However, that would be fiscally costly and raise controversial issues of health policy. While lower replacement rates would be desirable, there may be greater scope for improving the targeting of benefits to those genuinely incapable of work. For example, Autor and Duggan (2006) propose greater use of independent medical evaluations and providing legal representation of the taxpayers' interest at appeals. They argue that these reforms would raise the rejection rate of non-deserving claims, reducing adverse incentives, without hurting those in need.

Particular attention needs to be paid to the interaction of high replacement rates with the broadening of eligibility criteria to cover difficult-to-verify impairments such as back-pain and mental disorders. Either of these measures, on their own, need not be important.

Figure 2.8. **Disability benefit recipiency rates**[1]
Persons aged 15 to 64[2]

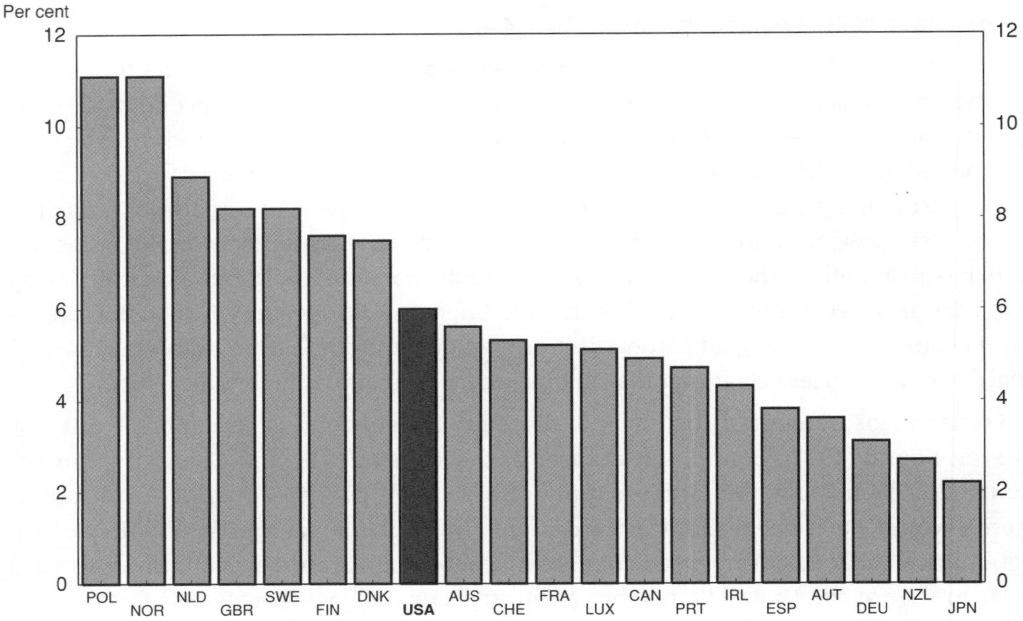

1. Data refer to 2004, except for the United States (2003), France (2003) and Canada (2002).
2. The age group is 20 to 64 for Australia, Denmark, Luxembourg, Norway, Poland, Sweden, Switzerland and the United Kingdom.
Source: OECD (2006b, 2007), Carcillo and Grubb (2006).

StatLink ᵐ⁵ℒ http://dx.doi.org/10.1787/008813844437

But together, they invite abuse. Thus the case for reducing replacement rates is strongest when impairments are difficult to verify. An explicit policy to this effect would seem unfair. However, a similar effect might be achieved by requiring successive levels of verification be passed before benefits are awarded. Those whose disability is obvious would then receive benefits earlier (and hence, in present value terms, higher) than those whose work eligibility is more doubtful.

The minimum wage

In mid-2007 Congress is expected to raise the federal minimum wage from its current level of $5.15 to $7.25 over the next two years, an increase of 41%. (At the time of writing, both Houses had passed bills to this effect, but with details that needed to be reconciled). The nominal change may sound dramatic, but it overstates the magnitude of the change in two respects. First, much of the increase represents a lagged catch-up to past inflation. Second, 29 states and the District of Columbia now have minimum wages that exceed the federal minimum. These higher minima will absorb much of the Federal increase. Based on the higher of Federal and state minima in each state, the average minimum wage is currently about $6.40 an hour.[6] The legislation under consideration by Congress would raise that to $7.40 (assuming no change in state legislation). That represents an increase from 37% of average hourly earnings of non-supervisory workers to 39% – assuming that average hourly earnings continue to grow at 4% a year. As shown in Figure 2.9, this would remain fairly low by historical standards.

OECD ECONOMIC SURVEYS: UNITED STATES – ISBN 978-92-64-03271-2 – © OECD 2007

Figure 2.9. **Minimum wage as fraction of average hourly earnings**

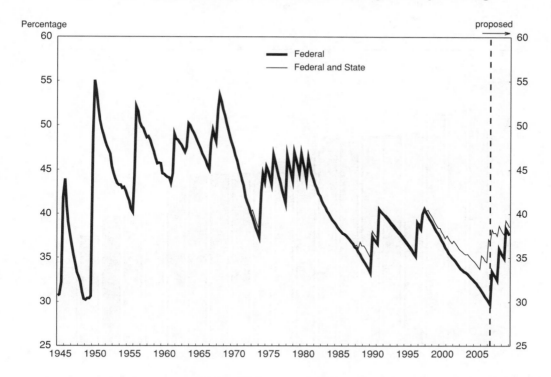

Source: OECD calculations based on Tulip (2004), Employment Standards Administration, Bureau of Labour Statistics.
StatLink ⬛ http://dx.doi.org/10.1787/008822815264

There is an academic debate about whether increases in the minimum wage do more harm than good. On one side are economists who stress adverse employment effects and the poor targeting of the minimum wage. Neumark (2006) provides a good statement of this view. The other side includes 650 economists who signed a petition calling for a higher minimum wage (Economic Policy Institute, 2006). Although these economists each have their own reasons, they appear to view employment consequences as modest and outweighed by favourable distributional changes.

However, from a policy perspective, the important question is whether the minimum wage is the best instrument for achieving its objectives. On this issue, expert opinion is much more settled. According to Gary Becker (2006) and N. Gregory Mankiw (2006), "Most knowledgeable supporters of a higher minimum wage do not believe it is an effective way to reduce the poverty rate". This is important because, among legislators, the most commonly provided argument for raising the minimum wage is to reduce poverty.

The ineffectiveness of the minimum wage arises for three reasons:

First, the minimum wage does not help many of the working poor. It does little for the temporarily unemployed, part-time workers or workers with large families. This contrasts with the Earned Income Tax Credit (EITC), the Federal Government's other main policy instrument for helping the working poor. This explicitly takes family size into account. Because the EITC is based on annual, rather than hourly, income, it helps those who are only able to find temporary or part-time work.

Figure 2.10. **Minimum wage as fraction of median wage**
2005

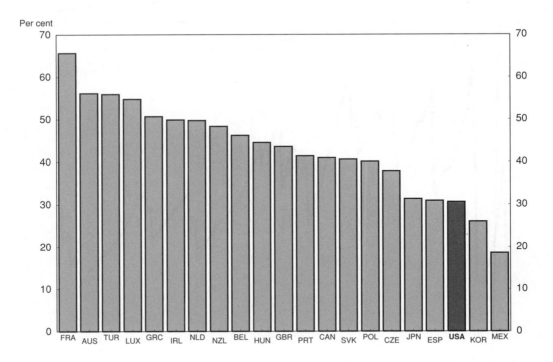

Source: OECD, Labour Force Statistics, 2006.

StatLink ᴹˢᴮ http://dx.doi.org/10.1787/008828672717

Second, the minimum wage helps many workers who are not poor. Many low-wage workers, such as teenagers and married women, come from middle-class families. In 2005, only 15% of the 12.8 million workers paid an hourly wage of less than $7.25 in 2005 were in poor families (Table 2.4). In contrast, 46% of these workers were in families with incomes more than three times the poverty threshold. Again, this contrasts with the distribution of recipients of the EITC. The same data source suggests that 39% of EITC payments went to poor families, with only 6% going to workers in families at more than three times the poverty level. Furthermore, 58% to 60% of the benefits of increases in the EITC (depending on which parameters of the programme are varied) would go to poor families.

Table 2.4. **Distribution of low-paid workers and EITC payments by family income (after taxes and transfers)**

Family income (after taxes and transfers)	Distribution of hourly workers paid less than $7.25 (%)	Distribution of EITC payments (%)
Less than poverty threshold	15	39
Between 1 and 1.5 times poverty threshold	13	29
Between 1.5 and 2 times poverty threshold	9	16
Between 2 and 3 times poverty threshold	18	10
More than 3 times poverty threshold	46	6
Total	100	100

Source: CBO (2007, Tables 2 and 4) based on data from March 2005 Current Population Survey. For earlier, more detailed estimates see Burkhauser and Sabia (2005).

Third, the minimum wage may significantly reduce employment. Some recent research (for example, Card and Krueger, 1995) has concluded that increases in the minimum wage have negligible effects on employment. This contrasts with previous research (as surveyed in Brown, 1999) that appeared to consistently find negative effects. However, the extent of any disagreement is easy to overstate. The previous consensus focussed on small pockets of the labour market, such as teenagers and the low-skilled. Hence in aggregate terms, it only implied very small impacts of the minimum wage. So the policy implications (as opposed to the theoretical implications) of the two streams of research were not obviously in conflict. That said, the thrust of recent research has been that direct employment effects of the minimum wage are negative, though probably small. For a comprehensive (150 page!) survey of this literature, see Neumark and Wascher (2006). Neumark (2006) provides an accessible (opinionated) overview.

Indirect employment effects may be larger. Tulip (2004), Grossman (1983), Spriggs and Klein (1994) and others have found that increases in the minimum wage flow on to other wages, boosting inflation unless unemployment increases. Juhn, Murphy and Topel (2002) find that wage increases for unskilled workers have large labour supply effects giving rise to unemployment unless employment increases. Other studies, surveyed by Brown (1999) and Neumark (2006) suggest the minimum wage impairs training, school enrolment, job mobility and matching in the labour market. There are reasons to be sceptical of much of this research, particularly with regard to the magnitude of these effects. Many of these effects could be small. However, there is little theoretical or empirical reason for expecting them to be positive. So the risks of unfortunate labour market outcomes seem clearly skewed to the downside. Given, the difficulty of identifying benefits from a high minimum wage, policy makers may wish to avoid these risks.

Again in contrast, the Earned Income Tax Credit (EITC) boosts rather than reduces employment. In principle, the employment effects of wage subsidies like the EITC might be either positive or negative, due to offsetting income and substitution effects and the increase in marginal tax rates as the subsidy fades out. In practice, studies find negative effects are difficult to discern while positive effects are substantial. Surveys by Holt (2006) and Eissa and Hoyes (2005) conclude (in Eissa and Hoyes words) "the overwhelming finding of the empirical literature is that the EITC has been especially successful at encouraging the employment of single parents, especially mothers". For example, Eissa and Leibman (1996) found that the expansion of the EITC in 1986 raised the workforce participation rate of single mothers by 1.4 to 3.7 percentage points. Studies have also found *negative* effects on the participation of women in two-earner families, but these results are smaller and harder to discern. Moreover, the research does not mean that the same favourable results would necessarily be obtained at higher levels of the EITC.

If the EITC achieves the objectives of the minimum wage more directly and effectively and with less risk of job loss, why do many policy makers prefer to raise the minimum wage? The most common answer is the visibility of the cost. A higher minimum wage is initially paid by employers, many of whom would presumably pass the cost increase on through higher prices. Many consumers may be unaware of the reason for those higher prices. In contrast, the EITC involves explicit budget transfers that are well understood by other taxpayers. It is sometimes said that "fiscal constraints", such as implicit or explicit PAYGO rules, make increases in the EITC more difficult than increases in the minimum wage. This assumes that households will be more accepting of a reduction in their real disposable income if it is brought about through higher prices than by taxes.

Box 2.1. **Recommendations on potential employment**

Increasing the social security retirement age would remove distortions favoring early retirement and move the Social Security system towards actuarial balance.

● Speed up the transition from age at which full social security benefits are paid from 65 to 67 and index it to further increases in life expectancy thereafter.

The disincentive effects of the disability insurance system have been unintentionally increasing due to declining relative wages for unskilled labour and the rising real value of medical benefits, discouraging a rising share of the population from staying in the workforce.

● Reduce high replacement rates.

● Tighten eligibility. In particular, delay awards for hard-to-verify impairments.

● Consider greater use of independent medical examinations and legal representation of the Social Security Administration at appeals.

The minimum wage is an ineffective and inefficient instrument for helping the working poor. It helps many workers who are not poor, fails to help many who are poor and risks sizeable job losses. In contrast, the Earned Income Tax Credit achieves the objectives of the minimum wage more directly with better employment effects.

● Future increases in state and federal minimum wages should be avoided.

● The Earned Income Tax Credit should be increased.

Notes

1. The OECD's decomposition differs from many others in that it does not distinguish between trends in the non-farm business sector and those in the overall economy. There are advantages in both approaches – that of the OECD's is that it is simpler, more transparent and facilitates international comparisons.

2. Some of the difference between the two measures reflects multiple job holding, which boosts the establishment survey relative to the household survey. Perhaps the largest source of difference is with regard to illegal immigration, which households may be less inclined to report than employers. For discussions, see Perry (2005) and Wascher (2005).

3. Another important cause of the OECD's revisions has been projections of the employment discrepancy. As household employment has continued to outstrip payrolls, the OECD has given more weight to the likelihood of this persisting (until the next Census rebenchmarking). This factor may be more specific to the OECD's particular accounting framework, as other forecasters give this much less emphasis.

4. OECD estimates now focus on economy-wide productivity whereas they used to be built up from estimates for the business sector (see endnote 1).

5. The recipiency rate in Figure 2.8 is higher than in Figure 2.7 due to the inclusion of veterans and SSI recipients and exclusion of the over-65 population.

6. The higher of the federal or state minimum for each state and the District of Columbia is multiplied by its share of national employment.

Bibliography

Aaronson, S., B. Fallick, A. Figura, J. Pingle and W. Washer (2006), "The Recent Decline in the Labor Force Participation Rate and its Implications for Potential Labor Supply", *Brookings Papers on Economic Actvity*.

Autor, D. and M. Duggan (2003), "The Rise in the Disability Rolls and the Decline in Unemployment", *Quarterly Journal of Economics*, February.

Autor, D. and M. Duggan (2006), "The Growth in the Social Security Disability Rolls: A Fiscal Crisis Unfolding", National Bureau of Economic Research, *Working Paper* No. 12436, August.

Becker, G.(2006), "On Raising the Minimum Wage", 26 November. *www.becker-posner-blog.com*.

Beffy P-O, P. Ollivaud; P. Richardson and F. Sédillot (2006) "New OECD Methods for Supply-side and Medium-term Assessments; A Capital Services Approach", *OECD Economics Department Working Papers* No. 482.

Bianchi, M., B.R. Gudmundsson and G. Zoega (2001), "Iceland's Natural Experiment in Supply-Side Economics", *American Economic Review*, 1564-79.

Blundell, R. and T. MacCurdy (1999), "Labor Supply: A review of alternative approaches", in O. Ashenfleter and D. Card (eds.), *Handbook of Labor Economics*, Vol. 3a, Chapter 27.

Bound, J., R. Burkhauser and A. Nichols (2001), "Tracking the Household Income of SSDI and SSI Applications", *University of Michigan Retirement Research Center, Working Paper* No. 2001-09.

Bound, J. and T. Waidman (2001), "Accounting for Recent Declines in Employment Rates Among the Working-Aged Disabled", *NBER Working Paper,* No. 7975, Cambridge, MA.

Brown, C. (1999) "Minimum wages, employment, and the distribution of income", in O. Ashenfleter and D. Card (eds.), *Handbook of Labor Economics,* Vol. 3b, Elsevier.

Burkhauser, R. and J. Sabia (2005), "Raising the Minimum Wage: Another Empty Promise to the Working Poor", Employment Policies Institute, August.

Carcillo, S. and D. Grubb (2006), "From Inactivity to Work: The Role of Active Labour Market Policies", OECD Social, Employment and Migration Working Papers, No. 36.

Card, D. and A.B. Krueger (1995), *Myth and Measurement: The New Economics of the Minimum Wage*, Princeton, NJ, Princeton University Press.

Chen, S. and W. van der Klauuw (2005), "The Work Disincentive Effects of the Disability Insurance Program in the 1990s", mimeo.

Congressional Budget Office (2006), "Projecting Labor Force participation and earnings in CBO's Long Term Microsimulation Model", Congressional Budget Office Background Paper, October.

Congressional Budget Office (2007), "Response to a Request by Senator Grassley about the Effects of Increasing the Federal Minimum Wage *Versus* Expanding the Earned Income Tax Credit".

Economic Policy Institute (2006), "Hundreds of Economists Say: Raise the Minimum Wage", at *www.epinet.org/content.cfm/minwagestmt2004*.

Eissa, N. and H. Hoynes (2005), "Behavioral Responses to Taxes: Lessons from the EITC and Labor Supply", *NBER working paper,* No. 11729, November.

Eissa, N. and J.B. Leibman (1996), "Labour Supply Responses to the Earned Income Tax Credit", *Quarterly Journal of Economics,* 111, May, 605-37.

Goldin, C., L.F. Katz (2002), "The Power of the Pill: Oral Contraceptives and Women's Career and Marriage Decisions", *Journal of Political Economy*, Vol. 110, No. 4.

Grossman, J.B., (1983), "The Impact of the Minimum Wage on Other Wages", *Journal of Human Resources*; 18(3), Summer, 359-78.

Gruber, J. (2000), "Disability Insurance Benefits and Labor Supply", *Journal of Political Economy,* 108, December.

Gruber, J. (2005), *Public Finance and Public Policy*, Worth Publishers.

Gruber, J. and D. Wise (1999), "Introduction and Summary", In *Social Security and Retirement around the World*, in J. Gruber and D. Wise (eds.), University of Chicago.

Holt, S. (2006), "The Earned Income Tax Credit at Age 30: What We Know", The Brookings Institution, February.

Jorgenson, D., M. Ho. and K. Stiroh (2007), "A Retrospective Look at the US Productivity Growth Resurgence", *Federal Reserve Bank of New York Staff Reports,* No. 277.

Juhn, C., K.M. Murphy and R.H. Topel (2002), "Current Unemployment, Historically Contemplated", *Brookings Papers on Economic Activity*.

Mankiw, N.G. (2006), "Minimum Wage as a Symbol", 27 November, *www.gregmankiw.blogspot.com*.

Neumark, D. and W. Washer (2006), "Minimum Wages and Employment: a Review of Evidence from the New Minimum Wage Research", NBER working paper series, No. 12663, November.

Neumark, D. (2006), "The Economic Effects of Minimum Wages", Show-Me Institute, Policy Study No. 2, October.

OECD (2003), *Transforming Disabilitiy into Ability*, Paris.

OECD (2006a), Sources and Methods of the *OECD Economic Outlook*.

OECD (2006b), *Sickness, Disability and Work: Breaking the Barriers, Norway, Poland and Switzerland*, Paris.

OECD (2007), *Sickness, Disability and Work: Breaking the Barriers, Australia, Luxembourg, Spain and the United Kingdom*, Paris.

Perry, G. (2005), "Gauging Employment: Is the Professional Wisdom Wrong?", Brookings Papers on Economic Activity, Fall, 285-312.

Spriggs, W.E. and B.W. Klein (1994), *Raising the Floor: The Effects of the Minimum Wage on Low-wage Workers*, Washington DC, Economic Policy Institute.

Tulip, P. (2004), "Do Minimum Wages Raise the NAIRU?", *Topics in Macroeconomics*, Vol. 4, Issue 1, The Berkeley Electronic Press.

Wascher, W. (2005), comment on "Gauging Employment: Is the Professional Wisdom Wrong?", by G. Perry, *Brookings Papers on Economic Activity*, Fall, 312-319.

ANNEX 2.A1

The OECD's decomposition of potential output

Potential GDP (GDPVTR) is assumed to reflect a Cobb-Douglas production function, with labour (LABOUR) and capital services (KTVS) as inputs, multiplied by total factor productivity (TFP):

$$GDPVTR = TFP * LABOUR^{0.68} * KTVS^{0.32}$$

Where 0.68 is the labour share* and most mnemonics are those used in the OECD's database. Taking logarithms and differencing shows changes in potential (approximately equal to percentage changes) as a function of growth in productivity, labour and capital.

$$\Delta\ln(GDPVTR) = \Delta\ln(TFP) + 0.68\Delta\ln(LABOUR) + 0.32\Delta\ln(KTVS)$$

Labour input, or aggregate hours, is the product of average hours (HRST) and potential employment (ETPT), the latter being measured as the trend in non-farm payrolls plus agricultural employment plus the self-employed.

$$LABOUR = HRST * ETPT$$

The household survey measure of potential employment (ETS) is the product of trends in population (POPT), the participation rate (LFPRS) and the employment rate at full employment (1 – NAIRU).

$$ETS = POPT * LFPRS * (1 - NAIRU)$$

Multiplying the household survey by the trend employment discrepancy (CLFS = ETPT/ETS) gives:

$$LABOUR = HRST * CLFS * POPT * LFPRS * (1 - NAIRU)$$

Taking logarithms, differencing and expressing as approximate percentage changes gives:

$$\Delta\%LABOUR \approx \Delta\%HRST + \Delta\%CLFS + \Delta\%POPT + \Delta\%LFPRS + \Delta\%(1 - NAIRU)$$

The elements of the right hand side are shown in Table 2.1.

* This is higher than the wage share shown in Figure 1.7 for several reasons, the most important of which is that it includes an estimate of the labour share of the self-employed.

ISBN 978-92-64-03271-2
OECD Economic Surveys: United States
© OECD 2007

Chapter 3

Ensuring fiscal sustainability

The recent improvement in federal government finances reflects surprisingly buoyant tax receipts rather than discretionary measures, with public spending as a share of GDP remaining on a rising trend. The new official target of balancing the unified federal budget by 2012 is the minimum, given the bleak longer-term fiscal outlook. Reintroduced budget rules may be helpful in achieving it. But reforming entitlement programmes is the main imperative. Under current law, public spending on retirement and health care is projected to approach by the middle of the century a fifth of GDP (equivalent to current total federal expenditure). Soaring budget deficits would entail a government debt that could reach twice the size of GDP at that time. The situation is particular worrying for health care programmes, where cost pressures compound the effect of population ageing. Whether revenues need to be increased will depend on the success in curbing spending. But tax reform is desirable in any case with a view to enhancing economic efficiency.

The recent decline in the federal government deficit reviewed in Chapter 1 does not indicate a substantial change in long-term budgetary challenges (Congressional Budget Office, 2007b). Rather, it seems likely to be "the calm before the storm" (Federal Reserve Board, 2007), as the current fiscal path is "both imprudent and unsustainable" (Government Accountability Office, 2007a). The reason for such alarming statements is the outlook for the major entitlement programmes, spending on which is projected to nearly double as a share of GDP in the coming two decades due to population ageing and cost pressures. To give a sense of the magnitudes involved: if total federal government expenditure relative to GDP were to be maintained at its current level, absent entitlement reform discretionary spending would have to be cut by more than half by 2030. And entitlement-related fiscal pressures will continue to rise in the following decades, although at a slower pace. Meanwhile, with little progress in addressing this issue and persistent budget deficits, the government's total reported liabilities, net social insurance commitments and other fiscal exposures have continued to grow, representing approximately four times the country's GDP last year. This highlights the importance of acting earlier rather than later. Restoring budget balance in the near term and putting the country on a sustainable fiscal course over the longer term will require increased budgetary discipline, but above all reforming entitlements and taxation as soon as possible. These issues are discussed below against the backdrop of the fiscal outlook.

The federal budget outlook

The Congressional Budget Office (CBO) is mandated by law to make budget projections for the coming ten years. Its latest baseline projection, shown in Figure 3.1, looks, at first glance, rather benign. The unified federal budget moves into a surplus of 1% of GDP early in the next decade and then remains broadly stable until 2017. However, the rules that govern the calculation of the CBO baseline – for instance, the assumption of unchanged legislation – tend to result in too rosy a picture for government finances. In the near term, budget deficits are understated by the fact that likely supplementary spending on military operations in Iraq and Afghanistan is not taken into account (the Administration has already asked for additional funds in 2007-08, see Chapter 1). Further out, the improvement in the fiscal position is strongly influenced by the assumption of unchanged tax law. If the Alternative Minimum Tax (AMT) is indexed (as it has been in the past) beyond 2007 and the Administration's tax cuts in recent years are extended beyond 2010 (their current expiration date), the budget deficit would remain broadly unchanged over the next ten years. Another CBO baseline assumption is that discretionary spending remains constant in real terms, growing in line with inflation. Relative to nominal GDP, it declines by 2 percentage points over the next ten years, with defence and non-defence spending equally contributing. So far this decade, both defence and non-defence spending have increased relative to GDP. If the AMT is indexed, tax cuts are extended and discretionary spending grows in line with nominal GDP (that is, less than in recent years), the federal budget deficit would rise gradually, exceeding 3% of GDP towards the end of the

Figure 3.1. **Projected federal budget balance**
Per cent of GDP

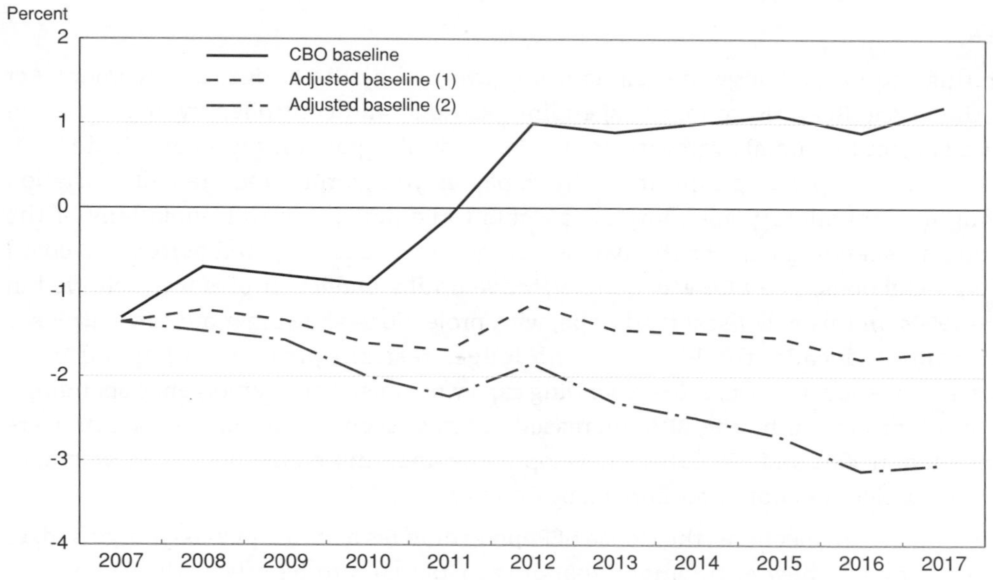

1. Including projected costs of extending the current Administration's tax cuts beyond 2010 as well as indexing the Alternative Minimum Tax (AMT).
2. In addition to extending the tax cuts, discretionary spending is assumed to grow in line with nominal GDP rather than inflation.

Source: Congressional Budget Office, The Budget and Economic Outlook: Fiscal Years 2008 to 2017 (January 2007).

StatLink ᴍᴸ🔲 *http://dx.doi.org/10.1787/010003115214*

projection period. To be sure, there are substantial uncertainties surrounding such estimates, but they show how difficult it will be to achieve budget balance or even budget surpluses, although a speedy improvement in the fiscal position would certainly be desirable in the light of longer-term budgetary pressures.

Over most of the 10-year projection period, the unified federal budget balance will still benefit from annual Social Security surpluses. Through 2016, Social Security is projected to collect more in cash receipts than it pays in benefits. The impact of deteriorating entitlement programme finances will be increasingly felt outside the projection window. Longer-term projections (Congressional Budget Office, 2005b, Office of Management and Budget, 2007), based on intermediate assumptions for retirement and health spending as well as constant revenues and discretionary spending relative to GDP, suggest that without policy changes the primary federal budget deficit would reach between 2% (OMB) and 9% (CBO) of GDP by 2030 and between 8% and 15% by 2050. This would imply a federal government debt between 24% and 100% of GDP by 2030, which then would more than double in the following two decades. Other projections show an even steeper rise in deficits and debt (see, for instance, Government Accountability Office, 2007a or Kogan *et al.* 2007). Such developments would have adverse implications for investment and growth and ultimately spark a fiscal crisis (Federal Reserve Board, 2007). A higher tax ratio, as in the CBO 10-year baseline projection (about 2 percentage points of GDP above the historical average), would still result in government debt in excess of nominal GDP. The same is true for lower discretionary spending growth (in line with inflation) alone. This suggests that some combination of changes in policies for spending and revenues is likely to be necessary to achieve fiscal sustainability in coming decades. In this context, it is worth noting that the US tax burden is low by OECD standards.

Budget rules

During the 1990s, budget decisions were governed by the Budget Enforcement Act (BEA). Under the BEA, discretionary spending provided and controlled by appropriation acts was subject to annual aggregate limits. Congress also periodically established multi-year discretionary spending caps. In addition, pay-as-you-go rules required all legislation involving new mandatory spending or tax cuts to be deficit neutral. Violations of the discretionary spending caps or the pay-as-you-go provisions triggered across-the-board spending reductions. The BEA was quite effective until a budget surplus was achieved in the late 1990s. In this new fiscal landscape, with projections showing mounting surpluses for the coming decade, the BEA could no longer restrain pressures to spend more (Congressional Budget Office, 2003). Spending caps were raised and "emergency spending", which was not limited by the BEA, increased sharply. Even before major tax cuts were implemented in 2001 and 2002, these developments undermined the budget enforcement framework, which was not re-authorised by Congress in 2002.

After the recent elections, the House of Representatives adopted pay-as-you-go budget rules requiring any new entitlement spending or tax cuts to be offset, that is, budget neutral. The rules are internal to the House, which can waive them at any time (they would have to be signed by the President to become statutory rules). While some have welcomed the House's move as an important acknowledgement of the country's serious deficit problems, others have argued that only restoring a statutory form of pay-as-you-go could bind Congress to follow its own rules. Moreover, the new budget enforcement rules have been criticised for not covering discretionary spending while favouring tax increases (any extension of expiring tax cuts would require offsets). In keeping with these concerns, the President's 2008 Budget proposes new statutory caps on distinct categories of discretionary spending each year through 2012 and a pay-as-you-go requirement that is limited to mandatory spending.

Although the House's new rules may enhance fiscal responsibility, only a statutory and comprehensive system, covering all spending as well as taxation, can be expected to be as effective as the budget enforcement procedures that existed in the 1990s (Anderson and Minarik, 2006). Experience has shown that even that framework could be strengthened in many ways (Congressional Budget Office, 2003). Caps on discretionary spending should be global, as separate sub-limits for specific areas (as sometimes applied in the 1990s) make it difficult to shift priorities and can undermine spending discipline. Emergency spending needs to be limited and the purposes for which it could be provided need to be restricted. The 2008 Budget proposal to define emergencies is welcome. But, in addition, explicit budgeting for emergencies based on average emergency spending in previous years should also be considered. While it would facilitate the extension of expiring tax cuts, exempting taxation from the pay-as-you-go rule narrows the focus to controlling mandatory spending, rather than budget deficits, which could still rise. Moreover, it would constitute an incentive to create "tax entitlements", with benefits that otherwise would be provided through an entitlement programme being funnelled through tax breaks instead.

The 2008 Budget also proposes a number of other budget reforms. They include a line-item veto, which would enable the President to cancel certain provisions of law providing targeted tax benefits or spending that is deemed wasteful or unnecessary. Apart from constitutional problems (previous legislation was invalidated by the Supreme Court), it is unclear whether such an instrument would lead to significant budget savings. Another proposal is to make the budget resolution, which sets the overall levels of spending, receipts and debt, a law, with a view to encouraging the President and the Congress to reach agreement on overall fiscal policy before individual tax and spending bills are considered. A statutory budget resolution might be a more effective means to pair new budget policies with the appropriate enforcement procedures, such as discretionary caps and a pay-as-you-go requirement. Views differ, however, about whether it would improve the budget process that has been characterised by increasing delay and gridlock. The same is true for the President's proposal to move to a biennial budget cycle. While it is hoped that this would ease the pressures on the budget process and permit better oversight and long-range planning, there are concerns that a two-year cycle might diminish Congressional control over the budget.

In principle, a longer-term orientation of budgetary policy is desirable, given the fiscal challenges described above. At the minimum, more use should be made of the information already provided by several government agencies. However, a more formal framework may be helpful. One of the first countries to introduce such a framework was New Zealand, where legislation defines principles for responsible fiscal management that have to be respected in the long run, while allowing some flexibility in the short term (New Zealand Treasury, 2006). They include the achievement and subsequent maintenance of prudent levels of debt, maintaining budget balance on average over time, achievement of net worth sufficient to provide a buffer against future shocks, and maintaining predictable and stable tax rates. These objectives have to be quantified. At the moment, in New Zealand, maintaining gross debt at around 20% of GDP is considered prudent for the coming decade. Some short-term variation would be consistent with responsible fiscal policy, but an ever-increasing level of debt would not. The legal framework also specifies reporting requirements, both concerning the achievement of objectives and the long-term fiscal position (40 years ahead). In recent years, many other OECD countries have adopted similar frameworks to encourage a better long-term orientation of budgetary policy.

In addition to requiring that the annual budget submission includes long-term fiscal goals, it would also be beneficial to focus on processes and presentational changes to increase transparency. While the budget has long held the spotlight in discussions of fiscal policy, the federal government's annual financial statements have been less prominent in the policy process. They are prepared using generally accepted accounting principles, with costs recorded on an accrual basis. For example, they record the costs of retirement benefits of federal workers when they are earned, while the budget partly reports them when pension payments are actually made (pension costs of workers hired since 1984 are recorded on an accrual basis, implying that this difference diminishes over time). The Federal Accounting Standards Advisory Board (FASAB) has recently drawn attention to the way social insurance programmes are treated. Some of its members have recommended that a large portion of future Social Security and Medicare benefits should be treated as current liabilities (Federal Accounting Standards Advisory Board, 2006), while its government members prefer to see them recorded as liabilities only when they are due and payable, which is how they are treated currently. Changing this would likely bring the federal government's long-term fiscal exposure to some $50 trillion, about five times what is currently shown in the financial statement's balance sheet (Government Accountability

Office, 2007b). This controversy raises the broader question to what extent budget policy should be informed by such accounting statements. In fact, although the budget largely uses cash accounting, an accrual approach has been introduced, for instance, for loans and loan guarantees to better reflect the actual costs of such programmes in the budget. The same logic does not apply to the social insurance programmes, however, as they are not contractual in nature. Furthermore, future Medicare benefits are highly uncertain and difficult to quantify. The Budget for many years has included a Stewardship Report that presents the long-term budget outlook and discusses a wide range of government financial obligations and assets and the other resources available to meet future challenges. Still, some changes to budget concepts may be helpful if fiscal challenges are to be addressed in a timely fashion (Congressional Budget Office, 2006b). The Government Accountability Office (GAO) has listed several areas where accrual accounting should be introduced to better represent the government's commitment; it has also recommended that a comprehensive statement of fiscal exposures should be included in the President's annual budget submission (Government Accountability Office, 2007a).

In summary, reinstituting and strengthening statutory budget controls for both spending and tax policies, as well as increasing transparency in financial and budget reporting to highlight long-term fiscal challenges, would be helpful in enhancing budget discipline. But these steps alone would not solve the problem. To return to a sustainable fiscal path, entitlement reform is inevitable.

Entitlement programmes

The large projected increases in future entitlement programmes have two principal sources. During the coming decades, the demographics of the United States will change markedly as the post-World War II baby boomers retire and increases in life expectancy continue, while fertility rates have settled at lower levels. The number of people age 65 or older is likely to more than double by 2050. This compares with a projected increase in the number of adults under age 65 by only about one-sixth. As a result, the ratio of people receiving retirement and health-care benefits will rise steadily over that period. At the same time, absent significant changes in policy, medical costs per beneficiary are likely to continue to grow faster than incomes. Even under the assumption that the growth differential between health expenditures per person and GDP per capita narrows considerably, federal spending on Medicare and Medicaid is projected to grow sharply in coming decades. Should the historical growth differential persist, federal health spending in 2050 would alone almost equal all federal spending (as a share of GDP) in 2006. By comparison, outlays for Social Security, which currently exceed those for health care, are projected to grow more moderately, but still significantly more than GDP and the system's revenues under current law. As will be shown further below, uncertainties surrounding long-term projections are considerable and they are very sensitive to underlying policy, economic and technical assumptions. Hence, the projections of entitlement spending in Figure 3.2 should be interpreted with caution. Indeed, the Administration's projections point to less pronounced, but still strongly mounting, spending pressures.

Social Security, Medicare and Medicaid are not the only entitlement programmes. Other mandatory spending covers an amalgam of programmes, including, for example, unemployment compensation, food stamps, refundable tax credits and veterans' benefits, as well as receipts recorded as negative outlays, such as contributions for federal retirement. However, compared to the major programmes, they are small and projected to

Figure 3.2. **Long-term projected federal entitlement spending**
Per cent of GDP

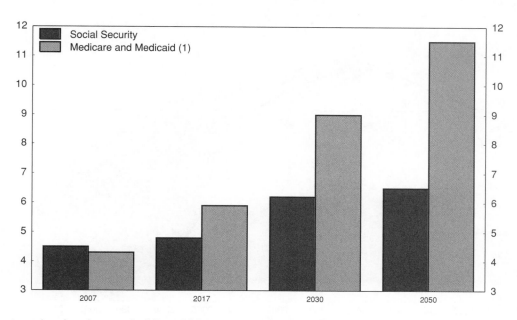

1. Assuming that the growth differential between per capita health cost and GDP narrows to 1% *per annum* after 2017.

Source: Congressional Budget Office, The Long-Term Budget Outlook (December 2005) and The Budget and Economic Outlook: Fiscal Years 2008-2017 (January 2007).

StatLink ⬛🖘 *http://dx.doi.org/10.1787/010005241562*

shrink gradually relative to GDP (to 1½ per cent by 2050, from 2½ per cent currently). The following discussion will therefore be limited to the large, rapidly growing programmes.

Social Security

Social Security – the federal old-age, survivors and disability insurance programme – was designed as a pay-as-you-go, self-financing system. It is largely funded through payroll taxes paid by beneficiaries and their employers. The combined tax rate has risen from 3% of taxable wages in 1950, when there were 16 workers for every beneficiary, to 12.4% currently, as the worker/beneficiary ratio has fallen to just over 3. Since the 1980s, Social Security has been running rising annual surpluses, which offset a portion of the deficit in the rest of the unified federal budget. The resulting Social Security Trust Fund holdings are invested in Treasury bonds. In about ten years, benefits for Social Security are projected to exceed revenues. At that time, Social Security will start to increase the primary deficit (or reduce the surplus, if one materialises). With the worker/beneficiary ratio falling towards 2, the gap between outlays and revenues is projected to rise for the rest of the century under current law. The effect on Social Security's finances is illustrated by the trust fund ratio, which indicates how many years' worth of benefits could be funded with a given balance. As Figure 3.3 shows, the ratio is likely to fall to zero in the 2040s, implying that the Trust Fund is exhausted, although there is a considerable uncertainty range surrounding such projections (Congressional Budget Office, 2006a). After the exhaustion date, fund ratios become increasingly negative. In fact, this is not possible under current law, because Social Security has no legal authority to borrow money. Thus, those negative balances represent

Figure 3.3. **Potential range of the OASDI trust fund ratio**[1]

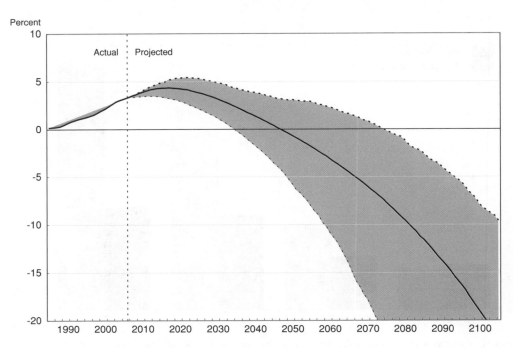

1. OASDI = Old-Age, Survivors, and Disability Insurance. The trust fund ratio is the ratio of the total trust fund balance at the beginning of a calendar year to total Social Security outlays in that year. The figure shows the range within which there is a 80% probability that the actual value will fall, based on 500 simulations from CBO's long-term model.
Source: Congressional Budget Office, Updated Long-Term Projections for Social Security, June 2006.
StatLink ⬛🖳▟ http://dx.doi.org/10.1787/010038140454

the cumulative amount of scheduled benefits that cannot be paid out of revenues. Despite the uncertainties surrounding the actual amount of unfunded obligations under Social Security and even though there is no impending crisis, it would be imprudent not to address this issue as soon as possible.

The reforms that could restore solvency to the Social Security system are well known and have been widely discussed (OECD, 2005). Options include: adjusting the age of retirement to reflect the fact that people are living longer (by accelerating the already legislated increase in the normal retirement age and indexing it to longevity thereafter); reducing initial benefits for the more affluent (by indexing them to inflation rather than wages) while maintaining current-law benefits for those with more modest means ("progressive" indexation); and raising payroll taxes (either by increasing the tax rate or the cap on payroll taxes). The effects of alternative measures have been quantified (see, e.g. Orszag and Shoven, 2005, or Reno and Lavery, 2005). For instance, completely removing the cap on wages subject to Social Security tax, generalised price-indexing of initial benefits or a rise in the payroll tax rate by 2 percentage points would each suffice to erase the system's unfunded liability. The same is true for a combination of "progressive" indexing and an accelerated increase in the full benefit age.

In February 2005, the Administration presented a plan for Social Security reform, which was reconfirmed in the latest Budget. One component not included in the proposed reforms but subsequently embraced by the Administration is "progressive indexing" of benefits, which would help restore the solvency of the system while protecting those who most depend on Social Security. More controversial is the Administration's proposal to allow workers to use a portion of the Social Security payroll tax to fund voluntary personal retirement accounts. In particular, there are concerns that the diversion of payroll taxes into private accounts would undermine the system; it has also been argued that "carve-out" private accounts do not address the fiscal challenges facing the current system, and instead would only make matters worse for a number of decades (see OECD, 2005, for a detailed discussion of the pros and cons of private accounts). In the 2008 Budget, the Administration also reconfirmed its opposition to raising payroll tax rates, given the associated negative effects on incentives to work. A compromise solution may be a package that combines adjusting the retirement age, "progressive" indexing and a broadening of the tax base. While relatively limited changes to programme parameters such as these should suffice to place Social Security on a more solid financial footing, the challenges facing the public health programmes are much more severe.

Health care

The federal government is one of the country's largest purchasers of health care, accounting for about one-third of the total health care spending that reached 16% of GDP in 2005. About one-half of federal healthcare is financed by Medicare, the programme for the elderly and disabled, one-third represents the federal contribution to Medicaid, the programme for the indigent, and the rest is for various other programmes (for instance, for veterans). Medicare is partly financed by payroll taxes, which are deposited in a trust fund, and partly by premiums and general tax revenues. While the projected deterioration in Social Security finances reflects mainly demographics and that in Medicaid mainly health cost pressures, Medicare bears the full brunt of both and therefore is the largest contributor to the overall growth in entitlement expenditures. Its unfunded obligation (the gap between projected receipts and costs) is more than four times as large as that of Social Security. The major challenge in the area of health care is to rein in cost pressures. The steepest curve in Figure 3.4 shows the path of federal health expenditure on the assumption that the historical growth differential of 2.5% between spending per enrolee and per capita GDP persists. In that case, health spending as a share of GDP is projected to exceed current total federal outlays by around 2045. However, this scenario is seen unlikely because it would imply drastic reductions in in per capita non-health consumption.

The options for slowing Medicare spending growth basically are a reduction in number of beneficiaries, the share of costs borne by government and/or the cost per beneficiary. Aligning the eligibility age with an increased normal retirement age for Social Security would seem logical because the two programmes largely affect the same population. However, cost savings would be relatively limited and partially offset by increased spending under Medicaid. The share of costs borne by the government could be reduced by raising premiums or increasing co-payments and deductibles. This could also raise the efficiency of health care by making enrolees more sensitive to service costs, provided that increased cost sharing is combined with restrictions on supplemental (private) coverage of beneficiaries (Congressional Budget Office, 2005a). A strategy that has regularly been used is lowering annual payments to providers below levels that would have otherwise applied (on the basis of automatic inflation adjustment). This could lower the budget cost but risks restricting access to care if providers cannot cover their costs (Medicare limits the amount that providers can charge enrolees over and above the programme's payment rates). As to

Figure 3.4. **Federal spending for Medicare and Medicaid
under different assumptions about cost growth**

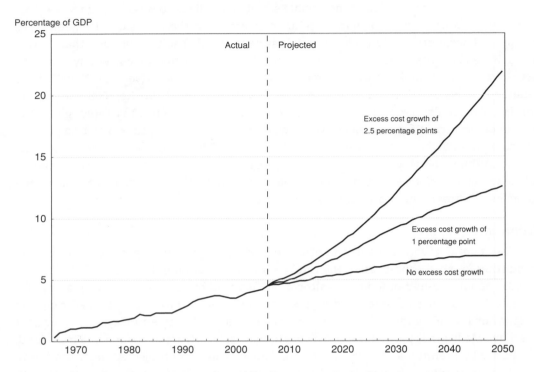

Source: Congressional Budget Office, The Long-Term Economic Outlook, December 2005.

StatLink ᴍᴉᶴᴾ http://dx.doi.org/10.1787/010054107208

Medicaid, the federal government could reduce its contribution through across the board cuts or by reducing the minimum matching rate of 50%, which applies to the wealthier states. Alternatively, it could restrict mandatory benefits and coverage groups or require greater cost sharing of beneficiaries. Nevertheless, all of these options involve difficult choices, since they concern health access or treatment of needy individuals.

In its 2008 Budget, the Administration proposes to restrain Medicare spending, in particular by reducing the automatic inflation adjustment for medical providers, encouraging them to take advantage of advances in medical technology and the delivery of care. The Budget assumes that Medicare physician reimbursement rates will be cut sharply over 2008-2012 owing to the Sustainable Growth Rate formula whose implementation has been delayed repeatedly in recent years. The aggregate impact of proposed reforms is estimated to slow the annual rate of growth of Medicare spending over the next ten years from 7.4% to 6.7%, which is still considerably above projected nominal GDP growth. The Administration also wants to limit the funding of Medicare expenditure through general tax revenues to 45%. Under current law, the Medicare Trustees have to issue a "funding warning" when that level is likely to be reached within six years, but there are no automatic consequences. According to the Administration's proposal, there would be automatic payment reductions to providers as long as the 45% threshold is exceeded (which is expected to be the case in 2012). Finally, the Budget proposes premium increases for higher-income Medicare beneficiaries. The House has recently adopted a bill that would require the Administration to negotiate with drug manufacturers on the prices of drugs covered by Medicare that could be charged to prescription drug plans. CBO estimates suggest that, in its present form, the legislation would have a negligible effect on federal spending (Congressional Budget Office, 2007a).

While some of these initiatives will improve the long-term outlook, the assumed persistent underpayment of providers is probably not viable and a more fundamental overhaul of the healthcare system will be required to reduce the looming budget pressures. In fact, many experts believe that it is not possible to substantially slow the cost of the public programmes without reforming the entire health-care sector (see, for instance, Frenzel *et al.* 2007, or Reischauer, 2007). Cost growth in Medicare and Medicaid tends to mirror – and is driven to a large extent by – cost growth in the health-care system as a whole, including care that is predominantly privately financed. As a result, trying to slow public-sector health-care cost without addressing private-sector health-care cost would require significant cuts in Medicare and Medicaid, with severe effects on the disadvantaged beneficiaries. The government has taken or proposed steps to improve the health system as a whole. For instance, it is promoting the use of health information technology to enhance the care delivery system, including the availability of price and quality information to individuals, with a view to encouraging better healthcare choices and cost-conscious spending. This is to be achieved by increased efforts of all responsible federal agencies in this regard and by co-ordinating public and private efforts to establish an interoperable health information network. To the same end, the Administration is promoting tax-favoured health savings accounts combined with high-deductible insurance plans, including making this option available to Medicare beneficiaries through Medical Savings Accounts. To promote higher quality and efficiency of care, Centers of Medicare and Medicaid Services is also exploring pay-for-performance and other value-based options. Finally, the government has proposed a significant change in the tax treatment of health care in order to eliminate the tax bias toward high-cost insurance (see below). But a comprehensive set of policies to curb health-care spending is still missing.

Taxation

Viewed in an international perspective, the United States has a relatively low tax burden (about 10 percentage points of GDP below the OECD average) and finances more of that burden by taxing personal income instead of consumption. Since the comprehensive tax reform in 1986, which broadened tax bases and lowered marginal tax rates dramatically, new tax expenditures have been added to the code, increasing its complexity, while many tax expenditures that had been retained have increased in value, adding to the distortions. To compensate for related revenue losses, this, in turn, required marginal rate increases, which were only partially reversed in 2001 and 2003. The narrowing of tax bases is evidenced by strongly rising tax expenditures. Federal tax expenditures are large. Estimates of their total cost differ because of definitional problems and possible interactions between them. What is important and undeniable is that they reduce tax revenues enormously and that they are moving back to their pre-1986 level. Table 3.1 shows the major federal personal income tax expenditures. To be sure, not all are of them are undesirable. In some instances, tax preferences may improve efficiency, such as incentives to increase retirement saving that offset distortions introduced by the tax system. By contrast, tax expenditures on housing and employer-sponsored health care, which each amount to around 1% of GDP, are both distorting and ill-targeted.

Table 3.1. **Selected personal income tax expenditures**

	Per cent of GDP, 2008
Net exclusion of pension contributions and earnings	
Employer plans	0.33
401 (k) plans	0.30
Deductibility of mortgage interest on owner-occupied homes	0.61
Capital gains exclusion on home sales	0.26
Exclusion of net imputed rental income on owner-occupied homes	0.24
Exclusion of employer contributions to health plan premia	0.89
Deductibility of state and local taxes	0.28
Exclusion of interest on public purpose bonds	0.16
Deductibility of charitable contributions	0.32
Child tax credit	0.22

Source: Office of Management and Budget, *Budget of the US Government, Fiscal Year 2008, Analytical Perspectives,* Washington DC, February 2007.

Frustration with the complexity of the tax system and dissatisfaction with its economic effects have led to calls for renewed fundamental tax reform. In response, in January 2005 the President created a bipartisan Advisory Panel on Federal Tax Reform that spent a year evaluating the current tax system and made a number of recommendations to make it simpler, fairer and more conducive to economic growth (Box 3.1). In particular, the Panel proposed to reduce a number of tax breaks, including those for mortgage interest payments, employer contributions to health insurance plan premiums, and state and local tax payments. In some cases, it recommended that tax deductions be phased out, in many others, that tax preferences be shifted from deductions, which tend to benefit high-income households, to tax credits, which benefit all taxpayers equally. To illustrate the trade-off, the Panel pointed out that, with a broader tax base, tax rates in all brackets could be reduced by about a third (The President's Advisory Panel on Federal Tax Reform, 2005). In addition to lowering top marginal rates on individuals and businesses, it supported the elimination of the Alternative Minimum Tax (AMT), another source of complexity. Indeed, a substantial simplification of the tax code, combining large-scale base broadening and a simpler rate structure with a repeal of the AMT, would be the most desirable route for reform within the current system. The Panel also offered an alternative plan, which mainly differs with respect to the taxation of businesses and capital income and would involve a move toward a consumption-based system. However, no consensus was reached on a progressive consumption tax plan, and on recommendations concerning a value added tax (VAT) or a national consumption tax.

In many respects, the Panel's proposals are in line with recommendations made in previous *Surveys,* which have repeatedly recommended wide-ranging simplification, substantial base broadening and reductions in marginal rates. The adverse effects of tax preferences for housing are discussed in more detail in Chapter 4. Chapter 6 argues that tax concessions for education purposes are also poorly targeted and other instruments would be more efficient in raising enrolment. Another long-standing OECD recommendation – to cap the exclusion of employer health insurance plan premiums – has been taken up by the Administration in its latest Budget, which proposes a standard deduction for health insurance, whether it is purchased individually or through an employer. It has been argued, however, that converting the current tax exclusion into a tax credit or a voucher would provide a bigger incentive for people to get an insurance while removing the incentive to have more generous insurance (Furman, 2006). Where

---

Box 3.1. **Recommendations of the President's Panel on Tax Reforms**

Households and families

- Eliminate the lowest and highest tax brackets.
- Repeal the Alternative Minimum Tax (AMT).
- Replace personal exemption and standard deduction with a Family Credit available to all taxpayers (additional credits for children and other dependents, itemised deductions eliminated).
- Replace the Earned Income Tax Credit with a Work Credit coordinated with the Family Credit.
- Reduce marriage penalty: all tax brackets, family credits and Social Security taxes for couples are double those for individuals.

Other major credits and deductions

- Replace home mortgage interest deduction with a Home Credit (home equity debt not deductible).
- Charitable giving deduction available to all taxpayers, but rules to address abuses.
- Non-group health insurance deductible up to the amount average premium; employer-paid premiums in excess of caps are taxable compensation.
- Repeal education credits and deductions (taxpayers can claim Family Credit for some full-time students, Save for Family Accounts).
- Eliminate deductibility of state and local taxes.

Individual savings and retirement

- Consolidate various defined contribution plans into Save at Work plans subject to current-law 401(k) limits.
- Replace various retirement savings plans with Save for Retirement Accounts available to all taxpayers.
- Replace education and health savings plans with Save for Family Accounts that would cover education, medical, new home costs and retirement savings needs. A refundable Saver's Credit would be available to low-income taxpayers.
- Either exclude dividends of US companies paid out of domestic earnings and a large part of capital gains from such companies, or tax them at a lower rate that would also apply to interest received.
- Replace three-tier tax structure for social security benefits with simple deduction.

Businesses

- Tax sole proprietors at individual rates (with a lower top rate) and other businesses at a uniform rate.
- Replace accelerated depreciation with expensing for small businesses, and eventually also for large businesses. In that case, interest paid would not be deductible.
- Repeal the corporate Alternative Minimum Tax (AMT).

recommendations in previous *Surveys* go beyond those of the President's Advisory Panel is greater reliance on consumption taxation to achieve further efficiency gains and address externalities. A broad-based federal VAT would allow reductions in personal and corporate income taxation. Raising taxes on carbon-based energy consumption would both improve environmental outcomes and could be used to lower other, more distorting taxes.

In summary, the appropriate level of the tax burden will depend on expenditure decisions. It would be desirable, however, to take these decisions well in advance, since stable and predictable tax rates are part of a growth-friendly economic environment. In any case, reform of the tax system is essential, both for efficiency reasons and for better targeting those in need.

Concluding remarks

The discussion has highlighted the long-term fiscal challenges stemming from population aging and medical cost pressures. Against this backdrop, accelerating budget consolidation would be desirable along with substantial entitlement reform in order to ensure fiscal sustainability over the longer term and avoid an excessive adjustment burden on future generations. Recommendations to this end are summarised in Box 3.2.

Box 3.2. **Recommendations regarding fiscal sustainability**

The federal government deficit has narrowed but persisted. It should be eliminated as soon as possible lest the longer-term fiscal pressures push it to unsustainable levels. Changes to the budget process could be helpful in this regard.

- Reinstate and strengthen the budget enforcement rules that expired in 2002. Statutory caps on discretionary spending and pay-as-you go requirements for increases in mandatory spending and revenue cuts would probably facilitate the return to budget balance.

- Consider the introduction of statutory long-term objectives for budget balance and public debt consistent with fiscal sustainability (such as exist in New Zealand).

- Adjust accounting rules and reporting requirements to better reflect the longer-term consequences of budget decisions.

The major entitlement programmes – Social Security, Medicare and Medicaid – are the main reason that government finances are on an unsustainable course. No reasonable amount of cuts in non-mandatory spending or revenue increases can fully address the longer-term fiscal challenge. Entitlement reform is therefore essential.

- Accelerate the already legislated increase in the normal retirement age and index Social Security benefits for rising longevity.

- Reduce replacement rates for higher earners and increase the taxable maximum amount of earnings subject to Social Security tax.

- Seek ways to improve efficiency in Medicare-related health delivery, and raise premiums for higher-income beneficiaries further.

- Promote cost-conscious decisions by eliminating the tax bias toward high-cost insurance and expanding individual health savings accounts.

The tax system is exceedingly complex, with a large number of ill-targeted and distorting exemptions. In principle, it would be desirable to use any revenue from tax base broadening to reduce marginal rates, but this will depend on the success in reining in spending growth.

- Reduce tax expenditures, in particular those concerning housing, employer-sponsored health plans, and state and local tax payments.

- Use the revenue from tax broadening for marginal rate cuts or well-targeted social measures.

- Shift the tax burden from income to consumption, including carbon-based energy consumption, to achieve further efficiency gains and take account of environmental externalities.

Bibliography

Anderson, B. and J.J. Minarik (2006), "Design Choices for Fiscal Policy Rules", *OECD Journal on Budgeting*, Vol. 5, No. 4, Paris.

Congressional Budget Office (2003), *The Expiration of Budget Enforcement Procedures: Issues and Options*, Appendix A of The Budget and Economic Outlook: Fiscal Years 2004 to 2013, Washington DC, January.

Congressional Budget Office (2005a), *Budget Options*, Washington DC, February.

Congressional Budget Office (2005b), *The Long-term Budget Outlook*, Washington DC, December.

Congressional Budget Office (2006a), *Updated Long-term Projections for Social Security*, Washington DC, June.

Congressional Budget Office (2006b), *The ABCs of Long-term Budget Challenges*, Opening Remarks by Acting Director Donald B. Marron at the Director's Conference on Budgeting and Accounting for Long-term Obligations, Washington DC, 8 December.

Congressional Budget Office (2007a), *H.R. 4, Medicare Prescription Drug Price Negotiation Act of 2007*, Washington DC, 10 January.

Congressional Budget Office (2007b), *The Budget and Economic Outlook: Fiscal Years 2008 to 2017*, Washington DC, January.

Federal Accounting Standards Advisory Board (2006), *Accounting for Social Insurance*, Washington DC, 23 October.

Federal Reserve Board (2007), *Longer-term fiscal challenges facing the United States*, Testimony of Chairman Ben S. Bernanke before the Committee on the Budget, US Senate, 18 January.

Frenzel W., C. Stenhom, W. Hoagland and I. Sawhill (2007), *Taming the Deficit*, Brookings Institution, Washington DC, January.

Furman, J. (2007), *Options to Close the Long-run Fiscal Gap*, Testimony before the the Committee on the Budget, US Senate, Washington DC, 31 January.

Government Accountability Office (2007a), *Long-term Budget Outlook. Deficits Matter – Saving Our Future Requires Tough Choices Today*, Testimony of Comptroller General David M. Walker before the Committee on the Budget, US Senate, 11 January.

Government Accountability Office (2007b), *Fiscal Stewardship: A Critical Challenge Facing our Nation*, Washington DC, January.

Kogan, R., M. Fiedler, A. Aron-Dine and J. Horney (2007), *The Long-term Fiscal Outlook is Bleak*, Center on Budget and Policy Priorities, Washington DC, 29 January.

New Zealand Treasury (2006), *Statement on the Long-term Fiscal Position*, Wellington, June.

OECD (2005), *Economic Surveys: United States*, Paris, December.

Office of Management and Budget (2007), *Budget of the United States Government*, Fiscal Year 2008, Washington DC, February.

Orszag, P. and J. Shoven (2005), "Social Security", in A. Rivlin and I. Sawhill (eds.), *Restoring Fiscal Sanity*, Brookings Institution, Washington DC.

Reischauer, R.D. (2007), *Defining Our Long-term Fiscal challenges*, Statement before the Committee on the Budget, US Senate, 30 January.

Reno, V.P. and J. Lavery (2005), *Options to Balance Social security funds Over the Next 75 Years*, National Academy of Social Insurance, Washington DC, February.

The President's Advisory Panel on Federal Tax Reform (2005), *Simple, Fair and Pro-Growth. Proposals to Fix America's Tax System*, Washington DC, November.

ISBN 978-92-64-03271-2
OECD Economic Surveys: United States
© OECD 2007

Chapter 4

Household debt

Household debt has risen particularly fast over the past decade in the United States. The outstanding amount of household financial liabilities increased from 89% of personal disposable income in 1993 to 139% in 2006, an unusually large rise by historical standards. Although similar run-ups occurred in other OECD countries, the increase was particularly substantial in the United States. The run-up in debt largely reflected the buoyancy of the housing market, the use of new financial instruments to extract equity from houses and the market entry of lenders willing to extend loans of lower credit quality. There has been recently a sharp rise of delinquencies among subprime borrowers, leading to financial difficulties among specialised lenders, which has so far not spread to other markets. US policies have traditionally played a key role in encouraging affordable homeownership. The tax system favours investment in housing, but at the expense of other household assets, and it mostly benefits high-income families rather than other house buyers. The government sponsorship of mortgage enterprises has also done little to promote affordable homeownership, but resulted in the accumulation of large mortgage loan portfolios, which pose a risk to financial stability and represent large contingent liabilities for the taxpayer. Policy recommendations are suggested to reduce these distortions.

There has been a large run-up of household debt in the United States since the early 1990s. The ratio of financial debt to personal disposable income rose from 89% in 1993 to 139% in 2006. Similar rises in household debts also occurred elsewhere in the OECD area, reflecting common determinants, but the rise in US household debt has been more substantial than in most of these countries and the current US debt ratio is consequently high by international standards (Figure 4.1 and Girouard *et al.* 2006). The transformation of the mortgage loan market by the use of new financial instruments and the entry of new lenders has played a distinctive role in this large rise in debt. More generally, US government policies have promoted investment in owner-occupied housing, at the expense of other household assets, possibly affecting capital formation elsewhere in the economy.

Household debt and the housing market

A well functioning and integrated mortgage market

While all categories of household debt have risen over the past decade, the largest contributor to the debt run-up has been home-secured debt. As shown by Table 4.1, mortgage debts have accounted for the bulk of the increase in financial liabilities. This expansion of mortgage loans reflected the buoyant housing market of the past decade, notably the high level of residential investment, which boosted the take-up of mortgage loans. Residential investment increased after the 2001 recession and reached high levels by

Table 4.1. **Rise in household liabilities: a decomposition**[1]

In per cent of personal disposable income

	2002	2003	2004	2005	2006
Net increase in liabilities, by origin (a + b − c − d)	12.6	13.7	17.8	17.7	15.1
a. Net acquisition of financial assets	8.1	12.2	14.2	10.8	7.8
b. Net investment in tangible assets[2]	4.6	5.1	5.5	5.5	6.1
c. Net capital transfers	−0.4	−0.2	−0.2	−0.2	−0.2
d. Personal savings, without durables[3]	0.5	3.8	2.2	−1.3	−1.0
Net increase in liabilities, by type of debt (1 + 2 + 3 + 4)	12.6	13.7	17.8	17.7	15.1
1. Mortgage debt on nonfarm homes	9.3	9.8	12.1	12.4	8.6
2. Other mortgage debt[4]	1.3	1.9	1.9	2.7	2.6
3. Consumer credit	1.4	1.3	1.3	1.0	1.2
4. Other liabilities	0.5	0.8	2.4	1.6	2.8
Memorandum items:					
Personal saving (NIPA definition)	2.4	2.1	2.0	−0.4	−1.1
Personal disposable income (billion $)	7 830.1	8 162.5	8 681.6	9 036.1	9 523.1

1. Based on the consolidated statement for household sector, non-farm, non-corporate business, and farm business.
2. Excluding consumption of durables. Consists mostly of residential investment and investment in corporate farms.
3. Flow of funds definition of personal saving, differs from the NIPA definition.
4. Includes corporate farms.
Source: Federal Reserve Board of Governors, Flow of Funds (8 March 2007).

Figure 4.1. **Household liabilities and assets**

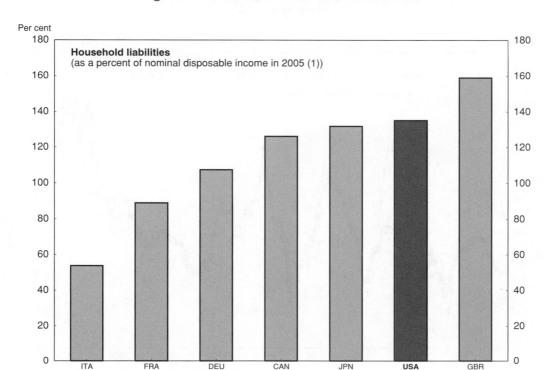

Per cent

Household liabilities
(as a percent of nominal disposable income in 2005 (1))

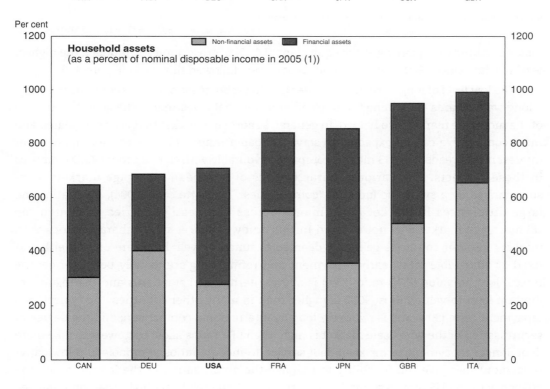

Per cent

Household assets
(as a percent of nominal disposable income in 2005 (1))

Non-financial assets   Financial assets

1. 2004 for Italy and Japan.

Source: Canada: Statistics Canada; France: INSEE; Germany: Deutsche Bundesbank; Italy: Banca d'Italia; Japan: Economic Planning Agency; United Kingdom: Office for National Statistics; United States: Federal Reserve.

StatLink ⫘⫘ *http://dx.doi.org/10.1787/010078731613*

Figure 4.2. **Household net borrowing and residential investment**
As a percentage of GDP

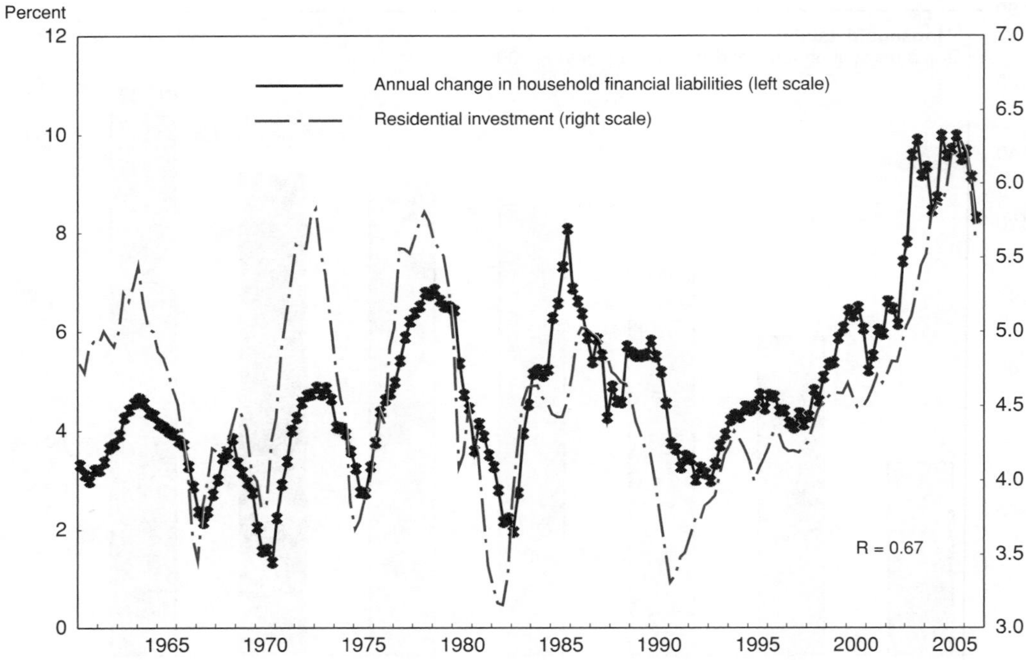

Source: Federal Reserve Board and Bureau of Economic Analysis.

StatLink ᴹˢ⁵ http://dx.doi.org/10.1787/010158227240

historical standards, peaking at the equivalent of 6.3% of gross domestic product, the highest level reached since 1960, and household debt closely followed this trend (Figure 4.2).

The low level of long term interest rates and the robustness of macroeconomic trends go a long way towards explaining the uptrend of residential investment. The good functioning of the mortgage market also helped. In general, a mortgage market that is less regulated and more competitive can be expected to serve a broader range of borrowers and apply lower interest rate spreads. The US market compares favourably with that of other OECD countries in these respects. The various characteristics of European mortgage markets were summarised by a synthetic index of "completeness" by Catte *et al.* (2004), illustrating the large differences in market performance across European countries. Although the US mortgage market was not covered in this study, it shares many characteristics with markets in other countries generally deemed to function well: loans are offered either at fixed or adjustable rates; early-repayment and refinancing are usually penalty-free; the typical loan-to-value (LTV) ratio (78%) is above international standards and the regulatory limit on loan-to-value ratios (90%) is higher than in many other countries; the typical loan repayment term (30 years) is relatively long by international comparison; and the degree of securitisation of the wholesale market is high. High LTV ratios allow borrowers to take more debt, longer repayment terms keep debt service-to-income ratios affordable and low early-repayment fees give the flexibility to manage the amortisation of the loan. Overall, the efficiency of the US mortgage market is considered to be relatively high: Diamond and Lea (1992) rank it above that of continental European countries (such as France) but lower than that of the United Kingdom and Denmark.

OECD ECONOMIC SURVEYS: UNITED STATES – ISBN 978-92-64-03271-2 – © OECD 2007

A specific feature of the US mortgage market is its high degree of geographical integration. The interventions of federal lending agencies and government-sponsored enterprises have contributed to a standardisation of mortgage products and helped harmonise lending practices. Loan originators have the assurance that they will be able to sell mortgage loans to a government-sponsored enterprise when these loans conform to pre-specified standards. As a result, the US mortgage market is more integrated than the euro area market, where institutional arrangements differ across countries. This is illustrated by a low dispersion of interest rates across US regions, compared to the dispersion prevailing across euro area members (ECB, 2005).

An important aspect of this standardisation is the prevalence of fixed-rate residential mortgage; in no year between 1990 and 2004 did the share of fixed-rate mortgages fall below 60% of new mortgage origination and in some years the fixed-rate share has been nearly 90% (Federal Housing Finance Board, Survey of Interest Rates, Historical Tables). The popularity of fixed-rate mortgages among lenders is explained by the presence of a very large secondary market, whose liquidity has been traditionally supported by government agencies. For borrowers, fixed-rate mortgages are attractive because they protect against rising interest rates, and the ability to refinance protects against falling interest rates. Nominal fixed-rate residential mortgages do not prevail internationally: for instance, they are almost unknown in the United Kingdom and Canada. However, nominal fixed-rate mortgage contracts contain inflation risk. In general, mortgage contracts have a prepayment option in the United States that protects the homeowner against the risk of a fall in nominal interest rates, because the homeowner can take out a new mortgage contract with a lower nominal rate. However this option does not come for free. Diamond and Lea (1992) put it at 73 basis points; this raises the interest rate on fixed-rate mortgages and leaves the homeowner with a contract that is expensive when inflation is stable (Campbell and Cocco, 2003).

Likewise, US mortgage lenders rarely offer the option of portability to transfer a loan from one property to another. Combined with the prevalence of fixed rates, the lack of portability may lessen labour force mobility: in an environment of rising mortgage rates, a borrower may decide not to move if, to buy a new home, he has to reimburse an existing low interest rate loan and take a new, higher interest rate loan. While the option of portability is offered in other English-speaking countries, it is rare in the United States.

New financial products and lending practices

The US mortgage market has been transformed over the past decade by the market entry of subprime lenders and the offering of home equity lines of credit. Table 4.2. shows that subprime mortgages and home equity lines of credit account for about 16% of outstanding mortgage debt.

The entry of lenders willing to provide mortgage loans to borrowers with lower credit quality has created the market for *subprime loans*. Subprime lending relies on risk-based pricing to serve borrowers who cannot obtain credit in the prime market. Technological innovation in loan application processing, notably the use of credit scoring models, has given lenders the information to price non-standard risk, including subprime credit risk (Bies, 2006). By one estimate, interest rates on subprime loans in 2001 ranged between 7.2% and 12.75%, compared with interest rates on conventional loans closer to 6%.[1] While they have reduced borrowing constraints and allowed less creditworthy households to access homeownership, such loans are characterised by high default rates. As noted below, there

Table 4.2. **Composition of mortgage market, 2003**
Billions of dollars

	Originations	Outstanding
First lien loans		
Prime loans, conventional	1 910	3 250
Other prime	550	1 175
Jumbo prime	660	1 470
FHA/VA	230	475
Atl-A	220	400
Subprime	310	650
Home equity credits		
Prime	110	190
Junior liens	290	480
Subprime	20	50
TOTAL[1]	**3 700/3 900**	**7 200/7 400**

1. The total differs from the sum of the above categories due to double-counting by lenders.
Source: Mercer Oliver Wyman (2005).

has been a sharp rise of delinquency among some categories of subprime borrowers, notably those having contracted adjustable-rate loan with low "teaser" rates, which sharply rose at the first reset period, thus causing large increases in monthly payment dues, pushing many borrowers on the brink of default. One problem with such subprime loans is that they fall outside the traditional federal regulatory framework for US banks and therefore cannot be easily monitored and regulated. Subprime mortgages are now about 12% of outstanding mortgage loans, with slightly more than half with adjustable rates.

Another market innovation is the emergence of *home equity lines of credit,* which are used by households to take advantage of the rise in house prices and increase their leverage. Such credits are attractive to borrowers who need extra cash and are better off taking out a smaller, higher-rate home-equity loan than refinancing their entire first mortgage, especially in an environment of rising interest rates. More than 80% of home-equity borrowers are of prime or even higher quality and typical loss rates for prime-only lenders are very low. This might change in the event of a significant house-price decline, because of the high leverage of some borrowers, but generally credit quality differs significantly from that of subprime loans. Besides home equity credits, other forms of home equity withdrawal have been used, including taking a second mortgage loan or reloading a loan to its initial value.[2]

Overall, the extraction of equity through various means was very substantial during 2004-06. As measured by the difference between the change in home-secured debt and net residential investment,[3] equity extraction reached a peak equivalent to 6-8% of personal disposable income in 2005 (Figure 4.3). The Tax Reform Act of 1986, by phasing out the tax deductibility of interest payments on traditional consumer debts (such as credit card balances and car loans) created an incentive to contract home-secured credits, which remained tax-deductible, and to consolidate all outstanding credits into a single tax-deductible home-secured credit. Thus, not all equity withdrawal increased the total amount of debt. Respondents to a Federal Reserve survey in 2001-02 allocated 26% of cash-outs from mortgage refinancing to the repayment of other debts, only 16% to consumer expenditures and most of the rest to various residential and financial investments. The

Figure 4.3. **Home equity withdrawal**[1]

In per cent of personal disposable income

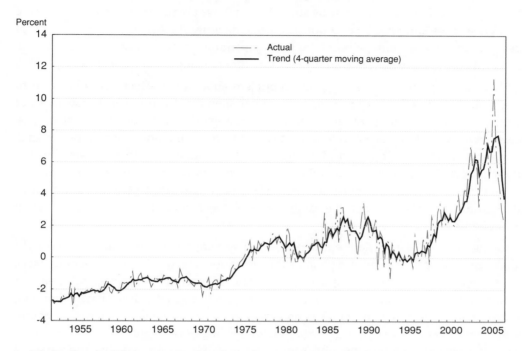

1. Calculated as the difference between the change in mortgage debt and net residential investment.
Source: Federal Reserve Board of Governors, Flow of Funds.

StatLink http://dx.doi.org/10.1787/010160264850

Federal Reserve's Survey of Consumer Finance of 2004 similarly found that 31% of borrowing against home equity lines of credit was used for debt consolidation, while 45% was for home improvement (Federal Reserve, 2006). The rise in home equity withdrawal therefore did not weaken markedly household balance sheets: it helped to repay high-interest credit card balances, financed the build-up of financial assets (including tax-deductible contributions to pension funds) and contributed to the maintenance of real estate assets.

Vulnerability of indebted households

The debt run-up of the past decade has triggered fears for macro and financial stability. A sharp fall in house prices would prevent households from extracting further housing equity and would put highly-leveraged borrowers under stress, with possibly large macroeconomic and financial consequences. Despite such fears, risks appear presently well contained.

Macroeconomic risks

A fall in house prices, or just their stagnation, would stop the growth of housing wealth and would prevent households from further extracting equity. There is, however, much uncertainty about the effects of equity extraction on consumption. Some researchers find a substantial impact; for instance, Catte *et al.* (2004) find that US consumers spend about 20 cents of each dollar of equity extracted (a marginal propensity to consume out of equity withdrawal of 0.20). IMF estimates by Klyuev and Mills (2006) find results within a very similar range in the long term (marginal propensity to consume of 0.18). On this basis, they estimate that a decline in the ratio of equity withdrawal to disposable income from 7% to the average of the last twenty years would depress the ratio of consumption to disposable income by about 1 percentage point. According to estimates of the Congressional Budget Office, a housing price decline of 10% would exert a drag of between 0.4 and 1.4 percentage points of GDP, depending on the marginal propensity to consume and using fairly neutral assumptions for other housing-related effects (CBO, 2007a).

Other empirical research expressed scepticism about such effects. An objection to them is that the causation may run from consumer spending to equity withdrawal rather than the other way around. In other words, borrowing against the value of a house may be a convenient way to finance a purchase that would have been made anyway, for instance by using another form of credit or drawing down financial assets. It could also be that equity withdrawal and consumer spending move together driven by a third factor, such as consumer confidence or expectations of future income growth. Overall, the impact of equity withdrawal on consumer spending may have been quite limited and its reversal could therefore also have small effects.

Judging from the few previous episodes covered by comprehensive data, a large outright decline in nominal prices of existing homes for the nation as a whole would seem unlikely. OFHEO's repeat-transactions house price index has not registered a four-quarter decrease at any point since 1975.[4] Nevertheless, for housing prices not to exert a drag on consumption, the ratio of housing wealth to nominal income would need to be stable, which would require continued housing price increases. A stagnation of housing prices would by itself mean that consumption would no longer benefit from rising housing wealth and that the personal saving rate would likely start to increase. A prolonged period with very sluggish home prices would be consistent with the previous US experience, and could be expected to result in sharply slower growth of mortgage debt and much lower residential investment compared with recent years. Judging from the relatively small effects from model simulations (as discussed above), this drag is likely to be of a small magnitude.

Financial stability

The accumulation of mortgage debt and the large withdrawal of equity means that real estate asset leverage is high both by historical and international comparisons (Girouard et al. 2006). Thus, some households could face difficulties in case of a decline in housing prices, which would imply further decline in equity – or indeed negative equity for the most exposed households. This might pose problems for households unable to wait until the housing market recovers, such as people facing a sudden loss of income and being forced to sell. Most households seem however to hold sufficiently large financial assets to cope with temporary difficulties. Indeed, the Federal Reserve's Survey of Consumer Finance does not indicate, until 2004, a deterioration in the net worth of households across various income groups, which would have happened if borrowers had increased their liabilities far more than their assets (Table 4.3).

Another source of vulnerability could result from the increase in debt service burdens, which may pose problems for the availability of disposable income required to meet both debt service obligations and consumption needs. Recent data from the Federal Reserve and the National Association of Realtors indicate that debt service payments increased rapidly during the period 2004-06 (Figure 4.4). Despite the rise in debt service payments, most households have been able to meet their payment obligations. However, delinquency rates in some market segments have risen in recent quarters. As measured by the Mortgage

Table 4.3. **Median net worth per household**

Thousands of dollars at 2004 prices

	1995	1998	2001	2004
All families	70.8	83.1	91.7	93.1
Percentiles of income				
Less than 20	7.4	6.8	8.4	7.5
20-39.9	41.3	38.4	39.6	34.3
40-59.9	57.1	61.9	66.5	71.6
60-79.9	93.6	130.2	150.7	160.0
80-89.9	157.7	218.5	280.3	311.1
90-100	436.9	524.4	887.9	924.1

Source: Survey of Consumer Finance, 2004, Federal Reserve Board of Governors.

Figure 4.4. **Household debt service indicators**

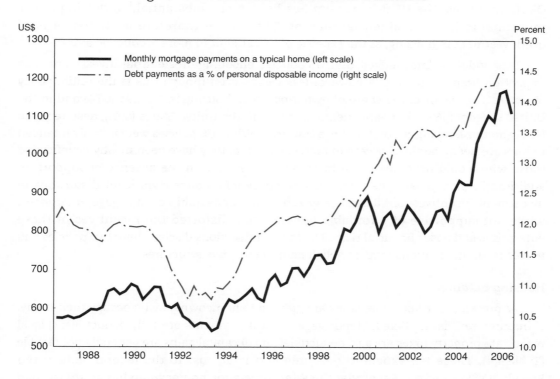

Source: National Association of Realtors and Federal Reserve Board.

StatLink 🔗 http://dx.doi.org/10.1787/010160453731

Bankers Association, the share of mortgages that are 60 or more days past due stood at 1.87% in the fourth quarter of 2006, showing a moderate increase from previous quarters.[5] Delinquencies and foreclosures increased more rapidly in the market segment of subprime adjustable-rate mortgage (ARM) loans, where the share of mortgages 60 days past due stood at 3.13% in the fourth quarter of 2006. While a number of subprime lenders have run into difficulties – with a few of them altogether exiting the market through bankruptcy – the relatively small size of the subprime ARM market (5% of total mortgage outstanding at the end of 2006) has been seen as a protection against systemic difficulties. At the time of writing, evidence of stress on the residential debt market was well contained: the share of mortgages past due had not increased in other markets, including in the market of subprime fixed rate mortgages. The effective shutdown of the subprime ARM mortgage market however meant a reduced demand for new homes and therefore lower residential construction activity.

The implication for US policies

The above discussion suggests that the US residential loan market has generally functioned well. Households have been able to take out large amounts of debts to finance their residential investment; they have gained further flexibility in financial management thanks to the emergence of instruments for equity extraction; lower-income households have seen their borrowing constraints diminished by the entry of subprime lenders; and the financial position of the household sector does not appear to be vulnerable. The relatively small market segment of subprime lending recently came under stress, but there is as of now no sign that this will spill over to other market segments. Compared to other OECD countries, the US debt run-up has been more substantial,[6] reflecting larger investments in the residential market. There have therefore been concerns of overinvestment in housing, at the expense of investment in more productive assets.

It is widely acknowledged that US policies encourage residential investment. The impact on homeownership is however less clear – even though this is the initial policy objective. For instance, the share of owner-occupied housing in Canada (66%) and in the United Kingdom (69%) in nearly identical to that in the United States (69%), despite much less generous housing support in these countries. While US policies were initially intended to improve needy families' access to homeownership, they have been mostly beneficial to those who would have been able to own a house, even in the absence of support. In addition, in their present setting, housing tax reliefs induce significant distortions in investment incentives. Similarly, the government-sponsorship of mortgage enterprises, while not supportive of affordable housing, has distorted the incentives of these enterprises and poses financial risks. The following sections discuss these two policies and makes recommendations to re-establish neutral incentive structures.

Housing taxation

At present, four tax concessions are granted to homeowners who occupy their home: a) imputed rent is not taxed; b) mortgage interest payments are fully deductible; c) local real estate property taxes are also deductible; and d) capital gains are generally not taxable (Table 4.4). These tax expenditures come at a large cost to the federal budget: the President's Tax Reform Panel identifies incentives for homeownership as the second largest tax expenditure (after health deductions), with a total cost of over $700 billion during FY2006-2010. As shown in Table 4.5, tax expenditures on housing are estimated to be substantial, in particular for the income tax deductibility of mortgage interest payment.

These tax concessions do not by themselves make the tax system favourable to owner occupation. For this assessment to be made, it is necessary to evaluate jointly all the taxation of owner occupation, such as the taxation of owner-occupied imputed rent, the treatment of mortgage interest, the taxation of capital gains, local property taxation and indirect taxes. In the United States, this mainly requires assessing the effects on personal income taxation and local property taxation, as there is no VAT or sales tax on the value of properties. Under tax neutrality, the net income derived from owner occupation should be taxed in a similar way as other capital income, with net income from owner-occupation

Table 4.4. **Main characteristics of housing-related tax concessions**

Tax concessions	Conditions
Exclusion of net imputed rental income on owner-occupied homes	If a person owns a house and rents it out, this person must pay taxes on the rental income (net of expenses). The owner also pays a tax on any capital gain when the house is sold. If, instead, the owner lives in the house, the tax code does not require the owner to report the rental value of the home as gross income.
Deductibility of mortgage interest and property taxes on owner-occupied homes	The owner can deduct mortgage interest and property taxes from his or her other income in computing income tax liability for debt secured by a taxpayer's first or secondary residence on up to $1 million in acquisition debt as well as interest on as much as $100 000 in other loans (such as home-equity loans) that the owner has secured with the home, regardless of the loans' purposes.
Capital gains exclusion on home sales	Up to $250 000 ($500 000 for a married couple filing jointly) of capital gains on the sale of real property. The owner must have used the house as primary residence for two of the five years before the date of sale.

Source: Based on CBO (2007b).

Table 4.5. **Tax expenditures on housing**

Tax expenditure	Revenue loss estimate (billions $)	Revenue loss estimate as a percentage of GDP (%)
Exclusion of net imputed rental income on owner-occupied homes	24.6	0.2
Deductibility of mortgage interest on owner-occupied homes	61.5	0.5
Deductibility of state and local property taxes on owner-occupied homes	19.9[1]	0.2
Capital gains exclusion on home sales	29.7	0.2

1. Estimates from the Department of the Treasury.
Source: GAO (2005).

defined as the difference between gross income (imputed rent plus any change in the value of the dwelling) and costs to obtain this income.

The deduction of mortgage interest, being a cost required to obtain an income, is normal under a neutral tax system, provided that the (imputed) income is taxed. As noted below, property tax rates, which are internationally high in the United States, could be considered a form of imputed rent taxation. Assuming that the income derived from a house reflects the user cost of capital (property value x interest rate), the average property tax rate of 1.7% would imply a taxation of about 27% with an interest rate of 6.1%. A two-earner family with an average income (combined income of $65 000), with $100 000 to invest either in government bond or in a larger house would face the following tax consequences: if the money is used to acquire taxable bonds earning 6% annually, taxes are increased by $1 500 (100 000 * 6% * 25%); if the money is used to purchase a larger house, property local taxes are increased by $1 700 ($100 000 * 1.7%) and federal income taxes are decreased by $425 ($1 700 * 25%), with net increased taxes of $1 275. In this example, the deductibility of mortgage interest and local property taxes from federal taxes results in a tax system that favours investment in housing over other investments. In other cases, such as in municipalities where property taxes are higher than the national average, these aspects of the tax system might not favour home ownership. On average, the tax exemption of capital gains on owner-occupied houses deviates from tax neutrality and favours investment in housing. It is important to note, however, that the US tax code also includes a variety of tax preferences for capital gains for investments other than housing.

As noted, in a neutral tax system (*i.e.* a tax system not distorting incentives), investment in housing would be treated the same way as financial investment (Box 4.1). It would make no difference, in terms of taxation, whether a person decides to invest in a

Box 4.1. **Neutral taxation of housing**

Although the main purpose of any tax is to raise revenues, the tax system is used in many countries to promote various socioeconomic objectives. Tax expenditures are commonly used to reach such goals through the allowance of income deductions, tax credits, special low rates and other special reliefs affecting incentives.

In the case of housing, the income deductibility of mortgage interest is frequently combined with tax relief typically granted when taxing the return from investment: capital gains on owner-occupied homes can be left untaxed, the income provided by the provision of housing services (imputed rent income) is often exempted, homes may not be subject to inheritance taxes, wealth taxes may apply to the value of the house, sales of new houses may be subject to value-added tax and local property taxes may apply to some or all of the value of the house. The United States is not the only OECD country to provide housing support through tax relief. As Table 4.6 shows, many governments provide a tax incentive on mortgage interest payments, although not all countries (Canada, Germany, France and the United Kingdom are notable exceptions).

The combination of various tax advantages makes the task of assessing the overall impact of the tax system on housing investment a complex undertaking (Wood, 1990). This complexity is enhanced when low-income taxpayers are not subject to income taxes and therefore do not receive the benefits from income deductions; likewise, complexity is increased in the US case by the fact that families in lower tax brackets generally take a standard deduction, rather than itemise their allowances, and thus do not directly feel the effects of the tax relief.

Starting from the principle that tax systems should be neutral with respect to incentives, how should housing be taxed? Considering that housing is an investment good, tax neutrality would imply that it be subject to the same taxation as a financial investment, *e.g.* purchasing bonds, so as to avoid distorting the incentive of investing in different assets. Investment in housing however implies lower tax revenue than investment in financial assets, due to the possible deduction of mortgage interest on debt-financed investments and the foregone tax revenue from bonds when undertaking equity-financed housing investments. In a neutral tax system, this lower tax revenue needs to be compensated by a taxation of the housing consumption and capital gain tax bases. For owner-occupied houses, neutral taxation can be obtained using various combinations of taxes on property values, imputed rent income or capital gains. Tax neutrality results from a symmetrical tax treatment of income and interest expenditure. This implies that the taxation of capital income (imputed rent) be accompanied by the deduction of mortgage interest. One of two models can be used to tax owner-occupied imputed rental income: i) Imposing a recurrent taxation on imputed rent (based on the real interest rate) and on accrued capital gains (based on housing price inflation); and ii) imposing a recurrent taxation on the imputed rent that corresponds to the nominal interest rate, instead of operating with a separate taxation of the housing consumption and the housing capital gains. Alternatively, neutrality can be obtained by replacing the imputed rent with property value taxation. In a tax system with progressive taxation, neutrality requires a corresponding progressive taxation of property. This can be obtained by imposing progressive taxation of the imputed rent – similarly to the progressive taxation of interest income. However, the deductibility of the property tax results in a regressive net property tax. This is, of course, not consistent with neutrality (in a system with progressive taxation of capital income), nor with equality.

> ### Box 4.1. **Neutral taxation of housing** (cont.)
>
> The first-best tax treatment of owner-occupied housing would be to have a combination of taxes on property value, imputed rent or capital gains that come as close as possible to neutral taxation. Many OECD countries, however, have a taxation of housing that significantly deviates from neutrality. This seems to result from implementation problems likely to appear in introducing a neutral system, even though such problems are not insurmountable.

government bond or a house: the tax implications would be the same. Tax neutrality and the absence of distortions would be a first-best situation. In practice, however, there are many distortions in the US tax system, which have been granted over time under a variety of programmes. The aim of tax policy, in a second-best environment, is therefore to minimise, rather than eliminate, the distortions stemming from existing tax reliefs. There is a concern, for instance, that a significant number of households could perform tax arbitrage by cutting back on their mortgage repayments and increasing their contributions to retirement savings accounts (Amromin *et al.*, 2006).

Imputed rental income is not taxed in the United States, unlike in some other OECD countries (Table 4.6) – at least not directly. However, local real estate property taxes could be considered as a form of imputed rent taxation that would be calculated as a constant fraction of the assessed house value. At around 3% of GDP, the amount of revenue collected from property taxes in the United States is high by international comparison (Figure 4.5). Real estate property taxes represent the bulk of local government revenues (an important funding source for schools) and between 14% and 25% of total state and local own-source revenues in most states. It is calculated in a predictable manner, as a fixed fraction of the assessed house value, with few deductions to specific groups.[7] Property tax revenues per capita vary widely across states, reflecting variations in house values but also differences in tax rates. Prevailing tax rates are influenced by the nominal tax rates and by the fraction of the house that governments decide to subject to tax. The effective tax rate, which combines these two ratios, varies across localities, with a national unweighted average of 1.7%.

The deductions of interest payments and property taxes have also been criticised on the grounds of equity, because they disproportionately benefit households in upper-income brackets. According to estimates from the Tax Policy Center (2005), 54% of the mortgage and local tax deductions go to taxpayers with income exceeding $100 000 and 72% go to those whose income exceed $75 000. It is therefore not surprising that the increase in mortgage debt is heavily concentrated among upper income households. As noted, the income tax deductibility of mortgage interest payment is acceptable in a neutral tax system as long as owner-occupied imputed rental income is taxed: upper-income households tend to have larger houses, higher outstanding debts, larger property taxes (a form of imputed rent taxation) and it is logical that they can deduct more interest payments. The deduction of interest payments nonetheless disproportionately benefits high-income households because it is subject to progressive rates, while local property taxes use a flat tax rate. As well, the deduction of property taxes is subject to progressive tax rates, making it regressive. These deductions are often justified on the grounds that some form of housing support is useful in view of existing externalities (Box 4.2), notably among lower-income families. However, tax relief is targeted toward high-income households and are therefore unlikely to improve socioeconomic outcomes for low-income families.

Table 4.6. **Taxation of residential property**

	Imputed rental income taxed	Tax relief on mortgages		Capital gains on housing assets taxable	Inheritance tax	Stamp duty
		Interest	Principal repayments			
Austria	N	Y (up to ceiling)	N	Y (if sold < 10 years)	Y	6%
Belgium	Y (with fixed deduction)	Y (up to imputed rental income)	Y (within limit)	Y (if sold < 5 years) POOD are exempt	Y	10%-12.5% (5%-6% for modest houses)
Canada	N	N	N	Y (on 50% of gains) POOD are exempt	N (but subject to capital gains tax)	n.a
Denmark	Y	Y	n.a.	POOD are exempt	Y	1.5% total trading costs 7.2%
Germany	N	N	N	Y (if sold < 10 years) POOD are exempt	Y (lower than for financial assets)	3.5%
Finland	N	Y (up to a ceiling)	n.a.	POOD exempt if sold > 2 years	Y	4% (first-time buyers exempt)
France	N	N	N	POOD are exempt	Y	2%-3%
Italy	N (for POOD)	Y (for POOD)	N	Y (50% for POOD)	Y (until 2001)	10% (3% for POOD)
Netherlands	Y	Y	N	N	Y (above tax free threshold)	6%
Norway	N	Y	N	Y (if sold < 10 years)	Y	2.5%
Spain	N (for POOD)	Y	Y	Y (exempt if reinvested)	Y	n.a.
Sweden	Y	Y	N	Y	N	1.5%-3%
Switzerland	Y	Y (up to total property income + fixed amount)	N	Y (cantonal only) POOD are exempt	Y (cantonal only)	n.a.
United Kingdom	N	N	N	POOD are exempt	Y	1%, 2% or 4% (depends on house value)
United States	N	Y (up to ceiling)	N	Y (until 2002) (deduction for POOD if held > 2 years)	Y (to be phased out)	n.a

Note: PPO = principal owner-occupied dwellings.

Source: Catte et al. (2004), ECB (2003), Contact group (2002), European tax handbook (2002).

Figure 4.5. **Tax revenue from property taxes**
As a percentage of GDP, 2005[1]

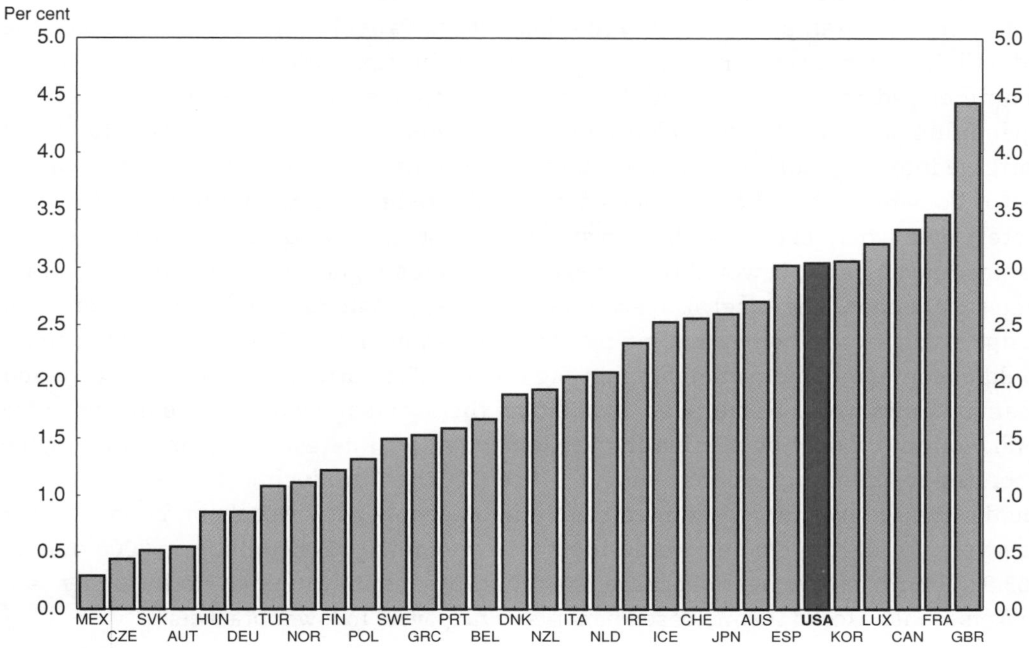

1. 2004 for Australia, Greece, Mexico, Poland and Portugal.
Source: OECD, *Revenue Statistics*, 2006.

StatLink ⛓ *http://dx.doi.org/10.1787/010178588437*

Box 4.2. **Externalities from housing support**

Proponents of policies promoting homeownership claim that there are socioeconomic benefits stemming from promoting homeownership. First, homeowners have an interest in making their community attractive to outsiders and therefore are likely to contribute to the production of public goods. This is for instance the case for schools: homeowners have an interest to contribute to the quality of schooling; several researchers find that children are more likely to graduate from college if their parents are homeowners, after controlling for other determinants. By contrast, renters have no financial stake in strengthening the local community and may even be interested to see the community stagnate and their rents decline. A policy resulting in positive externalities would therefore be to make it possible for households facing borrowing-constraints to access to homeownership. On the other hand, there are negative externalities from excessive investment in housing: this includes urban sprawl, migration of upper-income families to suburbs and depressed inner cities. Investment in secondary houses, which stay empty most of the time, also can create negative externalities. Overall, there appears to be some justification for limited, well-targeted housing support.

In a first-best system, there would be a neutral taxation of owner-occupied housing and any form of support to homeownership would be targeted, explicit and transparent. This first-best solution would require removing the deductibility of property taxes, harmonising the existing system of property taxation to reflect income from housing services and making housing capital gains subject to taxes. A second-best, more politically acceptable system would seek to reduce existing distortions with a combination of taxes and deductions that raise the overall level of taxes closer to that of a typical capital investment. For example, the President's Tax Reform Panel has suggested to reduce the deductibility of mortgage interest expense from the taxable income base. The Panel recommended that the existing deduction be replaced with a better targeted tax expenditure, a tax credit available to all homeowners, which would be equal to 15% of mortgage interest paid, but limited to the amount of the tax credit based on the average cost of housing within the taxpayer's area. A tax credit proportional to the amount of interest paid would benefit all homeowners, not just those who itemise; capped by the average housing cost, it would be less skewed towards higher income than the current interest deduction. The Panel also recommended to eliminate the deduction of interest on mortgages on second homes and interest on home-equity loans. Thus, the new tax credit would encourage home ownership, not big homes. The current subsidy for luxury and vacation homes would be curtailed. In addition, the tax credit would reduce the incentive to take out more debt by eliminating the deduction for interest on home equity loans. According to the Congressional Budget Office (2007b), introducing this reform in 2008 would increase taxes for an estimated 28.6 million people but lower them for some other taxpayers. In all, the change would increase revenues by $21.7 billion in 2008 and by $165.9 billion over five years because the reduced benefits to taxpayers in higher rate brackets would exceed the increased benefits to taxpayers in lower brackets.[8]

There has been reluctance to remove interest deductibility for fear that this would hurt the housing market. While the effect of tightening the deductibility of interest payment on the level of residential investment is uncertain, it would probably have a negative impact on prices, inasmuch as the tax advantage is capitalised in property values. Hence, it would be prudent to phase in gradually the reduction in the tax concession. Other countries have successfully downsized or dismantled their tax subsidies to mortgage loans, in many instances without damage to their housing markets (Box 4.3).

Government sponsorship of mortgage enterprises

US governments have repeatedly intervened in the mortgage market to encourage its good functioning, structure its operations, reduce transaction costs and facilitate securitisation – with the explicit goal of promoting homeownership (Green and Wachter, 2005). Another important policy measure to structure the US mortgage market was the establishment of two government-sponsored enterprises (GSEs), Fannie Mae and Freddie Mac (Box 4.4). These two institutions securitise pools of mortgages, thereby assuming their credit risk and allowing the resulting mortgage-backed securities (MBS) to trade as effectively AAA-rated securities. By standing ready to buy complying mortgages, they have diversified the funding sources of commercial banks and other mortgage originators. Also, by developing a secondary mortgage market, they have created a vast asset-backed securities market, which has contributed to the transfer of interest-rate risk from highly-leveraged originators of credit (banks and thrifts) to less-leveraged investors, notably insurance companies, pension funds and mutual funds. The policy intention is therefore to provide a direct financial channel between housing credit and capital markets, rather than have mortgage loans being financed by bank deposits.

Box 4.3. Tax subsidies for households with mortgage loans

In the following countries a reduction in tax deductibility of mortgage loan repayments has been implemented:

● Sweden reduced the tax deductibility of mortgage interest payments over a period of time (1985-91). The maximum deductible rate declined from 50% in 1985 to 30% in 1991.

● The United Kingdom fully phased out the tax deductibility of mortgage interest payments over the course of 25 years (1974-99). First, a nominal ceiling was introduced on the size of mortgages eligible for interest deductibility. Second, the rate at which interest on debt below the ceiling could be deducted was gradually lowered to zero.

● In Denmark, the tax value of interest deductibility was reduced in several steps during the 1980s and 1990s. As the marginal tax rates for capital income were reduced from 48-73% in 1986 to 33% from 2001 onwards, this reduces the tax value of deductible interest payments.

● In the Netherlands several steps have been taken to limit mortgage interest deductibility when owner-occupiers withdraw housing equity: since 1997, they have not been permitted to claim interest deductions on equity withdrawals from their existing residence except for home improvements; since 2001, the period during which mortgage interest payments could be deducted from personal income has been limited to 30 years and, more importantly, a cut in tax rates has effectively lowered tax subsidies for high income earners by about 20%; and, from the beginning of 2004, owner occupiers can only deduct interest on that part of the mortgage that is equal to the home's value minus the equity withdrawal from the former home.

● In France, the tax credit equal to 25% of mortgage interest payments, conditional on being the principal residence and only for the first five years after the purchase, was abolished in 1997.

Box 4.4. Benefits granted to government-sponsored enterprises

Fannie Mae and Freddie Mac are considered as government-sponsored enterprises because they follow charters granted by an act of Congress. They must serve public purposes, including contributing to stability in the secondary market for residential mortgages. For this purpose, they receive several benefits. They are exempt from state and local income taxes, exempt from the Securities and Exchange Commission's registration requirements and fees, and may use the Federal Reserve as their fiscal agent. In addition, the US Treasury is authorised to lend $2.25 billion to both Fannie Mae and Freddie Mac. GSE debt is eligible for use as collateral for public deposits, for unlimited investment by federally chartered banks and thrifts, and for purchase by the Federal Reserve in open-market operations. GSE securities are explicitly government securities under the Securities Exchange Act of 1934 and are exempt from the provisions of many state investor protection laws. Those advantages have not been granted to any other shareholder-owned companies.

The GSEs issue corporate debt to finance their purchases of mortgages and create mortgage-backed securities; increasingly, they have also issued debt to invest in large, highly-leveraged portfolios of financial assets, mostly in the form of their own mortgage – backed securities (MBS). Although GSE debt is not explicitly backed by the US government, investors worldwide have concluded that the government will not allow GSEs to default (Greenspan, 2005). Debt instruments issued by these enterprises and the MBS guaranteed by them are therefore perceived to be more secure than those issued by comparable institutions that do not operate under a federal charter (Quigley, 2006). The implicit guarantee has been interpreted as a subsidy to the GSEs, which various authors have measured based on the yield difference between the new debt issued by GSEs and that of other participants in the banking and finance industry. The estimated advantage is calculated to be 27-29 basis points over AA-rated banks and 37-46 basis points over AA-rated firms, close to the estimate of 41 basis points used by the CBO (2001) in estimating the annual federal subsidy to the GSEs and to the 40 basis points estimated by staff at the Federal Reserve Board.

Various views have been expressed regarding the benefits to homeowners from GSE operations. The most recent empirical research suggests that these benefits are small, if not negligible. The subsidy derived from the implicit guarantee could in principle flow on to mortgage borrowers. The structure of the mortgage market, however, notably its imperfect competition, means that the subsidy mostly accrues to the shareholders of the GSEs and the owners of financial institutions originating the mortgage loans, with management and other employees sharing the rents. A recent study using a reduced-form vector auto-regression model suggests that GSE portfolio purchases have essentially no short- or long-run effects on either primary or secondary mortgage rate spreads (Lehnert *et al.* 2006). An explanation of the absence of link between GSE operations and mortgage rates is that the latter are set in worldwide capital markets, like other highly-rated debts; henceforth, the operations of US agencies cannot influence mortgage rates.

Even if GSE operations had a small downward effect on mortgage rates, this would be unlikely to have a visible impact on the rate of homeownership. A survey of existing simulation studies finds that a reduction in mortgage rates by 2 percentage points increases the percentage of homeowners by only 0.5 percentage points (Eggers, 2005). Hence, a reduction in the mortgage rate of 7 basis points, as Passmore *et al.* (2005) estimate is the effect of GSEs, would raise the homeownership rate by 0.0175 percentage points, which seems negligible. A small effect of interest rates on homeownership is consistent with evidence that first-time home buyers tend to be liquidity-constrained and face difficulties in making a downpayment, rather than periodic loan reimbursements. The types of assessment criteria used by lenders (tenure in job of the borrower, amounts of assets, existing debts, loan-to-value ratio, debt-to-income ratio) appears to be a more important determinant of homeownership than the interest rate.

At the end of 2004, GSE-issued MBS totaled nearly $2.7 trillion, or nearly 35% of outstanding home mortgage debt. At the same time, GSE portfolios totaled over $1.5 trillion, or more than 20% of total mortgage debt. The extensive portfolio holdings of the institutions, mostly for commercial purposes, has little rationale for public policy. Such holdings, which are not entirely hedged, however pose risks for the financial system and result in a large contingent liability for the federal government (Bernanke, 2007).

It would therefore be prudent to reform the policies governing the GSEs. Because a repudiation of the implicit guarantee of GSE debt might be politically difficult, other actions would be important. For instance, the GSEs could be charged for the insurance provided by the government sponsorship, although this would make the guarantee more explicit, with possible new distortions (such as moral hazard). Thus, it might make sense to limit the coverage of GSE actions to first-time home buyers (about one-third of transactions), who are younger and more risky and therefore have greater difficult getting access to credit. The GSEs could take advantage of the financial benefits resulting from the implicit government guarantee to facilitate access to homeownership for these young homebuyers, by passing on some of the subsidy that they receive as a result of their special statute.

Following accounting problems at Fannie Mae and Freddie Mac in 2003-04, the Administration stepped up its supervision and investigation of the two GSEs, while Congress pursued the discussion of new legislation. The legislative issue at stake is the replacement of the current regulator (the Office of Federal Housing Enterprise Oversight in the Department of Housing and Urban Development) by a new regulatory agency responsible for the safety, soundness and mission regulation of these enterprises. In view of their rapid growth and systemic importance, their regulation and supervision needs to be tightened. The GSEs need a regulator with authority on a par with that of banking regulators, with a free hand to set appropriate capital standards, and with a clear and credible process for placing GSEs in receivership, should it be needed. The Administration has made proposals to this end, including relocating the regulatory authority with a new independent regulator.

As argued in OECD (2004), reforms should go beyond that by eliminating the GSEs' special status. Withdrawing government sponsorship would most likely raise the GSE borrowing cost but, as discussed, this would be too small to have a visible impact on homeownership. The Administration should also review the law treating GSE debt as government securities, including its eligibility for the Federal Reserve's open-market operations, so as to avoid sending signals to market participants about the special status of such debt. In addition, legislation should limit the size of GSE portfolios; without such action, investors may still perceive GSEs as being instruments of the government and consider their debt to be equivalent to government debt (Greenspan, 2005). Limits could be placed on the growth of their mortgage-related asset portfolios, so that mortgage-backed securities traded in public markets, and not GSE debt, become the dominant source of secondary-market funding for mortgages. Limiting the GSEs' holding to affordable housing assets would be a way to limit the growth of the portfolios; this would be consistent with the public purpose of these companies (Bernanke, 2007).

Conclusion

The rise in household indebtedness since the early-1990s has been unprecedented in many respects. This reflects a combination of interconnected factors including low real interest rates, robust growth, financial innovation and the market entry of subprime lenders. The risks linked to the debt run-up are notable, but should not be exaggerated. US policies have traditionally encouraged debt-financed access to homeownership. The tradition of exempting housing from a variety of taxes has encouraged investment into housing, especially among high-income families, without clearly promoting homeownership among needy families. The large portfolio of investments made by the two GSEs pose a risk to financial stability and to the taxpayer. Reforming these two policies would eliminate existing distortions and would not be detrimental to socio-economic objectives; there are even ways, as recommended in Box 4.5, to refocus government policies on promoting affordable housing.

Box 4.5. **Policy recommendations on household debt**

Reduce the disparity between the very low taxation of residential and other types of investment:

- Replace the interest tax deduction, which mostly benefits upper income households with little constraint to access homeownership, by a tax credit available to all homeowners, with a maximum amount reflecting the average cost of housing.

- Eliminate the interest deductibility on home equity loans and on second homes.

- Increase the minimum occupancy of the primary residence required to benefit from capital gains exemption from the current period of two out of five years.

- Adopt pending legislation on government-sponsored enterprises (GSEs).

- Limit the coverage of GSE actions to mortgages loans contracted by first-time home buyers. Other activities should be market-based, with official guarantee explicitly denied.

- Provide for the creation of a new, independent regulator in charge of the oversight of GSEs.

- Limit the holdings of mortgage-based securities assets by GSEs.

- Review the law considering GSE debt as government securities.

Notes

1. Cutts and Van Order, 2005.

2. Home equity withdrawal is defined by Federal Reserve researchers as "the discretionary initiatives of homeowners to convert equity in their homes into cash by borrowing in the home mortgage market".

3. The calculation used here (difference between the change in mortgage debt and residential investment) is an approximation of equity extraction. This estimate comes close to, without totally equalling, the calculations of Greenspan and Kennedy (2005). Some researchers prefer to focus on "active equity extraction", which only covers equity-withdrawers who stay in their homes.

4. Based on the OFHEO index of prices on repeat sales. Although no annual declines have been observed in nominal terms, there have been declines in real terms.

5. Based on data from the Mortgage Bankers Association, which track a sample of about 43 million loans of conventional, FHA and VA mortgages. No disaggregate figure is available for non-traditional loans.

6. During the period 1994-2005, the US ratio of household liabilities to personal disposable income increased by 3½ percentage points annually on average; by contrast, the increase was limited to about 2 percentage points in Canada and Italy and to about 1 percentage point or less in France, Germany and Japan. Only in the United Kingdom was the debt run-up faster than in the United States (among G7 countries).

7. For instance, the so-called homestead deduction exempts a specified proportion of the house value from property taxes, based on age or disability.

8. The Congressional Budget Office also notes that another advantage of limiting mortgage interest deduction is that it would discourage taxpayers from borrowing against their homes to fund tax-favoured retirement. That practice takes advantage of tax savings on both transactions and thus provides an incentive for people to pay down their mortgage debt more slowly and contribute more to retirement accounts than they would if mortgage interests were not deductible. Such transactions reduce tax revenue without increasing net saving.

Bibliography

Amromin, G., J. Huang and C. Sialm (2006), *The Tradeoff Between Mortgage Prepayments and Tax-Deferred Retirement Savings*, NBER Working Paper No. 12502, Cambridge, MA.

Bernanke, B.S. (2007), *GSE Portfolios, Systemic Risk, and Affordable Housing*, Remarks before the independent community bankers of America's annual convention and teachworld, Honolulu, Hawaï (*via* satellite), 6 March 2007.

Bies, S.S. (2006), "A Supervisor's Perspective on Mortgage Markets and Mortgage Lending Practices", Remarks at the mortgage bankers association presidents conference, 14 June.

Campbell, J.Y. and J.F. Cocco (2003), *Household Risk Management And Optimal Mortgage Choice*, NBER Working Paper No. 9759, Cambridge, MA.

Catte, P., N. Girouard, R. Price and C. André (2004), "The Contribution of Housing Markets to Cyclical Resilience", *OECD Economic Studies* No. 38, 2004/1.

Congressional Budget Office (2001), "Federal Subsidies and the Housing GSEs", CBO, Washington DC.

Congressional Budget Office (2007a), "Housing Wealth and Consumer Spending", CBO Background Paper, Washington DC.

Congressional Budget Office (2007b), *Budget Options*, Washington DC.

Contact Group on Asset Prices (2002), "Turbulence in Asset Markets: the Role of Micro Policies", Bank for International Settlements, Basle, September.

Cutts, A.C. and R.A. van Order (2005), "On the Economics of Subprime Lending", *The Journal of Real Estate Finance and Economics*, 30:2.

Diamond, D.B. and M.J. Lea (1992), "Housing Finance in Developed Countries: An International Comparison of Efficiency", *Journal of Housing Research*, Vol. 3, Fannie Mae, Washington.

Eggers, F.J. (2005), "Homeownership Gains During the 1990s: Composition Effects and Rate Effects", *Study prepared for US Department of Housing and Urban Development*.

European Central Bank (2003), "Structural Factors in the EU Housing Markets", March.

European Central Bank (2005), "Inter-Regional Comparison of Mortgage Rates in the Euro Area and in the United States", *Annual Report 2005*, Box 11, pp. 127-128.

Federal Reserve Board of Governors (2006), "Recent Changes in US Family Finances: Evidence from the 2001 and 2004 Survey of Consumer Finances", Board of Governors of the Federal Reserve System, Washington DC.

Federal Reserve Board of Governors (2007), *Monetary Policy Report to the Congress*, Board of Governors of the Federal Reserve System, February, Washington DC.

Feldman, R. (2001), "Mortgage Rates, Homeownership Rates and Government-Sponsored Enterprises", *Federal Reserve Bank of Minneapolis Annual Report*.

Girouard, N., M. Kennedy and C. André (2006), "Has the Rise in Debt Made Households More Vulnerable?", *OECD Economics Department Working Papers*, No. 535.

Government Accountability Office (2005), Government Performance and Accountability, Tax expenditure represent a substantial government commitment and need to be re-examined, Washington DC.

Green, R.K. and S.M. Wachter (2005), "The American Mortgage in Historical and International Context", *Journal of Economic Perspectives*, Vol. 19, No. 4, Fall.

Greenspan, A. (2005), "Government-Sponsored Enterprises", Remarks to the conference on housing, mortgage finance and the macro-economy, Federal Reserve Bank of Atlanta, Georgia.

Greenspan, A. and J. Kennedy (2005), "Estimates of Home Mortgage Originations, Repayments, and Debt On One-to-Four-Family Residences", *Finance and Economics Discussion Series Paper* 2005-41, Washington DC.

International Bureau Of Fiscal Documentation (IBFD) (2002), *European Tax Handbook*, 13th annual edition, Amsterdam.

Klyuev V. and P. Mills (2006), "Is Housing Wealth an 'ATM'? The Relationship Between Household Wealth, Home Equity Withdrawal and Savings Rates", *IMF Working Paper* WP/06/162, June, Washington DC.

Lehnert A., W. Passmore and S.M. Sherlund (2006), "GSEs, Mortgage Rates, and Secondary Market Activities", *Finance and Economics Discussion Series* 2006-30, Federal Reserve Board, Washington DC.

Mercer Oliver Wyman (2005), The US Residential Real Estate Market: Economics and Outlook, Report, April.

OECD (2004), *OECD Economic Surveys: United States*, Vol. 2004, Issue 7.

Passmore, W., S.M. Sherlund and G. Burgess (2005), The Effect of Housing Government-Sponsored Enterprises on Mortgage Rates, *Real Estate Economics* 33(3), 427-463.

President's Advisory Panel on Federal Tax Reform (2006), *Simple, Fair, and Pro-Growth: Proposals to Fix America's Tax System,* Report of the Panel, Washington DC.

Quigley, J.M. (2006), "Federal Credit and Insurance Programs: Housing", *Review,* July/August 2006, Federal Reserve Bank of St. Louis.

Urban-Brookings Tax Policy Center (2005), How to better encourage homeownership, *Tax Policy Issues and Options*, No. 12, June.

Wood, G.A. (1990), "The tax treatment of housing: economic issues and reform measures", *Urban studies*, Vol. 27, No. 6.

ISBN 978-92-64-03271-2
OECD Economic Surveys: United States
© OECD 2007

Chapter 5

Improving primary and secondary education

The average educational attainment of US students is weak by international comparison. For example, mean results of PISA test scores are below the OECD average. This is despite substantial resources devoted to the schooling system. One partial explanation for this is that academic standards, curriculum and examinations are not sufficiently challenging in most US states. In 2001, Congress enacted the No Child Left Behind Act (NCLB) to raise achievement levels, especially of certain groups that perform badly. The Act requires states to establish clear content standards as to what students should know, to regularly assess performance and to set thresholds for adequate yearly progress; it also requires schools where students are failing to meet such thresholds to improve or close, while enhancing options for parents of children in such schools to place their children elsewhere. The law appears to be well conceived, addressing key problems in a sensible manner. Preliminary indications are consistent with it raising school performance and closing achievement gaps. The NCLB legislation should therefore be reauthorised. Moreover, the NCLB framework of standards, assessment and accountability should be extended through upper secondary education. That said, there are a number of areas in which improvements could be made. Though the federal government cannot set standards, it could strengthen incentives for more states to make their standards more challenging. As well, the federal government should help states and districts to better test student achievement and assess progress.

A centrepiece of the Administration's domestic policy agenda is the No Child Left Behind Act. Against a background of disappointing education performance, the act aims to raise standards and hold schools accountable for results. Specifically, it calls for nationwide annual testing in grades 3 to 8, greater accountability requirements (while preserving local control), and increased parental choice if schools are failing. This chapter discusses the background, implementation and effects of these measures, with a focus on standards. Given space limitations, the treatment is selective. Important policy issues such as teacher quality and school choice are not discussed.

Dimensions of the problem

Determining what school students can and should learn is difficult. Accordingly, international comparisons provide a useful and interesting benchmark. Unfortunately, the performance of US students in international tests is not especially good. For example, the 2003 Programme for International Student Assessment (PISA) tested 15-year olds in four broad areas. (In the United States, most 15-year olds are in 10th Grade). As shown in Figure 5.1, US students performed near the OECD average in reading and below the average in science, mathematics, and problem solving. These results are disappointing given that many Americans expect their school students to outperform those of other countries. This expectation seems a reasonable one, considering the stellar performance of the United States in other educational fields and the many advantages US students enjoy (discussed below).

Other international comparisons show similar results. Table 5.1 reports the rank of US students relative to other OECD countries, as measured by PISA, the Progress in International Reading Literacy Study (PIRLS) and the Trends in International Mathematics and Science Study (TIMSS). For comparability and simplicity, the table restricts the sample to OECD countries. So the often-superior performance of the United States relative to many poor non-OECD countries is not reflected, but neither is the inferior performance relative to Singapore, Hong Kong and Chinese Taipei. The relative US performance is not as disappointing in TIMSS and PIRLS as in PISA, yet a common finding is that US students fall below international best-practice. In most studies, the US performance varies between middling and poor.[1] These results are also in line with international comparisons of adults. The Adult Literacy and Lifeskills (ALL) Survey assessed the literacy and numeracy skills of 16-65 year olds in six countries in 2003. US participants did worse than those from Norway, Bermuda, Switzerland and Canada, but better than Italy (OECD, 2005).

This unimpressive performance is not new. PISA results for 2000, TIMSS results for 1995 and 1999, as well as earlier, less representative, results from the International Assessment of Educational Progress also showed qualitatively similar results. Hanushek (1998, Chart 1) shows a series of international comparisons from 1963 to 1991. In five of the six tests the United States lies below the mean. What is new is that this under-performance in terms of quality is no longer being masked by the superior performance in

Figure 5.1. **The US performance in international tests is unimpressive**[1]

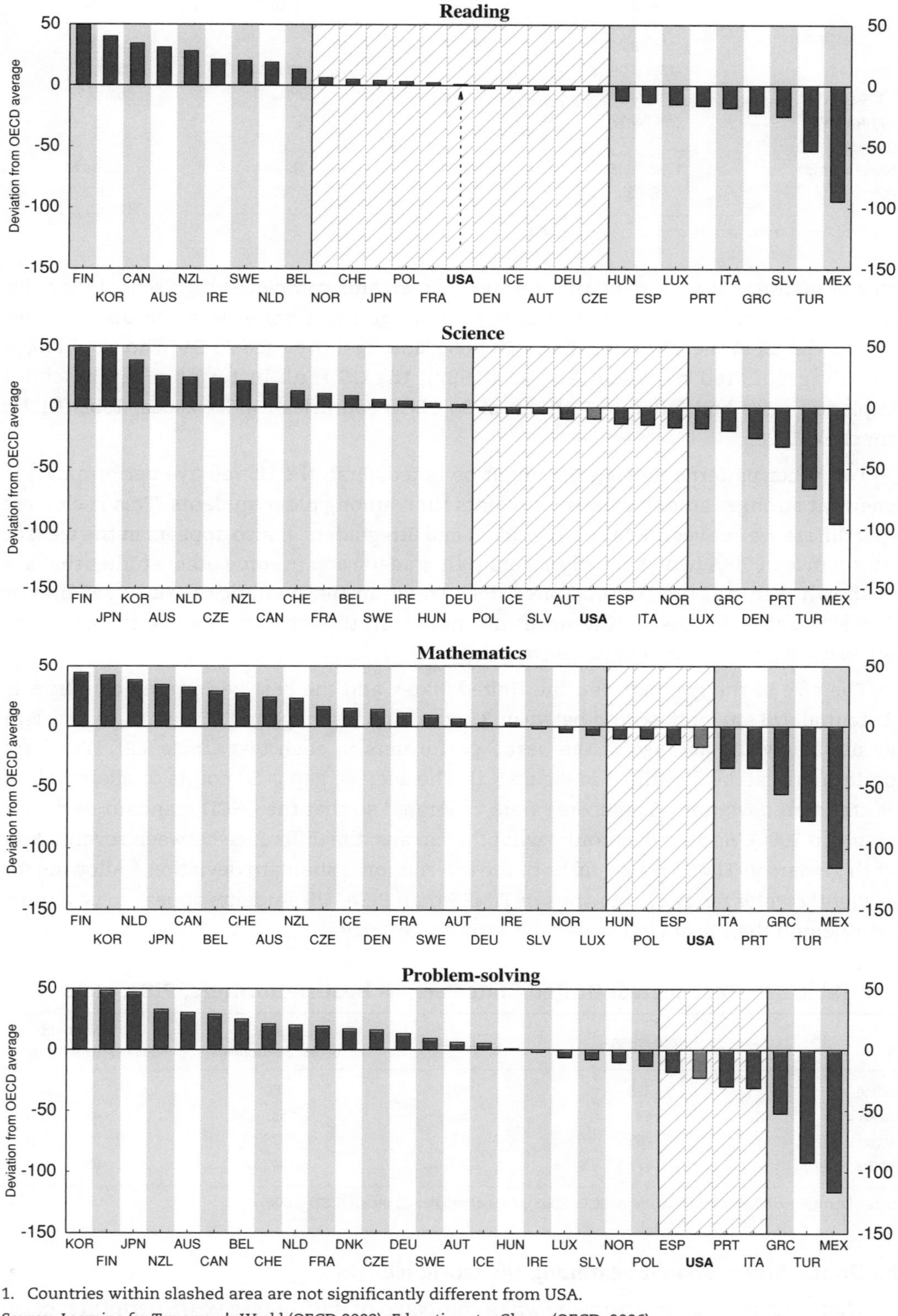

1. Countries within slashed area are not significantly different from USA.

Source: Learning for Tomorrow's World (OECD 2003), *Education at a Glance* (OECD, 2006).

StatLink ᴍᴸ http://dx.doi.org/10.1787//010181740022

Table 5.1. **International comparisons of student performance**

Rank of US students relative to other OECD countries

	PISA	PIRLS	TIMSS	TIMSS
Reading	15th of 29	6th of 17		
Science	18th of 29		3rd of 11	5th of 13
Mathematics	24th of 29		6th of 11	8th of 13
Problem solving	24th of 29			
Memo items:				
Students tested	15-year-olds	Grade 4	Grade 4	Grade 8
Date	2003	2001	2003	2003

Source: Adapted from Lemke and Gonzales (2006).

terms of quantity. It used to be that far more Americans completed high school than did their counterparts in other countries. But other countries began to catch up with and overtake the US in the 1970s and 1980s. By 2004, among those aged 25-34 (who would have typically graduated between 1988 and 1997), the US rank in terms of high-school completion rates had fallen to 11th out of 30 OECD countries (OECD, 2006a, Table A1.2a; Hanushek, 1998).

Two other patterns in Table 5.1 might be noted. First, the US relative performance is somewhat stronger among younger students than among older students. This is clearest in the difference between TIMSS 4th graders and 8th graders. It also appears in the weaker performance in PISA (which mostly covers 10th graders) and in some other studies that are not shown. Second, the United States does worse in mathematics than in reading or science. Reasons for these differences are not clear, though they may be important to diagnosing why the United States disappoints.

The size of the gap between the United States and the best performing countries is substantial. US students scored between 35 points (in reading) and 65 points (in problem solving) below the average of the best 5 performers in each test (Table 5.2). (The best 5 performers can be identified in Figure 5.1). The average gap is 50 points or about half of one standard deviation. (Test scores were calibrated so that the OECD standard deviation was 100 in 2000). As an indication of what this means, the difference between seventh and eighth graders in TIMSS is two-fifths of the international standard deviation.[2] Allowing for the slightly wider range of countries in TIMSS than PISA, US students appear to be almost a year behind their peers in the best-performing countries.

Table 5.2. **Test scores: United States *versus* best-performers, PISA 2003**

	US mean	OECD average	Average of best 5 performers	Gap between US and best performers
Reading	495	494	530	35
Science	491	500	537	46
Mathematics	483	500	538	55
Problem Solving	477	500	542	65

Source: *Learning for Tomorrow's World* (OECD, 2003), *Education at a Glance* (OECD, 2006).

The United States should be among the world leaders

These test results are surprising when compared to the impressive US performance on many other social and economic indicators. In particular, the performance of

US universities, noted in the following chapter, suggests that education is something Americans can do exceptionally well. Consistent with this, the United States has a highly skilled workforce (whether measured by wages or credentials) and it leads the world in many technologically-advanced industries.

The test results are all the more puzzling in view of the advantages US school students enjoy. On average, and relative to other OECD countries, US students come from well-educated, wealthy families and they go to schools that are unusually well-financed. Given any of these factors, US students might be expected to be among the world leaders. But no. Figure 5.2 compares PISA test scores with GDP per capita, educational attainment of 35-54 year olds (a proxy for parental education) and cumulative spending per student from the age of 6 through age 15.

The strength of these relationships has been the subject of substantial research. In general, this suggests that income and parental education are strongly correlated with educational performance, whereas spending is not. But for present purposes, the key point is how badly US students do, relative to their resources. In each of the three panels, the United States is one of the largest negative outliers. If one believes that inputs should bear some relationship to outputs, the US test results are a puzzle.

Inequality

It is widely believed that the variation in performance among US students is much greater than variation within other countries. That belief is consistent with results from some earlier international education comparisons and with other social and economic indicators. However, as shown in Table 5.3, it is not supported by the most recent data from PISA. The United States does have marginally more variation than many other OECD countries, but not strikingly so. The difference from the average within-country standard deviation is small – of the order of a few achievement points. Standard deviations within the United States are similar to those of the OECD as a whole.

Differences in dispersion within countries, such as those shown in Table 5.3, are small relative to differences in means (Table 5.2). Closely related to this, the lagging US performance can be seen at all levels of achievement. For example, in mathematics US students at the top 5th percentile scored below students at the 5th percentile in 22 out of 29 other OECD countries – about the same ranking as for other percentiles and the mean (*Learning For Tomorrow's World*, Table 2.5c). This contradicts the popular view that the disappointing results of US students reflects a high-performing elite being dragged down by a long tail. Rather, top US students are outperformed just like average and struggling US students.

As another way of showing this, Figure 5.3 shows the distribution of students at each level of proficiency for the United States, the OECD average and the average of the 5 best-performing OECD countries in each subject. The right hand side of the top panel, for example, indicates that only 8% of US 15-year-olds performed at the highest level of proficiency in reading. This was about the same as the OECD average. In contrast, an average of 15% of 15-year-olds from Finland, Korea, Canada, Australia and New Zealand performed at this level. The United States does not just have a larger percentage of bad students – it also has a smaller percentage of good students.

It is sometimes suggested that the poor US performance reflects failings of disadvantaged inner-city schools, while more prosperous schools do relatively well. Again, this hypothesis does not seem consistent with the latest PISA results. The students tested

Figure 5.2. **US students should do better**

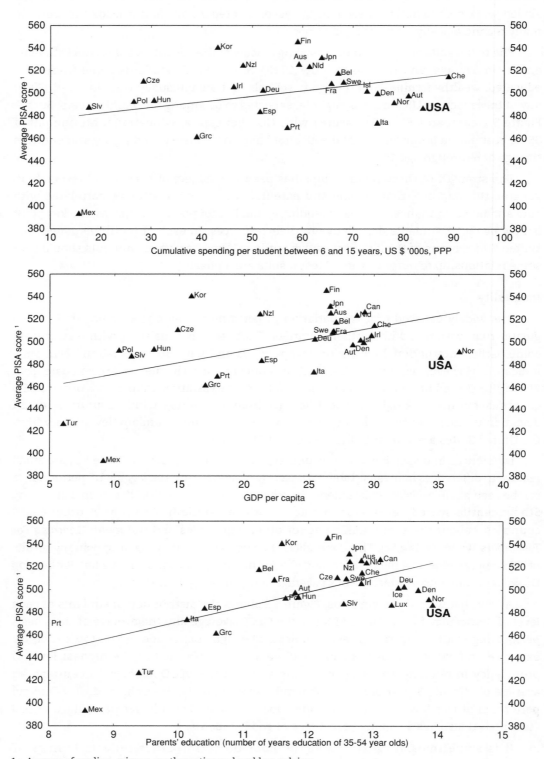

1. Average of reading, science, mathematics and problem solving.

Source: Learning for Tomorrow's World (OECD 2003), *Education at a Glance* (OECD, 2006).

StatLink ᐱ᎒ᏩᎤᓯ *http://dx.doi.org/10.1787/010186872080*

Table 5.3. **Dispersion of test results, PISA 2003**

	US standard deviation	Average within-country standard deviation	Rank of US standard deviation among 29 OECD countries
Reading	101	96	8th
Science	102	101	15th
Mathematics	95	94	10th
Problem solving	98	93	6th

1. the standard deviation of the whole OECD (with each country having equal weight) was set to 100 in 2000. This reflects both within-country variation (shown in the table) and between-country variation.
Source: OECD calculations based on *Learning for Tomorrow's World* (OECD 2003), *Education at a Glance* (OECD, 2006).

in PISA are asked about their parents' occupations, and these responses are mapped into an internationally comparable index of socioeconomic status. As shown in Table 5.4, when the mathematics performance of well-off US students is compared with that of well-off students in other countries, they lag in the same way as that of students from disadvantaged backgrounds. Measuring family background by parental education or number of books in the home gives essentially the same result (Hampden-Thompson and Johnston, 2006, Table 2). The relatively poor United States performance (for mathematics in PISA) is evident among all socio-economic groups.

Table 5.4. **Rank of US students in mathematics by parental occupation**

Socioeconomic background	Rank of US among 29 OECD countries
Bottom quarter	24
Second quarter	22
Third quarter	23
Top quarter	23
All	24

Source: Lemke (2004), p. 109.

Why do US school students perform below the international average?

It is not clear why US school outcomes are disappointing, relative to expectations. Part of the explanation is that academic standards in the United States appear to be lower than elsewhere. That is, less is asked of US students. Evidence on this comes from detailed comparisons of mathematics and science curricula as part of TIMSS (see for example, Schmidt *et al.* 1998, 2001, 2002). William Schmidt, the US TIMSS National Research Coordinator, summarises differences in mathematics curricula:

> By the middle grades the top achieving countries … begin the transition to the study of algebra, including linear equations and functions, geometry and even in some cases, basic trigonometry. By the end of eighth grade in these countries children have mostly completed US high school courses in algebra I and geometry. By contrast, most US students are destined to mostly continue the study of arithmetic. In fact, we estimate that at the end of eighth grade US students are some two or more years behind their counterparts around the world (Schmidt, 2003 p. 1).

Similarly, while US middle-school students are still focussed on basics of elementary science that are strong on description (for example, earth sciences), students in other countries are shifting to beginning concepts in chemistry and physics that are more analytical (Schmidt, Houng and Cogan, 2002, p. 3).

Figure 5.3. **Distribution of students by proficiency**

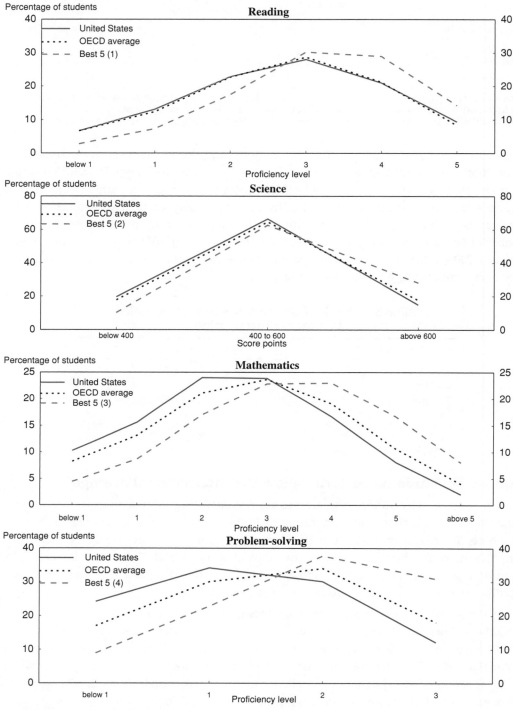

1. Australia, Canada, Finland, Korea, New Zealand.
2. Finland, Japan, Korea, New Zealand, Netherlands.
3. Belgium, Japan, Korea, Netherlands, Switzerland.
4. Belgium, Finland, Korea, Japan, New Zealand.

Source: Learning for Tomorrow's World (OECD 2003), *Education at a Glance* (OECD, 2006).

StatLink ᵐˢᴸ *http://dx.doi.org/10.1787/010382423056*

Consistent with this, students who move between countries report that US schools are easier. Loveless (2002) surveyed high school students from other countries who had recently studied in the United States. Eighty-five percent reported that US classes were easier while 11% thought US classes were harder. US students who had studied abroad agreed, though less emphatically. Fifty-six per cent thought US classes were easier while 30% thought they were harder. Apart from being interesting in itself, this suggests that the correlation between standards and performance is less likely to reflect reverse causation. One reason why standards are low in the United States may be that they have been lowered to accommodate low performance. But if that were all, one would expect to find students having difficulty with the material. Instead, they find it easier – suggesting that standards have been lowered by more than student ability warranted.

The astonishing self-confidence of US students also suggests standards are lax. Although they rank 24th out of 29 OECD countries in mathematics performance, US students more strongly agree with the statement "I get good grades in mathematics" than students from any other country. Similar self-confidence is reflected in their responses to statements "In my mathematics class, I understand even the most difficult work", "I learn mathematics quickly", "I have always believed that mathematics is one of my best subjects", and "I am just not good at mathematics". Although cultural differences may underlie these responses, one interpretation is that US students are being commended for work that would not be acceptable in other countries.

This matters, but perhaps in a different way to what is often thought. Contrary to widespread hopes that promotion of self-esteem and confidence will encourage learning, grade inflation seems to lower performance. The PISA index of self-confidence in mathematics (on which the United States ranks highest) is negatively and significantly correlated with mathematics performance across countries.[3] More persuasively, Figlio and Lucas (2004) track students through *longitudinal* data across different teachers. Their data set has observations on third, fourth and fifth graders in a large school district in Florida. Controlling for class-room composition and school and student fixed effects, they find that improvements in test results are about 20% greater in math and one-third greater in reading for students who are assigned to teachers who are tough graders.

In short, one reason why US students perform worse than their international counterparts seems to be that they are not being challenged. For teachers, principals, textbook authors and the like, some remedies for this are probably obvious. For policy makers, it is important to determine *why* standards are low.

The TIMSS research noted above (Schmidt *et al.* 1998, 2001, 2002) suggested that US students lag behind their peers overseas because of weaknesses in US curricula. Following detailed comparison of standards, textbooks, surveys of teachers and classroom observation in different countries, Schmidt and his colleagues concluded that US courses were "a mile wide and an inch deep". For example, whereas eighth-grade mathematics textbooks in Japan cover 10 topics in depth, US eighth-grade textbooks cover 30 topics superficially. (The correlation between textbook coverage and what teachers teach is about 0.95). A lack of focus promotes memorisation rather than depth of understanding. Either because of this, or because little sinks in, the content is reviewed in subsequent years. Whereas high-achieving countries often teach specific topics in mathematics in three consecutive years, they are typically taught over six years in the United States. Because of the time devoted to repetitive review, progress is slow.

These findings have been very influential. For example, the recently released guidelines by the National Council of Teachers of Mathematics (2006) propose clearer focus in mathematics curricula with more depth and less breadth. They emphasise the TIMSS research in motivating the changes. As a parallel development, many school districts have been adopting foreign curricula. For example, some 300 school systems in the United States have adopted "Singapore Math" (Hechinger, 2006) – Singapore being the highest ranked country in TIMSS. Educators have likewise been looking closely at how mathematics and science are taught in other high-performing countries, such as Finland and Taiwan.[4]

It may be that the problems of US curricula simply reflected poor information: educators may have been unaware that they could do better. If so, developments such as those noted in the previous paragraph are very encouraging. Or it may be that the problems are more fundamental. Schmidt *et al.* (1998) for example, attributed the breadth and consequent lack of depth to the decentralised nature of educational planning in the United States, which leads to curricula that attempt to keep everyone happy. In that case the appropriate policy remedy would presumably be increased centralisation of standards.

Another prominent explanation for the low standards of US schools relative to those overseas is the absence in the United States of Curriculum-Based External Exit Exams (CBEEEs). In other countries it is common for students to sit an exam at the end of high school that tests what they have learned – their success in this exam determines success in employment applications, what college they may attend, and what courses at college they may enrol in. Examples include the baccalauréat in France, and the GCSC and A-levels in Great Britain. Table 5.5 shows CBEEEs in mathematics and science across the OECD. Within the United States, New York State and North Carolina have general CBEEEs, and Advanced Placement courses fulfil similar functions for advanced students. Many US states have other exit exams but these need not be curriculum-based, nor external.

Table 5.5. **Curriculum-based external exit exams, OECD, 1997**

Both Mathematics and Science	Mathematics but not Science	In some states or provinces but not others	None
Czech Republic	France	Australia	Belgium
Denmark	Iceland	Canada	Greece
Hungary	Norway	Germany	Portugal
Ireland		Switzerland	Spain
Japan		**United States**	Sweden
Korea			
Netherlands			
New Zealand			
Slovak Republic			
United Kingdom			

Source: Bishop (1997, p. 261). Unfortunately, this reference is somewhat dated and does not provide information on other OECD members. OECD (2006a, Table XI.3) provides recent information on all OECD countries and Center on Education Policy (2006) describes differences across US states, but in neither case is the focus on exams that are curriculum-based and external.

Bishop (1997, 2006) and Fuchs and Woessman (2003) argue that CBEEEs raise performance in many ways. When testing is external, the performance of the school and teacher can be assessed, raising incentives. Students compete against their peers in other schools, so they have less incentive to discourage/disrupt their co-students. Students and parents will encourage teachers to set high rather than low standards. Curriculum-based tests require mastery of the subject matter taught. This is in contrast to aptitude tests like the SAT-I or ACT which are designed so as to be difficult to study for.

In simple cross-country regressions, the effect of CBEEEs is often large and statistically significant. For example, comparing PISA countries, Bishop (2006) found the existence of a CBEEE raised performance by 40 points in mathematics, 32 points in science and 25 points in reading.[5] Differences of that magnitude would be enough to raise the US performance to close to (though still below) the best performing countries (see Table 5.2, last column). Similar results have been found in TIMSS (at both country and micro level), PIRLS, across German Länder and across Canadian provinces. Students from New York State and North Carolina have been found to outperform students of the same ethnic and social background in other US states. Bishop (2006) provides a survey of this research. However, not all research is as positive. Perhaps the most thorough and sophisticated study is that of Fuchs and Woessman (2004). This used micro-level PISA data, controlling for student social background (something not possible in the other international studies) and found effects for mathematics and science that were half as large as Bishop's estimates (and only marginally significant) and an effect on reading scores that was close to zero (albeit positive).

Within the United States, there is a debate over whether high-school graduates should be required to pass an exam. Empirical research (see, for example, Center on Education Policy, 2006) has not found this requirement, of itself, to be especially advantageous. The international literature, in contrast, has focussed on exams that are curriculum-based and external, where the results are clearer. Overall, CBEEEs are strongly correlated with performance in a wide range of data sources. That said, there are still substantial uncertainties. For example, it is not clear that this effect is causal or robust to alternative specifications. Furthermore, some of the favourable effect of CBEEEs may come from their high stakes. In a decentralised economy like the United States, where the federal government cannot direct colleges or employers to use exam grades in their admission decisions, it is not clear that the success of CBEEEs could be easily transplanted.

In addition to the above references there have been many other assessments of international differences in education performance. For example, many policy advocates argue that international comparisons vindicate their particular policy positions, though formal evidence in support is typically weak. Multivariate analysis is at a stage that might be described as exploratory rather than conclusive. Three recent econometric investigations of PISA data (in addition to the research cited above on CBEEEs) include *Learning for Tomorrow's World* (OECD, 2003); Carey and Ernst (2006) and Willms (2006). However, none of these include the factors discussed above (low expectations, curriculum design, CBEEEs, etc) in their specifications. Nor do they examine other topical policy issues, such as teacher quality or school choice. These studies, like the work cited above on CBEEEs, and many other less formal international comparisons, do not compare their conclusions with those of others. Although there is strong agreement that some background factors matter (for example, income or parental education), this does not extend to policy instruments. Consistent with this, many academics attribute much of the variation to "culture" (shorthand for factors that we cannot identify or measure). In particular, we have very limited information on why the United States does so poorly. International comparisons indicate there is considerable scope for doing better, but do not provide precise guidelines. Nevertheless, they do support calls to raise standards, give curricula more focus and coherence, and place greater emphasis on curriculum-based external exams. These issues are explored below.

Centralisation and academic schooling standards

As noted above, the comparative weakness of US academic standards may stem in part from the highly decentralised administration of the school system and from the absence of central steering (through central curriculum or external exams). Responsibility for schooling in the United States rests primarily with the states.[6, 7] The fifty state governments, territories and the District of Columbia establish the framework within which the approximately 13 000 local education authorities organise schooling from kindergarten through year 12.[8] Within that decentralised structure, there is a high degree of variability across states in the extent to which states themselves provide central direction.

The degree of decentralisation in the governance and administration of schools and lesson planning found in the United States (that is, control over inputs) is not exceptional by international comparison. A 2003 OECD survey of decision making in lower secondary education found that in 11 of the 25 countries or sub-national regions covered, schools had control over half or more of the decisions related to the organisation of instruction. Schools have authority to choose textbooks in nearly all countries and, in nearly half of the countries covered, had a say in the definition of course content and the range of subjects taught. Moreover, there has been a clear trend internationally towards decentralisation of decision making. Between 1998 and 2003, the percentage of decisions taken at the school level increased in 13 of the 17 countries for which data were available; centralisation of decisions occurred only in 4 countries. These shifts towards decentralisation of decision making extend to administrative matters as well (e.g. budgeting and hiring of teachers).[9] They have been motivated for similar reasons as those in the United States, particularly with regard to enhancing accountability. As school "league tables" have become more widely available, there have been stronger incentives for educators at the school level to exert more control over schooling. Classroom teachers and school administrators are in a good position to take stock of individual learning needs and they need the autonomy to adapt instruction accordingly. Decentralisation has occurred also as part of a continuing trend towards increasing parental say in local school affairs (Glenn and de Groof, 2005).

Whereas many countries have decentralised decision-making with regard to inputs, decisions over outcomes, such as the academic performance standards, are more centralised. In this regard, the US is unusual. The international trend towards decentralisation coincides with a stronger central role in the design of curricula, standards and testing. Thus, although schools in 19 out of 25 countries decide on textbooks, those decisions are typically guided by a framework established at a higher level (usually central government). In most countries overall academic programme design is either set or guided by the state or central level of government. Even in countries where schools define course content, this usually is done within a framework of learning objectives established by state or central government. Also, the use of external exit examinations in many countries should be seen as an integral element of comprehensive approaches to building quality into schooling systems. They are the last of a series of independent assessments for monitoring progress towards educational targets that are set at a higher (often central) level; educators decide – often with a high degree of autonomy – how to achieve those targets.

Decentralisation of decisions on outcomes is a worry because if individuals are able to evaluate their own performance, they will tend to assess it too favourably, particularly if doing so increases financial payments or reduces penalties. As educational decision-making is decentralised down to a district or town level, these incentives may not change, but the control that individuals (students, teachers and parents) have, and hence the distortions arising from subjective assessments, increases. To prevent grade inflation, some central control over the "measuring rod" is needed. Furthermore, decentralisation seems likely to lead to more dispersion of results.

Indeed, a state-by-state analysis of standards carried out by the Thomas B. Fordham Foundation provides direct evidence of shortcomings in state standards and the high degree of variability between states. Starting in the late 1990s the foundation organised teams of experts to review state standards, first in language, and later in US history, mathematics, science and world history. They judged standards according to their clarity and rigour and whether they were "right-headed about content". Based on this, they graded states (on a scale from A to F – highest to lowest) and ranked them. The results of this analysis were published in 1997, 2003, and 2006 (Finn *et al.*, 2006). By their assessment, they found in 2006 only 9 states to be doing very well (grade of B or better) and 26 states to be doing poorly or failing (grade of D or F). Testing practices reveal important differences as well. Until the end of the 1990s, a large majority of states did not have final examinations. By 2004, only 20 states had compulsory exit exams, with as few as 10 with exams based on standards (*i.e.* linked to a curriculum and course requirements guided from the state level).[10] As a result, in many states there is considerable discretion at the local and school levels with regard to the number of courses that students are required to take, what it is that students are expected to know at different grade levels, and whether and how student performance is judged. The prevalence of low standards found by the Fordham Foundation implies that that discretion is often exercised poorly.

Past attempts to improve schooling performance fell short

The weaknesses in schooling discussed above are not new. In 1964, Congress enacted the Elementary and Secondary Education Act (ESEA) to strengthen what was perceived as weak performance in schools serving large numbers of disadvantaged children. It channelled federal money to support programmes aimed at improving education opportunities, quality and attainment. Yet by the early 1980s it was evident that schools were failing not only in hard-pressed inner cities and poor rural areas, but more generally. The National Commission on Excellence in Education concluded in 1983 that "... *the educational foundations of our society are presently being eroded by a rising tide of mediocrity that threatens our very future as a Nation and a people. What was unimaginable a generation ago has begun to occur-others are matching and surpassing our educational attainments*". The Commission recommended higher and more challenging standards; proficiency in reading, mathematics, science, social studies, computer science, and foreign language; regular testing of achievement; and that students meet rigorous achievement standards to graduate (National Commission on Excellence in Education, 1983). The report drew attention to weaknesses in American education and raised their visibility and importance in national debate. Following publication of the report, some states launched initiatives to implement the Commission's recommendations. In 1989, in an unprecedented "education summit", the President and governors agreed to set national goals to be met by the year 2000. These were later spelt out to include raising high school graduation rates, demonstrating mastery of "five core subjects"[11] at the end of 4th, 8th and 12th grade. When the ESEA was reauthorised in 1994 it introduced a requirement that every state introduce a "standards-based education system that would apply to all students". The law required states to specify standards for each year and to develop tests to measure progress; it required poor children (those covered by ESEA Title I) to be tested at least once in grades 3-6, 6-9, and 10-12.

However, as in the past, the federal government was able to play only a limited role in overseeing implementation and compliance (Hess *et al.* 2006, pp. 14-15). In 1996, following a second education summit it was noted that "*[g]raduation rates are up, and the number of students taking a core of academic subjects increased from 13% to 47%. But there's still cause for concern. In 1994, only a third of 12th grade students could master rigorous reading passages. Only 11% showed a strong grasp of history, and standards of US schools pale in comparison to those of other industrialised nations*". (Bracket 1996).

A stronger federal role to raise academic standards

In 2001, Congress enacted the No Child Left Behind Act[12] (NCLB) because of the persistent ineffectiveness of state and school districts and earlier federal legislation to effectively address the problem of poor outcomes. NCLB aims to strike a balance between the federal interest in setting stronger standards, and the authority of states to define such standards, without impinging on autonomy of schools (Box 5.1). Specifically, the Act redefines the authority of the federal government in schooling matters by establishing a framework for strengthened accountability of school performance. It requires states to put in place assessment systems to increase the availability and quality of information on student and school performance; it requires states to establish *content standards,*[13] as well as *achievement standards*[14] that, when met, will ensure that by 2013/14 all pupils are functioning at or above the level each state determines to be proficient. It requires that such standards be met for all sub-groups in the population. The strengthened framework for accountability breaks with earlier federal legislation by extending coverage of such requirements from just those schools receiving ESEA funding, to all schools in any state receiving ESEA funding. In most important respects the goals of NCLB and instruments for achieving them are in line with the trend in federal education legislation, as well as with initiatives in several American states to improve education quality by strengthening standards and accountability for outcomes. They also parallel developments in other countries referred to above (see also OECD, 2006b).

Five years after NCLB was signed into law, different aspects of the legislation are in different stages of implementation; some remedies and sanctions have not even been applied for the first time because of their phased escalated nature.[15] So far, all states and the District of Columbia have put in place accountability plans and reading and mathematics assessments for all students in grades 3-8 and at least once in high school. The proportion of teachers who are highly qualified has risen to 91%.

Early signs of progress

The real tests of NCLB will be whether it raises overall achievement levels and closes the achievement gap facing certain sub-groups in the population. The US Government believes that "the NCLB Act is working" (US Department of Education, 2006). In the January 2007 State of the Union speech, President Bush said "Five years ago, we rose above partisan differences to pass the No Child Left Behind Act… Because we acted, students are

Box 5.1. **Main provisions of the No Child Left Behind Act (NCLB)**

State assessments

States must implement annual assessments in reading and mathematics in grades 3-8 and at least once in grades 10-12, and in science at least once in each of three grade spans: 3-5, 6-9 and 10-12. Assessments must be aligned with challenging state content and academic achievement standards. States must provide for participation of all students, including students with disabilities and limited English proficient (LEO) students. States must provide for the assessment of English language proficiency of all LEP students.

Adequate yearly progress

States must set annual targets that will lead to the goal of all students' reaching proficiency in reading and mathematics by 2013-14. For each measure of school performance, states must include absolute targets that must be met by key subgroups of students (major racial/ethnic groups, low-income students, students with disabilities, and LEP students). Schools and districts must meet annual targets for each student subgroup in the school, and must test 95% of students in each subgroup, in order to make "adequate yearly progress". States also must define an "other academic indicator" that schools must meet in addition to proficiency targets on state assessments.

Schools identified for improvement

Schools and districts that do not make adequate yearly progress (AYP) for two consecutive years are identified for improvement and are to receive technical assistance to help them improve. Those that miss AYP for additional years are identified for successive stages of interventions, including corrective action and restructuring (see below). To leave "identified for improvement" status, a school or district must make AYP for two consecutive years.

Public school choice

Districts must offer all students in identified schools the option to transfer to a non-identified school, with transportation provided by the district.

Supplemental educational services

In schools that miss AYP for a third year, districts also must offer low-income students the option of supplemental educational services from a state-approved provider.

Corrective actions

In schools that miss AYP for a fourth year, districts must also implement at least one of the following corrective actions: replace school staff members who are relevant to the failure to make AYP; implement a new curriculum; decrease management authority at the school level; appoint an outside expert to advise the school; extend the school day or year; or restructure the internal organisation of the school.

Restructuring

In schools that miss AYP for a fifth year, districts must also begin planning to implement at least one of the following restructuring interventions: reopen the school as a charter school; replace all or most of the school staff; contract with a private entity to manage the school; turn over operation of the school to the state; or adopt some other major restructuring of the school's governance. Districts must spend a year planning for restructuring and implement the school restructuring plan the following year. Schools that miss AYP for a sixth year should be closed down.

Box 5.1. **Main provisions of the No Child Left Behind Act (NCLB)** *(cont.)*

Highly qualified teachers

All teachers of core academic subjects must be "highly qualified" as defined by NCLB and the state. To be highly qualified, teachers must have a bachelor's degree, full-state certification, and demonstrated competence in each core academic subject that they teach. Subject-matter competency may be demonstrated by passing a rigorous state test, completing a college major or coursework equivalent, or (for veteran teachers) meeting standards established by the state under a "high, objective uniform state standard of evaluation" (HOUSSE).

Source: Reproduced from *Institute of Education Sciences* (2006) *National Assessment of Title 1: Interim Report,* Executive Summary, Washington DC, Department of Education, p. 12.

---

performing better in reading and math, and minority students are closing the achievement gap". Other observers are more cautious, noted that such improvements were underway before NCLB was enacted and that it may be too early to draw clear lessons about its effectiveness.

The main evidence on changes over time in educational performance is the National Assessment of Educational Progress (NAEP), often referred to as the "Nation's Report Card". This provides a robust measure of progress using a survey that is administered by the Federal government on a regular basis.[16] Table 5.6 shows trends in the first few years in overall scores in reading and mathematics. As can be seen in the final column, 4th graders have improved in both mathematics and reading. 8th graders have improved in mathematics while showing little change in reading performance.

Table 5.6. **Changes in reading and math achievement, during early years of NCLB, as measured by NAEP**[1, 2]

	Early score	2005 score	Change
Mathematics 2000-05			
4th graders	226	238	12
8th graders	273	279	6
Reading 1998-2005			
4th graders	215	219	4
8th graders	263	262	−1

1. All results for accommodation permitted.
2. Data are presented in terms of scale score. A score, derived from student responses to NAEP assessment items, that summarises the overall level of performance attained by a group of students. NAEP does not produce scale scores for individual students. NAEP subject area scales typically range from 0 to 500 (reading, mathematics, history, and geography) or from 0 to 300 (science, writing, and civics). When used in conjunction with interpretive aids, such as item maps, they provide information about what a particular aggregate of students in the population knows and can do.
Source: National Assessment of Educational Progress. *http://nces.ed.gov/nationsreportcard/nde/statecomp.*

Table 5.7 presents data from NAEP on trends in the proportion of students who are functioning at the "proficient level", a particular concern of both policy and the legislation. This paints a very similar picture to Table 5.6. The proportion of all 4th graders who were proficient in mathematics rose strongly, from 22% in 2000 to 35% in 2005. Trends in proficiency for 4th grade reading and 8th grade mathematics have been mildly positive, while 8th grade reading proficiency has deteriorated slightly. Overall, these results are encouraging, though not quite as good as might be hoped. In particular, the improvements do not seem fast enough to achieve the key objective of bringing all students up to or above the "proficient" level by 2013-14. Annex 5.A1 provides further details on test results, including against achievement standards set by individual states.

Table 5.7 also provides information on select population groups. Disaggregated trends tend to track those for the national average. That is, whites, blacks and Hispanics all show substantial improvements in 4th grade mathematics, moderate gains in 4th grade reading and 8th grade mathematics, and little change in 8th grade reading. Overall, Blacks and Hispanics have shown slightly more improvement than Whites (especially when measured in percentage rather than absolute changes). Gaps seem to be narrowing, though they remain wide. Again, Annex 5.A1 has further details and discussion.

Table 5.7. **Trends in proportion of students at proficient level in reading and mathematics before and after implementation of NCLB, as measured by NAEP**

	1998	2000	2002	2003	2005
Results for 4th grade					
Math					
Total		22		31	35
White		31		43	47
Black		5		10	13
Hispanic		7		16	19
Reading					
Total	28		30	30	30
White	37	38	41	41	41
Black	10	10	12	13	13
Hispanic	13	13	15	15	16
Results for 8th grade					
Math					
Total		25		27	28
White		34		37	39
Black		5		7	9
Hispanic		8		12	13
Reading					
Total	30		31	30	29
White	39		41	41	39
Black	13		13	13	12
Hispanic	14		15	15	15

Source: National Center for Education Statistics (2006a,b).

These early test results suggest that overall performance is improving. However, the extent to which this can be attributed to NCLB is unclear. Whether progress is sufficient to reach the target of universal proficiency by 2013/14 is also unclear. Though it is too early to determine the net impact of NCLB, the initiative appears to be well conceived, addressing key problems in a sensible manner that is consistent with the role of the federal government in education. It appears to be well suited as a means for introducing the kind of system-level features that are associated with strong performance in other countries. Hence, the NCLB legislation should be reauthorised, and the NCLB framework of standards, assessment and accountability should be extended through upper secondary education. That said, the framework that NCLB provides is necessary, but by itself insufficient for improving American schooling. States and school districts need to do more. The most urgent need is in the area of introducing more challenging standards. Without more challenging standards it is difficult to see how the system can ever hope to get all students functioning at a proficient level.

The urgent need for challenging standards

The NCLB mandate to introduce challenging content standards is prompting changes. The analysis of the Fordham Foundation referred to above found that, between 2000 and 2006, 37 states had revised or replaced standards in at least one subject area, and 27 states had revised all standards (Finn *et al.*). But, in the view of the Fordham report authors, standards were no better in 2006 than they were in 2000, before NCLB (Finn *et al.* 2006, p. 9). Another study by the American Federation of Teachers (AFT)[17] to determine how well states met NCLB requirements was more positive.[18] It found that more than a third (18 states of 51) fully met criteria AFT used for defining strong standards, and an additional 24 states met 80% or more of the criteria.

But if these changes are leading to results, the results seem intolerably modest and slow in coming. So far the federal pressure on states to raise content and achievement standards does not appear to have much effect on student performance. It was anticipated that regular publication of NAEP results would make it possible to "name" states that performed badly against that nation-wide benchmark. In cases where student performance as measured by state assessment systems was inflated in comparison to NAEP because of lax state standards, it also was anticipated that the publication of NAEP results would "shame" states into improving content standards and raising the NCLB-mandated "cut-off point" – the minimum score required for satisfactory performance. In fact states do not appear to be raising the cut-off points in their state assessments to reflect the changes. This blunts the impact of NCLB as a tool for identifying under-performing schools.[19] Progress towards wider adoption of challenging content standards is slow at best. The discrepancies discussed in Annex 5.A1 between limited improvement according to NAEP, and marked improvement according to state assessment programmes are a troubling sign that, at a minimum, states hold divergent views as to what constitutes satisfactory levels of proficiency. A number of observers have suggested that the differences between NAEP and state assessment measures in the proportion of students found to have low levels of achievement provides further evidence that some states have adopted cut-off points[20] that are too low to be challenging.

> *Because states have considerable leeway to decide how aggressively to raise the AYP (adequate yearly progress) bar … NCLB may invite gaming of the system by states that wish to minimise the number of schools that fail to make AYP … [B]y 2005, some states had virtually no schools identified as needing improvement while other states identified more than 70% of theirs as failing to clear the bar … "universal proficiency" will have very different meanings in different states (Hess et al., 2006, p. 35).*

Recent developments regarding exams at the exit of high school are a symptom of the problem of unevenness between states in the strictness of standards. For years, the US high school diploma has been criticised for being little more than an attendance certificate, as states rarely required students to pass a central exam as a condition of graduation (Achieve, 2006). Minimum competency exams introduced in the 1970s and 1980s did little except to establish (low) thresholds for minimum accepted performance; few states required students to pass them to graduate. NCLB requirements[21] have pushed many states to introduce exit exams that high school students must pass in order to graduate. In 2006, it was reported that 26 states had put in place exit exams or planned to have them in place by 2012. But only 11 of them plan to use the same cut-off points that are required by NCLB. Most of the rest plan to use lower scores; some plan to use an entirely different test. As a result, only a small majority of states will be able to ensure that high school graduates reach or exceed "proficient" levels of achievement (CEP 2006). An earlier study of exit exams in six states (Florida, Maryland, Massachusetts, New Jersey, Ohio and Texas) found that the level of proficiency required to pass exit exams was low by international standards. The threshold for passing maths tests was found to correspond to what students in other countries typically learn in 7th or 8th grade and that for passing English language to what 8th and 9th graders should know. The subjects covered by such exams, though essential, were a relatively small slice of the areas in which students should be proficient (Achieve, 2004).

More challenging exit exams are not enough, however. If curriculum and schooling experience of students do not prepare students adequately, exit exams simply "inspect in quality" by identifying students who perform badly, rather than "building in quality" by providing a solid schooling experience. States should be implementing curriculum-based external exit exams that meet or exceed NCLB standards. They should be guided by the experience that states such as New York and Texas have had with exit exams.

It is not feasible for the federal government to prescribe common standards and curriculum, and central testing. However, it can strengthen incentives for states and districts to adopt proven standards-driven programmes. There is long history of *de facto* national schooling programmes such as the Advanced Placement Program and International Baccalaureate. These are programmes that match high standards for required level of performance with fully developed curricula and centralised examinations; they also have their own requirements for teacher preparation (independent of state requirements). Though far from universal, they are national in character and widely available in school districts throughout the United States. They have demonstrated capacity for addressing an increasingly broad spectrum of learning needs, with the result that total enrolments in these programmes have grown and are increasingly representative of the US student population. Moreover, because of the success of the Advanced Placement program in upper secondary education (years 10-12), it is being used increasingly to guide the restructuring of standards, curriculum and testing at lower grades (Box 5.2). States and districts need to implement more challenging curricula and levels of performance. Advanced Placement and the International Baccalaureate provide models of standards that could be adopted more widely.

Conclusion

United States education performance has slipped comparatively. As the international edge in high-school completion rates has disappeared, the weaknesses in quality of schooling have become particularly apparent. Lagging performance is evident across the board, including among affluent and academically successful students. The United States does not just have more students performing badly – it also has many fewer students performing well. The weak performance appears to be due in large part to system-level weaknesses. Resources do not appear to be at the root of the problem because the system is comparatively well-financed at an aggregate level, though how those resources are

Box 5.2. *De facto* national standards:
the example of the Advanced Placement Program

For legal and political reasons the federal government steers clear of establishing anything that could be interpreted as a national content standard, curriculum or examination. In the 1990s the Department of Education laid the groundwork for a discussion involving employers, trade unions and educators to discuss national targets for learning outcomes, but little came of that. However, *de facto* national standards do exist. One of the most successful is the Advanced Placement Program (AP).[1] Established in 1955 it consists of an intensive, high quality curriculum in 35 subject areas starting at the 10th year and geared to the entrance standards of selective higher education institutions. The AP curriculum is taught by teachers who are specially trained for the program. Students must get a passing grade to receive credit. AP exam results are used by higher education institutions in the US and more than 30 countries for purposes of admission decisions, award of higher education credit, and placement in higher-level studies (College Board 2006, *Advanced Placement: Report to the Nation, apcentral.collegeboard.com*, p. 1).

The AP program was designed to ensure that the last years of high school prepared students adequately for higher education. Originally developed with the standards of highly selective schools in mind, AP started out as a program targeted on students with strong academic records and demonstrated proficiency. As such it was an attempt to fill gaps in school standards that higher education admission offices found to vary greatly between and within states in terms of how challenging they were and how strictly they were applied in evaluating student performance. Its use has expanded as participation in higher education – and the need for remedial education for higher education students – has risen. Over time AP has evolved into a *de facto* national (though by no means universal) standard. It is found in schools in all states of the US, territories, and in overseas education facilities such as those operated by the Department of Defence for military dependents. Although AP emerged as a programme that heavily benefited students from the best high schools going to elite higher education institutions, it has evolved into a programme for any student going on to higher education, which comprises a large and growing share of high school graduates. Enrolment trends (see Table 5.8) reveal remarkable growth in the proportion of students enrolled in AP courses and scoring well on AP exams. Overall enrolments more than doubled during that time, with particularly large rises among Blacks (up 164%) and Hispanics (209%). During this time the number of examinations that were passed by graduating classes rose by 135%. Expansion of participation has increased to such an extent that for the high school class of 2005, 14.1% of graduating seniors had scored well on at least one AP examination during high school.

Table 5.8. **Advanced placement – trends in coverage, overall enrolments and enrolments of key subgroups, 1995-2005**

	1995		2000		2005		1995-2005
	Number	Share of total AP enrolments	Number	Share of total AP enrolments	Number	Share of total AP enrolments	Change in AP enrolments
Total enrolments (grades 10-12)	494 335	...	741 603	...	1 009 662	...	104%
Black	21 951	4%	35 480	5%	57 939	6%	164%
Hispanic	37 961	8%	72 996	10%	117 439	12%	209%
Females	271 646	55%	411 316	55%	572 796	57%	111%
Exams passed with score of 3 or better, for the class graduating in the year indicated	321 889	...	509 358	...	758 828	...	136%

Source: College Board.

Box 5.2. *De facto* national standards:
the example of the Advanced Placement Program *(cont.)*

One of the earlier criticisms of AP was that its imposition of high content standards penalised students enrolled in school systems with weak programmes at lower grade levels, thus limiting the extent to which AP could be adopted. Developments over the past several years suggest that in fact the robust AP high school programme can be used as a guide to reforming education at lower grades. As part of systemic strategy to address this problem, Montgomery County School District in the state of Maryland set out to determine what level of proficiency students in 9th grade needed in order to start AP courses in the 10th grade, and then what level of proficiency 8th graders needed to reach the level needed for 9th grade. School district officials have carried out this process of "backward mapping" and adjusted curriculum, teaching (including hiring and career development) and testing accordingly down to the level of 3rd grade. There are encouraging results in terms of enrolment in AP courses and passing AP examinations. During the current school year 20% of high school students are enrolled in AP courses, and 54% of seniors have taken at least 1 AP course in high school (three times the national average). School district authorities, recognising that high school assessment does not measure up to what higher education needs, have pursued this strategy in order to ensure that Montgomery Country students get into higher education. In Montgomery County the local community colleges typically admit high school graduates, but will not place them in courses for academic credit until they pass the remedial courses that have become a permanent part of higher education for many students. The political impetus for the strategy has come from the evidence that schooling outcomes are cumulative and that strengthening high school results requires strengthening lower levels of education. In Montgomery County this strategy now extends to the pre-school level (Maeroff 2006).

College Board, developers of the Advanced Placement Program have adapted the logic of "backward mapping" in developing a new initiative called "Springboard"[2] It is designed to put in place the curriculum, teacher preparation, and assessment practices (including guidance for formative assessment to evaluate progress and diagnose learning needs) needed to align studies starting in 6th grade with the requirements for starting Advanced Placement high school courses in 10th grade. Launched in mid-2004, the Springboard program now enrols more than 400 000 pupils in 524 schools (information provided by College Board).

1. AP was developed by the College Board, a private non-profit corporation widely known for the development of standardised examinations that are used for entrance to university under-graduate and graduate study.
2. *www.collegeboard.com/springboard*.

allocated between and within schools probably does matter. There is strong evidence that teacher quality and performance also matter. However this chapter has focused on the prior fundamental question of what is expected of primary and secondary education in the United States. Academic standards, curricula and testing are insufficiently challenging, in part because they are set at a de-centralised level.

Concerns about these weaknesses in the system are not new and many reforms at the state and federal level have aimed to address them. But results of regular nation-wide assessments carried out by the federal government indicate that the earlier reforms have not been especially effective: overall achievement levels remain low and the performance gaps facing some groups remain large. The No Child Left Behind Act of 2002 is the most recent federal initiative to strengthen schooling. It combines measures to prod states to raise standards and set performance targets, with requirements for better and more freely available information on school performance and remedies where schools under-perform. It appears to be a sound approach to improving schooling, but, because of the pivotal role of states and localities, is not enough by itself. Challenging education programmes do exist in the United States, but their take up is far from universal. Recommendations for building on the No Child Left Behind Act are outlined in Box 5.3.

Box 5.3. **Recommendations on schools**

Although there are considerable uncertainties regarding policy for schools, the Federal government's No Child Left Behind (NCLB) initiative appears to be well conceived, addressing key problems in a sensible manner. Preliminary indications are consistent with it raising school performance and narrowing achievement gaps. Hence:

● The NCLB legislation should be reauthorised.

● The NCLB framework of standards, assessment and accountability should be extended through upper secondary education.

That said, there are a number of areas in which improvements could be made. Educational content standards and curricula in the US appear to be less challenging than those found in other countries. No Child Left Behind requires states to formulate challenging content standards, but they vary and show no signs of reaching the levels needed. Tests are often testing the wrong things and failing to provide relevant information. Hence:

● States and districts need to implement more challenging curricula and levels of performance. For example, Advanced Placement and the International Baccalaureate provide models of standards that could be adopted more widely.

● The objective of bringing all pupils to high levels of proficiency should not be watered down.

● States should consider implementing curriculum-based external exit exams, like those in New York or North Carolina. NCLB should require curriculum-based external exit exams.

Notes

1. A possible exception is TIMSS 4th grade science, where the United States came third out of 11 OECD members. In the full sample, the United States ranked 6th out of 25 economies, behind Singapore, Chinese Taipei, Japan, Hong Kong and England.

2. A similar calculation (with the same result) can be done with PISA data (*Learning For Tomorrow's World* p. 60, 310-312) but as only 15-year olds are tested, the difference is likely to reflect differing performance of grade-repeaters.

3. Closely related to this, there is a strong negative correlation across countries between *enjoyment* of mathematics and performance. As Whitehurst (2003) points out, this suggests that mathematics does not need to be made fun.

4. For an account of how one school district (Montgomery county, Maryland) adjusted its mathematics curriculum in response to the TIMSS research, see Larson (2001).

5. The dependent variable was the country level mean of native-born students. Other regressors were per capita GDP and a dummy for East Asia. Coefficients on the CBEEE dummy were significant at the 1% level.

6. Under the US Constitution those responsibilities that are not specifically assigned to the federal government are left to the individual states. Australia, Austria, Canada, Germany, Spain,

Switzerland, and the United Kingdom have similar federal systems or other governance arrangements under which states/province/regions have primary responsibility for schools.

7. Until recently the federal role in schooling has been limited to federal responsibilities, such as national defence (the National Defence Education Act of 1958 was enacted to strengthen mathematics and science instruction in schools), areas where the Federal constitution supersedes state law or federal law addresses gaps in state law (Federal constitutional guarantee of equal protection or federal legislation guaranteeing access of students with disabilities to quality education), and support of educational research.

8. Education in America is delivered in schools that run from Kindergarten for 5-year olds through elementary schools (typically grades 1-6), middle schools (grades 7-9), and high schools (grades 10-12). A high school diploma is awarded at the end 12th grade. About half of US children participate in optional pre-school programmes (average for the OECD is); education is compulsory from age 5 through 15 or 16 (depending on the state); the upper secondary graduation rate in 2004 was 75% (the OECD average was 81%).

9. OECD, 2004, pp. 423-438. Also see OECD, 2006b for a discussion of changes in policy and practice to increase responsiveness of schools to parental and community preferences.

10. National Center for Education Statistics, 2005.

11. Among the following: English, mathematics, science, foreign languages, civics and government, economics, art, history, and geography.

12. Signed into law in January 2002 by President Bush *The No Child Left Behind Act of 2001* (Public Law 107-110) amends *the Elementary and Secondary Education Act of 1964*. ESEA was the original framework legislation for federal education law related to improving academic achievement of disadvantaged children (including pre-school education); improving instruction for limited English proficient and immigrant students; libraries; and Indian, Native Hawaiian, and Alaska native education.

13. What students are expected to know at each grade level in the main subject areas, including mathematics, reading and science.

14. These are targets defining levels of proficiency – basic, proficient and advanced – and the scores that students are expected to reach each level.

15. Later this year there will be available results of a comprehensive evaluation of implementation, as well as results of the 2006 round of the National Assessment of Education Progress (NAEP) results. In the meantime there are available results of recent tests of student achievement, as well as interim assessments of various aspects of the legislation.

16. The *National Assessment of Educational Progress* (NAEP), is carried out in all states receiving Title I funds. NAEP was developed under the auspices of the National Assessment Governing Board (NAGB); it measures achievement in reading, mathematics, science, writing, US history, civics, geography and the arts. NAEP is the only nationally representative and continuing assessment of what America's students know and can do in various subject areas.

17. One of the two main teachers unions in the US.

18. The AFT study judged standards according to criteria different from those used by Finn *et al.* In the AFT study state standards were considered to be 'strong' they met the following criteria: i) be detailed, explicit, and firmly rooted in the content of the subject areas to lead to a common core curriculum; contain particular content; provide attention to both content and skills; to be articulated for grades and subject and not contain excessive repetition across grade levels (AFT 2006).

19. NAEP cannot be used to evaluate the performance of individual schools. That can be done only through the state assessment programmes, mandated by NCLB, that specify, among other things, the cut-off point below which student performance is considered to be unsatisfactory. But states have an incentive to *not* raise the cut-point in order to minimise the number of schools liable to be found to be under-performing.

20. That is, the *achievement standards* that states are supposed to set to indicate the scores that correspond to the basic, proficient, and advanced level of achievement.

21. In particular the requirement that by 2014 all students be performing at a level of proficient or better, and that students be tested at least once between years 10 and 12.

Bibliography

Achieve, Inc. (2004), *Do Graduation Tests Measure up? A Closer Look at State High School Exams*, Washington DC, Achieve, Inc., *www.achieve.org*.

Achieve, Inc. (2006), *Closing the Expectations Gap 2006* (American Diploma Project), Washington DC: Achieve, Inc., *www.achieve.org*.

AFT Teachers (2006), "Smart Testing: Let's Get it Right", *Policy Brief*, No. 19, July.

Bishop, J. (1997), "The Effect of National Standards and Curriculum-Based Exams on Achievement", *AEA Papers and Proceedings*, Vol. 87, No. 2, May, pp. 206-264.

Bishop, J. (2006), "Drinking from the Foundation of Knowledge: Student Incentives to Study and Learn" Chapter 15 in *Handbook of the Economics of Education Vol. 2*, in E.A. Hanushek and F. Welch (eds.), North-Holland Publication, Netherlands.

Brackett, E. (1996), *Ready for Work: National Education Summit*, On-line Backgrounders, transcript, 27 March, Public Broadcasting System, *www.pbs.org/newshour/bb/education/summit_3-27a.html*.

Carey, D. and E. Ernst (2006), "Improving Education Achievement and Attainment in Luxembourg", OECD Economics Department Working Papers, No. 508, OECD Economics Department.

Center on Education Policy (2006), *From the Capital to the Classroom: Year 4 of the No Child Left Behind Act*, Washington, Center on Education Policy.

Figlio, D.N. and L. Kenny (2006), "Individual Teacher Incentives and Student Performance", *NBER Working Paper*, No. 12627, Cambridge, National Bureau of Economic Research, October.

Figlio, D.N. and M. Lucas (2004), "Do High Grading Standards Affect Student Performance?", *Journal of Public Economics 88*.

Finn, C. Jr., L.J. and M.J. Petrilli (2006), *The State of State Standards*, Washington DC, Thomas B. Fordham Foundation.

Fuchs, T. and L. Woessman (2004), "What Accounts for International Differences in Student Performance? A re-examination using PISA data", *CESifo Working Paper*, No. 1235, July.

Glenn, C. and J. de Groof (2005), *Balancing Freedom, Autonomy and Accountability in Education*, Nijmegen: Wolf Legal Publishers.

Hampden-Thompson, G. and J.S. Johnston (2006) "Variation in the Relationship Between Nonschool Factors and Student Achievement on International Assessments", National Center for Education Statistics, Institute of Education Sciences *Statistics in Brief*, NCES 2006-014.

Hanushek, E. (1998), "Conclusions and Controversies About Effectiveness of School Resources", *FRBNY Economic Policy Review*, March.

Hechinger, J. (2006), "New Report Urges Return to Basics in teaching Math", *Wall Street Journal*, 12 September, p. A1.

Hess, F.M. and M.J. Petrilli (2006), *No Child Left Behind: Primer*, New York, Peter Lang.

Hoxby, C.M. (2006), *School Choice: The Three Essential Elements and Several Policy Options*, Keynote speech, New Zealand Association of Economists, 46th Annual Conference 2005, Christchurch.

Institute of Education Sciences, (2006), *National Assessment of Title I: Interim Report – Executive Summary*, NCEE 2006-4000, Washington DC, US Department of Education, February.

Larson, J. (2001), "International Performance Standards in Montgomery County Public Schools" Montgomery County Public Schools office of Shared Sccountabiltiy, April.

Lemke, M. (2004), *International Outcomes Of Learning in Mathematics Literacy and Problem Solving: PISA 2003 Results from the US Perspective*, National Center for Education Statistics.

Lemke, M. and P Gonzales (2006) *US Student and Adult Performance on International Assessments of Educational Achievement; Findings from the Condition of Education 2006*, National Center for Education Statistics.

Loveless, T (2002), *The Brown Center Report on American Education*, 2002, The Brookings Institution.

Maeroff, G.I. (2006), *Building Blocks: Making Children Successful in the Early Years of School*, New York, Palgrave Macmillan.

Montgomery, L.and J. Mathews (2006), "The Future of D.C. Public Schools: Traditional or Charter Education", in *Washington Post*, 22 August, *www.washingtonpost.com/wp-dyn/content/article/2006/08/21/AR2006082101758_5.html*.

Murnane, R. (1996), "Staffing the Nation's Schools with Skilled Teachers", in E. Hanushek and D. Jorgenson (eds.), *Improving America's, Schools: The Role of Incentives,* Washington DC, National Academy Press.

National Center for Education Statistics (2006a), The Nation's Report Card: Mathematics 2005, Washington DC, *http://nces.ed.gov/nationsreportcard/pdf/main2005/2006453.pdf*.

National Center for Education Statistics (2006b), The Nation's Report Card: Reading 2005, Washington DC, *http://nces.ed.gov/nationsreportcard/pdf/main2005/2006451.pdf*.

National Council of Teachers of Mathematics, (2006), "Curriculum Focal Points for Prekindergarten through Grade 8 Mathematics: A Quest for Coherence".

National Science Board (2004) "Science and Engineering Indicators 2004", May, *www.nsf.gov/statistics/seind04/start.htm*.

OECD (2003), *Learning for Tomorrow's World*, Paris.

OECD (2004), *Education at a Glance*, Paris.

OECD (2005) *Learning a Living: First Results of the Adult Literacy and Lifeskills Survey*, Paris, OECD.

OECD (2006a), *Education at a Glance*, Paris.

OECD (2006b), *Demand-Sensitive Schooling: Evidence and Issues*, Paris.

Schmidt, W., R. Houang and L. Cogan (2002), "A Coherent Curriculum: The Case of Mathematics", *American Educator*, Summer 2002.

Schmidt, W. (2003), "Presentation to Mathematics and Science Initiative", 4 February, *www.ed.gov/print/rschstat/research/progs/mathscience/schmidt.html*.

Schmidt, W.H., C.C. McKnight, P.M. Jakwerth, L.S. Cogan, S.A. Raizen, R.T. Houang, G.A. Valverde, D.E. Wiley, R.G. Wolfe, L.J. Bianchi, W.-L. Yang, S.-H. Kang and E.D. Britton (1998), *Facing the Consequences: Using TIMSS for a Closer Look at United States Mathematics and Science Education*, Kluwer Academic Publishers.

Schmidt, W.H., C.C. McKnight, R.T. Houang, H.C. Wang, D.E. Wiley, L.S. Cogan and R.G. Wolfe (2001), *Why Schools Matter: A Cross-national Comparison of Curriculum and Learning*, Jossey-Bass, Indianapolis IN.

US Department of Education (2006) No Child Left Behind Act Is Working, *www.ed.gov/nclb/overview/importance/nclbworking.html*, December 2006.

Whitehurst, G. (2003), "Research on Mathematics Education" Presentation to Mathematics and Science Initiative, 6 February, at *www.ed.gov/print/rschstat/research/progs/mathscience/whitehurst.html*.

Willms, J.D. (2006), "Learning divides: ten policy questions about the performance and equity of schools and schooling systems", UNESCO *Institute for statistics, Working Paper*, No. 5.

Woessmann, L. (2006), "Public-Private Partnership and Schooling Outcomes across Countries", *CESifo Working Paper* No. 1662, February.

Woessmann, L.R. (2005), "The Effect Heterogeneity of Central Examinations: Evidence from TIMSS, TIMSS-Repeat and PISA", *Education Economics*, Vol. 13, No. 2, pp. 143-169, June.

ANNEX 5.A1

Further evidence on school performance

Another measure of performance is the trend in the proportion of students that reaches the proficient level as defined by state achievement standards, and as measured by the state assessments that are mandated by NCLB. This is somewhat cruder than NAEP. It does not shed light on absolute levels of achievement or on trends in achievement gaps between different population sub-groups. The Department of Education surveyed state education officials and compared results from the time just before implementation of NCLB to the first full year after implementation. The results (Table 5.A1.1) suggest that overall trends are in the right direction, but with certain groups such as migrants, those with limited English proficiency and disabled students faring less well. Results for mathematics are stronger. The Center on Education Policy (an independent think-tank) collected more aggregated information from states and school districts on changes in achievement during the first few years of NCLB. Those results (Table 5.A1.2) suggest that states are having more success in raising performance in mathematics than in reading, and that results for 4th graders are generally better than results for 8th graders.

Table 5.A1.1. **Number of states showing an increase in the percentage of 4th grade students performing at or above the state's proficient level from 2000-01 to 2002-03**

	Reading	Mathematics
All students	11/23 states	17/23 states
White	7/7 states	7/7 states
Black	5/7 states	5/7 states
Hispanic	6/7 states	5/7 states
Low-income	12/16 states	10/10 states
Limited English proficiency	12/20 states	15/20 states
Migrant	11/15 states	12/16 states
Students with disabilities	14/20 states	16/20 states

Source: Reproduced from *Institute of Education Sciences* (2006), p. 14.

Table 5.A1.3 presents further details from NAEP, disaggregating national data on trends in reading and mathematics scores by selected population groups. Encouragingly, improvements have been strongest among some of those with the weakest performance. Among 4th graders, scores of Black and Hispanic students roughly doubled the gains of White students in mathematics between 2000 and 2005. Reading gains were smaller, but Black and Hispanic students still managed to improve slightly more than White students.

Table 5.A1.2. **Summary of results of selected surveys of achievement trends in states (per cent of states)**

	CEP 2003/04-2004/05	Education week 2002/03-2004/05 4th grade	Education week 2002/03-2004/05 8th grade	Education trust 2001/02-2003/04 4th grade	Education trust 2001/02-2003/04 8th grade
Reading					
Improving	81	79	64	71	59
Same	14	3	14	11	11
Declining	5	18	22	18	30
Math					
Improving	84	84	86	97	86
Same	12	5	3	0	14
Declining	5	11	11	3	0
Total states reporting	43	38	36 reading; 35 math.	28 reading; 29 math.	27 reading; 28 math.

Source: Centre on Education Policy (2006), p. 43.

Table 5.A1.3. **Trends in reading and mathematics results, during early years of NCLB, as measured by NAEP[1]**

Average scale scores

	1998	2000	2002	2003	2005
Results for 4th grade					
Math					
Total		226		235	238
White		234		243	246
Black		203		216	220
Hispanic		208		222	226
Reading					
Total	215	213	219	218	219
White	225	224	229	229	229
Black	193	190	199	198	200
Hispanic	193	190	201	200	203
Results for 8th grade					
Math					
Total		273		278	279
White		284		288	289
Black		244		252	255
Hispanic		253		259	262
Reading					
Total	263		264	2 631	262
White	270		272	272	271
Black	244		245	244	243
Hispanic	243		247	245	246

1. All results for accomodations permitted; race/ethnicity used in NAEP results after 2001.
2. Data are presented in terms of scale score. A score, derived from student responses to NAEP assessment items, that summarises the overall level of performance attained by a group of students. NAEP does not produce scale scores for individual students.

Source: National Assessment of Educational Progress. *http://nces.ed.gov/nationsreportcard/nde/statecomp.*

These differential gains that are evident in Table 5.A1.3 led to widespread reductions in achievement gaps. Table 5.A1.4 summarises data on the trends in gaps between White and Black students, as well as between White and Hispanic students, indicating the number of states where such gaps have increased and decreased. The improvements were

Table 5.A1.4. **Changes in reading and math achievement gaps for selected groups during early years of NCLB, as measured by NAEP[1,2]**

	White-Black gaps			White-Hispanic gaps		
	Overall change	States with increasing gap	States with decreasing gap	Overall change	States with increasing gap	States with decreasing gap
Mathematics 2000-2005						
4th graders	−4.38	8	26	−5.59	6	17
8th graders	−6.32	11	19	−4.74	7	14
Reading 1998-2005						
4th graders	−2.71	7	29	−5.07	6	18
8th graders	1.16	15	16	−2.35	10	11

1. All results for accommodations permitted.
2. Data are presented in terms of scale score. A score, derived from student responses to NAEP assessment items, that summarises the overall level of performance attained by a group of students. NAEP does not produce scale scores for individual students. NAEP subject area scales typically range from 0 to 500 (reading, mathematics, history, and geography) or from 0 to 300 (science, writing, and civics). When used in conjunction with interpretive aids, such as item maps, they provide information about what a particular aggregate of students in the population knows and can do.
Source: National Assessment of Educational Progress. http://nces.ed.gov/nationsreportcard/nde/statecomp/.

most noticeable for 4th graders. Nationwide the achievement gaps between White students and Black and Hispanic students diminished, and the number of states showing shrinking gaps outnumbered those showing an increasing gap. Gains were larger for Hispanic students. The picture is different for 8th graders: sharp improvements in mathematics results for Black students sharply reduced their gap with White students by more than 6%, but the reading gap actually increased.

The NAEP results (Tables 5.6 and 5.7, as well as Tables 5.A1.3 and 5.A1.4) parallel the results based on the state assessments (Tables 5.A1.1 and 5.A1.2) in certain important respects. Improvements in math are more widespread than improvements in reading, and improvements among 4th graders are more widespread than among 8th graders (except for results from Education Week). However some of the state assessments paint a brighter picture than NAEP concerning results for 8th graders. NAEP as well as the Department of Education data show 8th grade reading achievement levels to be declining in more states than they are rising; results from Education Week and Education Trust show results to be rising in more states (64% and 59% respectively). There are a number of reasons for the apparent discrepancies. The robustness of reported improvements is not certain. The state educational assessment programs are not necessarily uniform over time and the dates of administering the tests does vary from year to year in some states. Changes in federal regulations regarding permissible testing practices (e.g. different tests and standards for disabled students and re-testing for students who perform poorly initially; see Riddle, 2006a), may diminish the comparability of achievement data over time. The "achievement standards" or "cut-off points" that state assessment programmes set for determining the threshold of proficient achievement appear to be less challenging than those of NAEP. If this is in fact so, the same achievement levels would look higher when measured using state assessments than they would when measured using NAEP.*

* In 2007 the National Center for Education Statistics will publish results of the 2006 round of NAEP that will include state-by-state comparisons of the proportion of students testing at the proficient level according to NAEP, and according to state assessment programmes and the cut-points they establish for determining proficiency.

ISBN 978-92-64-03271-2
OECD Economic Surveys: United States
© OECD 2007

Chapter 6

Financing higher education

America's higher education system is among the best in the world but there are, nevertheless, areas for improvement. In particular, there appear to be substantial financial barriers to higher education despite large government expenditures aimed at promoting access. Policy makers have proposed addressing these barriers by increasing student grants. However, grants are fiscally costly, they have unattractive efficiency and equity implications and research does not show them to be effective. Income tax concessions and state government subsidies suffer from similar problems. In contrast, international best practice seems to be converging on student loans with repayments that vary according to income. Income-contingent loans facilitate access to college at low fiscal cost and without the inefficiency and inequities that accompany grants, subsidies or tax concessions. At the same time, they do not discourage risk-averse or uninformed students in the way that conventional loans do. The United States has an income-contingent loan programme that should be expanded. While the design of repayments could be improved, the main problem with this programme is that lending limits are too low. Higher limits, especially for unsubsidised direct loans, would benefit students and promote access at little cost to the government. Were a good system of loans in place, then less cost-effective means of promoting access, such as grants and tax concessions, should be cut back.

In contrast to its high schools, the United States system of higher education[1] is widely seen to be the best in the world. Objective measures of quality are open to alternative interpretations but are arguably consistent with this favourable assessment. For example, United States colleges and universities offer more choice, their graduates receive greater wage premiums, and they attract more than twice as many foreign students as any other country. 17 of the best 20 research universities in the world are in the United States, according to the Shanghai Jiao Tong University.

The success of the US system of higher education is often attributed to its competitive and decentralised structure. These features distinguish it (in varying degrees) from both higher education in other countries and from primary and secondary education in the United States. Hoxby (1999) provides a discussion. Any changes need to build on these strengths.

There appears to be scope for improvement, however. The United States' lead is more obvious in research than in teaching (though this may reflect difficulties in measuring the latter). And in some areas other countries are overtaking. For example, whereas the United States had the highest tertiary attainment rate in the OECD a generation ago, it is now ranked 8th in tertiary attainment among 25-34 year olds. Enrolment rates are now below the OECD average.[2] The recent report of the Secretary of Education's Commission on the Future of Higher Education (2006), known as the Spellings Commission, "found … much that needed urgent reform". The Commission and others have pointed to serious problems in the areas of accountability, quality, transparency, cost control, diversity and many other aspects of higher education. Box 6.1 outlines the Administration's response to the report. Furthermore, the newly elected Congress has its own priorities.

Against this background, this chapter addresses the issue of how governments, particularly the federal government, should be involved in the financing of higher education. The focus is on the efficiency and equity of support rather than its level. This is not to say that financing is necessarily the most important issue facing higher education. For example, it can be argued that inadequate prior academic preparation is a greater problem. However, Chapter 5 has already discussed the performance of US high schools. Moreover, governments spend about two percentage points of GDP on higher education, primarily to promote access. How well that money is spent seems worth considering. Especially so, given that policy-makers plan to substantially expand current programmes and that international experience suggests better approaches are possible.

Background

International comparisons of tertiary education are difficult, because institutional structures vary greatly across countries. Nevertheless, the available data indicate that the United States spends much more on higher education than other countries. In 2003, it devoted 2.9% of its GDP to tertiary education, about twice as much as the OECD average. As shown in Figure 6.1, this reflected unusually large private expenditures, with public

Box 6.1. **Secretary Spellings' action plan for higher education**

In September 2006, the Commission on the Future of Higher Education, known popularly as the Spellings Commission delivered its final report, *A Test of Leadership*. The Commission comprised 19 diverse and prominent experts on higher education. It found that "US higher education needs to improve in dramatic ways" changing from "a system primarily based on reputation to one based on performance." In responding to the Commission's report, Secretary of Education Margaret Spellings announced an Action Plan. The Secretary's proposals were as follows:

Accessibility

- Strengthen K-12 preparation and align high school standards with college expectations.
- Work with Congress to expand the successful principles of the *No Child Left Behind Act* to high schools.
- Redesign the 12th-grade NAEP (Nation's Report Card) test to provide state-level estimates of college and workforce readiness.
- Raise awareness and mobilise leadership to address the issue of adult literacy as a barrier to national competitiveness and individual opportunity.
- Develop a federal research agenda for adult literacy to identify strategies, models and programmes that work.

Affordability

- Simplify the process by partnering with states to use existing income and tax data to help students complete the Free Application for Federal Student Aid (FAFSA) in half the time.
- Notify students of their estimated aid eligibility before spring of their senior year in high school.
- Work with Congress to provide new funds for need-based aid through the federal financial aid system.
- Commission an independent management consultant review of the federal financial aid system.
- Revitalise the Fund for the Improvement of Postsecondary Education (FIPSE) to promote innovation and productivity.
- Encourage organisations that report annual college data to develop consistent affordability measures.

Accountability

- Work with a consortium of states to build on and link together the 40 existing, privacy-protected higher education information systems.
- Explore incentives for states and institutions that collect and report student learning outcome data.
- Convene members of the accreditation community to recommend changes to the standards for recognition that will place a greater emphasis on results.
- Redesign the Department of Education's college search website to allow consumers to weigh and compare institutions based on their individual interests and needs.

spending being in line with other countries.[3] The high level of expenditure reflects near-average enrolments but very high per-student expenditure. In 2003, the United States spent $19 500 on core tertiary educational services per student, more than twice the OECD average of $7 800.[4] Most of the high per-student spending reflects high US income. Across

Figure 6.1. **Expenditure on tertiary education institutions**
Percentage of GDP, 2003

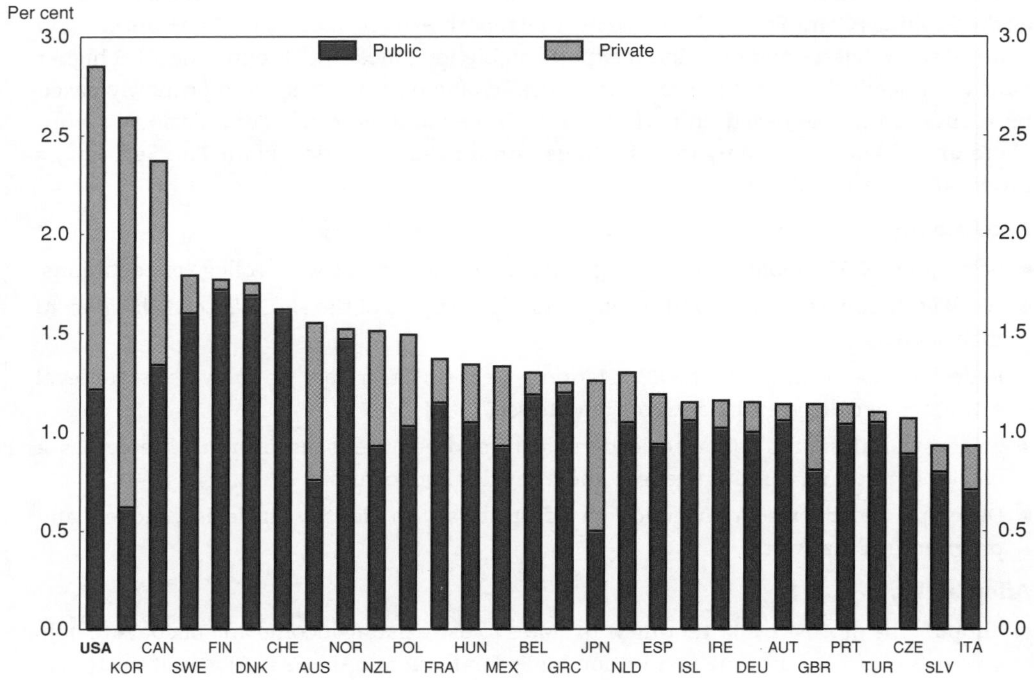

Source: OECD, *Education at a Glance*, 2006, Table B2.1b.

StatLink ⬛ᵢₛₗ http://dx.doi.org/10.1787/010418744654

countries, spending on tertiary education increases steadily, though non-linearly, with GDP per capita. (*Education at a Glance*, Chart B1.6).

High private expenditures reflect unusually high tuition fees (Figure 6.2). The average published tuition fee in the United States, at $8 700 a year in 2003, was almost five times the OECD average of $1 800.

Another striking feature of US higher education is its diversity. About three-quarters of full-time undergraduates attend public institutions, about one-fifth attend private non-profit institutions and a small fringe attend private for-profit institutions. The public sector is divided between 4-year institutions and 2-year community colleges – the latter are more vocationally oriented and most students attend part-time. Public institutions receive most of their funding from state governments and set tuition fees that are relatively low by US standards. At private schools, fees are higher and more variable, with top-tier schools (such as Harvard, Chicago and Stanford) charging between $32 000 and $34 000 a year. However, published fees (referred to as the "sticker price") overstate actual costs due to discounting, grants and tax benefits. These reduce costs at private 4-year institutions by an average $9 000, with smaller reductions at public institutions. Table 6.1 shows one measure of fees before and after grants, as estimated by the College Board (2006a).[5]

On top of net tuition charges, students need to pay for room, board and other living costs, which often amount to around $10 000 and $11 000.[6] Putting these together, a student considering going to college faces the prospect of spending an average $10 000 to $23 000 a year, depending on the institution. This "cost" is the relevant barrier for liquidity-

Figure 6.2. **Average tuition fees**[1]
Tertiary type-A institutions, 2003[2]

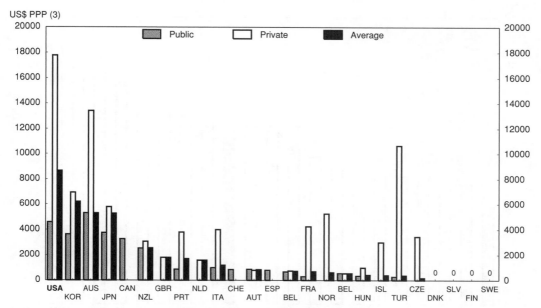

1. Countries are ranked by average tuition fee, weighted by full-time enrolment.
2. In the US, Tertiary type-A institutions mainly comprise bachelor's degree programmes, but also include master's and professional degrees and some academically-oriented associate's degrees.
3. Where data is provided as a range, the midpoint is used.

Source: OECD, *Education at a Glance*, 2006, Table B5.1.

StatLink ᴍᴤᴸ *http://dx.doi.org/10.1787/010430446512*

Table 6.1. **Average tuition and other expenses: 2006-07 academic year**

	Share of full-time enrolment (%)	Average published tuition and fees ($)	Average net price[1] ($)	Living expenses[2] ($)	Total ($)
Private four year	20	22 200	13 200	11 100	23 300
Public four year	45	5 800	2 700	10 500	13 200
Public two year	25	2 200	100	10 000	10 100

1. Average net price is calculated by subtracting average grant aid from all sources and tax benefits per full-time student from the published price.
2. Living expenses include room and board, transport, books, supplies and miscellaneous expenses. Estimates are for residents at four-year institutions and commuters at two-year public institutions.

Source: College Board (2006a) *Trends in College Pricing.*

constrained students worried about whether they can afford to enrol. An alternative measure of cost recognises that living expenses would be incurred anyway. For students with ready access to finance, the decision is not whether they *can* go but whether they *should*. For this decision, the relevant cost is foregone earnings plus net tuition. The median annual earnings of a 20-year-old high school graduate was $22 000 in 2005. On this basis, the average cost of enrolment varies from $22 000 to $35 000, depending on the type of institution. Note that regardless of whether the cost is measured using living expenses or foregone earnings, either of these elements far exceeds net tuition charges. Contrary to the popular misapprehension, it is only at a small number of very expensive institutions that tuition and charges represent the major barrier to college attendance. For the large

Figure 6.3. **Internal rates of return to tertiary education,**[1] **2001**[2]

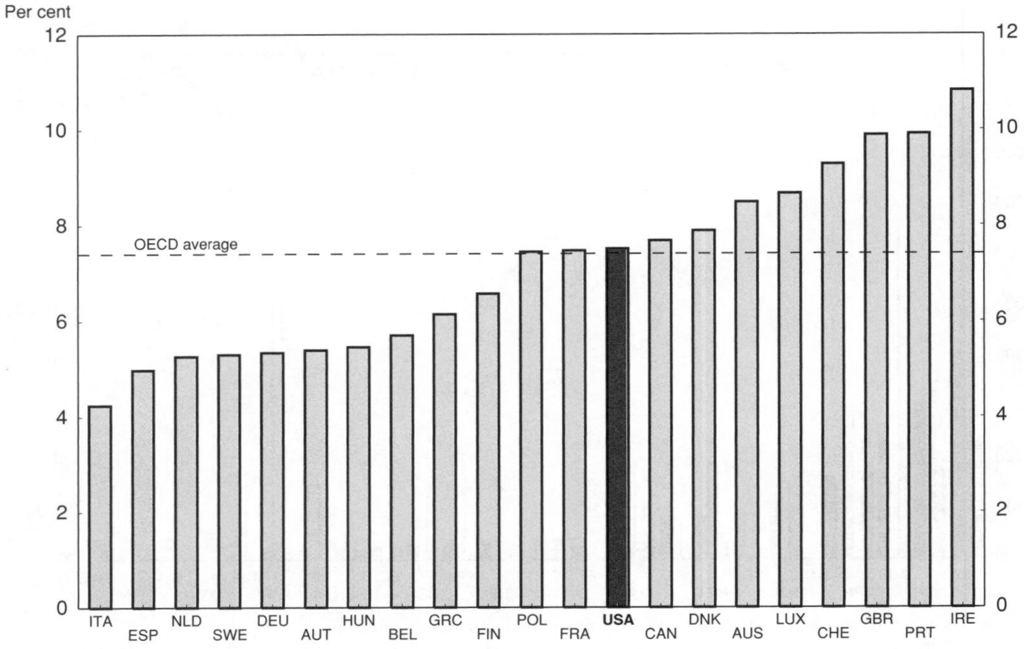

1. Average of estimates for men and women. Labour productivity is assume to grow at 1.75%.
2. Except Poland and Switzerland: 2000 and Hungary: 1997.
Source: OECD (forthcoming).

StatLink ⫘ *http://dx.doi.org/10.1787/010445480808*

majority of college students, the main barrier is the need to cover living expenses while forgoing normal paid employment.

In return for these investments, college graduates then receive a much higher salary. In 2005, the median 35-44 year old bachelors degree holder earned $54 800 – some 70% more than the median earnings ($32 200) of a 35-44 year old with only a high-school diploma. (College Board, *Education Pays*, 2006c) When allowance is made for taxes, financial assistance, different employment probabilities and so on, OECD estimates suggest that the average return to tertiary education is 7½ per cent a year, in real terms (Figure 6.3). This is close to the OECD average return, with the effect of high tuition fees being offset by relatively high wage premiums.

For policy purposes, the more interesting benchmark is the domestic real interest rate. Students earn a much greater return on their investment in education than they do on alternative investments. For example, the real pre-tax return on government bonds is about 2% in the United States. For borrowers, no prevailing interest rate serves as an obvious benchmark (arguably due to market failures discussed in the following section). The most common rate, on federal government Stafford loans (discussed in detail below) has a real after-tax rate of about 2%. Hence for the average student, going to college represents a very profitable investment in human capital.

Given that the estimated returns substantially exceed available interest rates, why do not more students go to college? Part of the reason is that the estimates above refer to the average student. Some potential students may expect to receive lower than average returns. However, the more common explanation, discussed in more detail below, is financial barriers. There is a widespread perception that many students do not have the resources to undertake college education.

Private markets, on their own, do not efficiently finance investments in education. Private loans are usually not available unless the borrower has a guarantee from the government or credit-worthy co-signer. This failure partly reflects the difficulty of ensuring repayment – unlike physical capital, human capital cannot be used as collateral. Wealthy families have traditionally dealt with this market failure by financing education through accumulated savings. However, this option is not available to potential students with poor or ungenerous parents. Even middle class parents find this difficult, particularly if they have several children or tuition fees are high.

The inability of poor families to fund their children's education is a problem in terms of both efficiency and equity. Accordingly, governments intervene to rectify this. In the United States, this intervention has many forms, of which the main ones are: state provision, grants, student loans, and tax concessions. (Governments also intervene in higher education for other purposes, such as research). Figure 6.4 provides some perspective on the size of these four programmes, though data availability makes

Figure 6.4. **Selected government support for higher education**

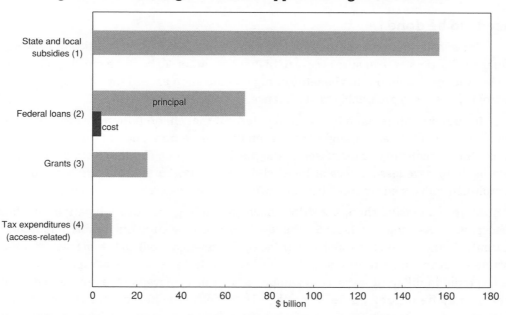

$ billion

1. State and local subsidies represents payments to institutions (not students) for 2001-2002 (*Digest of Education Statistics*, 2005, Table 28).
2. The $69 billion of federal loans received by students in 2005-06 (College Board, 2006b, Table 1) came with an *ex post* budgetary cost of $33 billion (most of which reflected increased subsidies for previously originated loans). Without unanticipated falls in short-term interest rates and their consequent cost of consolidations, the *ex ante* cost of student loans is budgeted to be $3 to 5 billion a year for the next decade (CBO, 2007, Table 3-3).
3. Grants reflect Federal and State (but not institutional) grants for 2005-06, from College Board, 2006b, Table 1.
4. Tax expenditures are for fiscal year 2006 from OMB (2006). Related expenditures are listed in Table 6.5 below.
Source: See above.

StatLink ᴍᴨᴾ *http://dx.doi.org/10.1787/010527652174*

comparisons inexact. Moreover, loans can be valued either at principal or at budgetary cost (subsidy value), depending on the purpose. Valuing loans at cost and ignoring differences of timing, expenditure on these four programmes sums to about $200 billion a year or 2% of GDP. This is somewhat higher than the estimates in Figure 6.1, due to differences in timing, coverage and definition. For example, Figure 6.1 excludes tax expenditures and grants for living expenses. Direct provision through locally and state-supported colleges and universities is by far the most expensive government intervention.

This chapter discusses these four programmes in rough order of the importance of the policy recommendations. So, after discussing the adequacy of current policy, the discussion below leads with loans, and then considers grants, tax concessions and subsidies.

The focus is on the effect of these policies on financial barriers, as issues of access dominate the US debate and are used to justify substantial government expenditures. That contrasts with debates in other countries, where externalities are often emphasised and the key question is the level of funding. In the United States it is often assumed that current levels of support substantially exceed levels justified by relevant externalities. Surveys of higher education financing in the United States (Gruber, 2005; Kane, 1999; or McPherson and Shapiro, 2006) attach minimal importance to them. Whether that assessment is valid is difficult to say – empirical research providing little guidance. That makes it difficult to make strong recommendations on the overall *level* of support. In contrast, there is a great deal to be said about *how* governments should intervene. Because existing forms of support are inefficient, better policy could deliver more access at lower cost.

More needs to be done

The substantial expenditures shown in Figure 6.4 do not appear sufficient to overcome financial barriers or to ensure access to higher education. To be more precise, there appear to be students for whom the benefits of higher education exceed the cost, but who do not enrol because they are unable to get finance.

In support of this claim it is often pointed out that children from wealthy families are much more likely to attend higher education than those from poorer families. But in itself, this is not convincing. As discussed in the previous chapter, children from poorer families are likely to have less success at high school. So it may be that the difference in college enrolment reflects educational barriers rather than short-term financial constraints.

More persuasive then, are differences controlling for both education and family background. As shown in Table 6.2 the lowest performing students from rich families had essentially the same enrolment rate (77%, the upper-right cell) as the highest performing students from poor families (78%, the lower left cell). These comparisons can be interpreted in different ways. For example, academic achievement, as measured in these tests, may be a poor guide to college-readiness (Heckman). However, the usual interpretation is that "poor and smart" students are more qualified for college than their "rich and dumb" counterparts, but a lack of financial resources turns them away.

Further evidence comes from differences in the sensitivity of enrolment rates. Enrolments appear to be relatively insensitive to future benefits or costs. For example, the dramatic widening of wage differentials over the 1980s raised the net present value of a college degree by over $100 000.[7] But the college enrolment rate rose only rose a modest 7 percentage points, from 65% to 72% (NCES, *Condition of Education, 1997*, p. 64). In contrast,

Table 6.2. **College enrolment rates by income and achievement levels, 1994**

Percentage of high school graduates attending post-secondary education with two years

Achievement levels (in quartiles)	Low-income	Middle-income	High-income
First (low)	36	49	77
Second	50	66	85
Third	63	79	90
Fourth (high)	78	89	97

Source: USDoE, NCES Condition of Education 1997 p. 64. Based on National Educational Longitudinal Study for High School Class of 1992.

a wide body of research finds much greater sensitivity to most determinants of current cash-flow. For surveys, see Kane (2002), Dynarski (2002) or Long (2007). This research suggests that to achieve a 7 percentage point increase in enrolments would only require a reduction in net cost per year of $1 000 to $2 000. The insensitivity to longer run returns, coupled with responsiveness to short-term cash-flow, is consistent with the view that many marginal students are constrained by limited finance.

There are many other pieces of evidence that point to limitations on the availability of finance. This includes the above-normal returns to higher education, the higher-still returns to marginal students (such as those living far from colleges), students working part-time for low pay (postponing graduation), and much greater sensitivity to costs by students with low family incomes (see Kane, 1999, 2006; Card, 2000). However, all of these are subject to alternative interpretations. Cameron and Heckman (1998) and Carneiro and Heckman (2002), for example, express scepticism.

One common response to this research is to point out that private loans for higher education have grown quickly. (For information on private loans, see Institute for Higher Education Policy, 2006). Some commentators assume that this has solved the problem of access. However, although private loans are now widespread, they are not universal. They typically require a credit-worthy co-signer, such as a parent. Many students, such as "independent" Pell grant recipients, cannot provide this. Some loans are available without a guarantor, but these are for professional students, not the typical undergraduate. So the popularity of private loans does not remove the need for policy measures to ensure access.

Admittedly, these issues are controversial. The important point may be that there is a large body of research that supports with the view that financial barriers prevent many students from undertaking worthwhile study. However, the extent to which this research clearly establishes that hypothesis is subject to debate.

In addition to the formal research there is also a great deal of anecdotal evidence. Financial aid advisors, career guidance counsellors and others who deal with high-school leavers suggest that financial barriers are decisive in preventing many students going to college. And many policy makers say they are personally aware of examples. That kind of evidence may not persuade researchers, but it appears to be influential within the higher education community and broader policy circles. At that level, there seems to be a consensus that financial barriers to education are important and that more needs to be done about this. Although the academic debate may not be resolved, the political debate seems more settled.

The most recent expression of this consensus is the report of the Spellings Commission. It concluded that "Access to higher education in the United States is unduly limited by … persistent financial barriers … There is ample evidence that qualified young people from low-income families are far less likely to go to college than their similarly qualified peers from high-income families" (Commission on the Future of Higher Education, 2006, p. 7). Accordingly, it called for an enormous increase in needs-based financial grants. In particular, "to increase the purchasing power of the average Pell Grant to a level of 70% (from 48% in 2004-05) of the average in-state tuition at public four-year institutions over a period of five years" (p. 18). This would involve a real increase of about two-thirds in Federal Pell grant expenditure, at a total cost of perhaps around $8 billion (assuming tuition continues to increase at recent rates). The Administration and Congress have responded very positively to these proposals. At the time of writing, it is expected that large increases in Pell grants will be included in the next budget.

The political reality is that there are strong pressures on policy makers to ameliorate perceived financial barriers. The important question is not *whether* policy should aim to reduce financial barriers, but *how*. The following subsections discuss the four main ways in which governments support higher education.

Loans

Raising the Stafford loan limits

The US government has several student loan programmes, of which the most important are "Stafford" loans. These come in two varieties. "Direct" student loans are from the federal Department of Education, while "guaranteed" student loans are from private banks for which the government guarantees repayment. In 2005, 23% of Stafford loans were made through the direct student loan programme. Stafford Loans may be "subsidised" or "unsubsidised" the difference being that no interest is charged on subsidised loans until 6 months after graduation. Legislation currently before Congress would substantially lower the interest rate on subsidised loans. About half the Stafford loans originated in 2005-06 were subsidised. Other loan programmes include PLUS loans made to parents and Perkins loans distributed by schools. Individual loans (including loans from different programmes) can be "consolidated" or joined together in one loan.

The Stafford loan programme has many attractive features relative to loan programmes in other countries. Loans are available for both tuition fees and living costs. They are available to almost all students, albeit up to differing limits. Subsidy levels vary but tend to be light. And repayments can vary with post-graduation income. Several of these features, particularly the last two, are discussed below.

The cost to the government of Stafford loans varies. Loans originated since July 2006 have an interest rate of 6.8%. This is about 2 percentage points above the current government 10-year bond rate of 4¾ per cent. Costs of administration and of default are difficult to estimate, but may each add about 1½ percentage points a year (CBO, 2005), which is partly offset by a one-off origination fee of up to 3%. The overall cost to the government of direct unsubsidised Stafford loans is small and possibly negative. Costs for subsidised loans, guaranteed loans and loans originated before July 2006 are higher.

In assessing subsidy levels, the tax deductibility of interest payments may also be relevant. This deduction reduces interest payments (for those below an income threshold) by the marginal income tax rate. Assuming a marginal (federal, state plus local) rate of say 35%,[8] the effective interest rate is about 4.4%, which would seem significantly subsidised. But arguably, the tax deduction should not be seen as a subsidy but as a counterpart to the tax on the return from the investment. Viewed that way, the subsidy is small. That is important because it means fiscal constraints are not an argument against expansion of this aspect of the programme.

Student loans have been found to modestly increase college attendance, persistence and choice (GAO, 2005, p. 29). For example, Long (2004, cited by GAO, 2005) found that a $1 000 increase, in 1977 dollars, resulted in a 4.3 percentage points increase in college enrolment among dependent students with family incomes below $15 000. Dynarski (2003) found a similar response among wealthier students to increases in the subsidy value of loans. These results contrast with research on Pell grants which, as discussed below, has often found little if any effect. In international comparisons, countries with large student loan programmes tend to have above-average enrolment rates (Figure 6.5) and graduation rates. It is not clear in which direction the causation of this relationship runs, but it is consistent with the view that loans facilitate access to college.

Figure 6.5. **Student loans and enrolment rates, 2003**

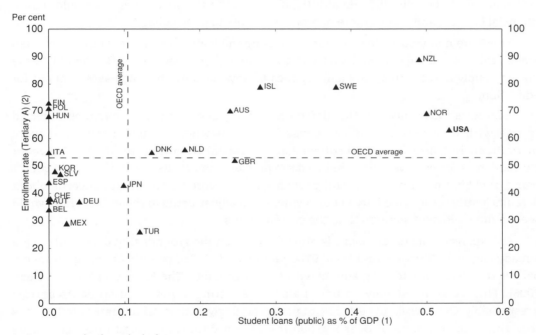

1. Loans are valued at principal.
2. US enrolment is for both Tertiary-type A and type-B institutions.

Source: OECD, *Education at a Glance*, 2006, Tables C2.1 and (except USA) A3.1. US loans are taken from College Board (2006b).

StatLink ⫶⧉⧉ *http://dx.doi.org/10.1787/010535355245*

Perhaps the main problem with the Stafford loan programme is that there are low limits on how much students can borrow, as set out in Table 6.3.

These limits fall far short of the total cost of study for most students, especially undergraduates. They do not cover living expenses, let alone tuition. Accordingly, they are often binding. Among the 33% of dependent students who took out Stafford loans in 2004, about 60% borrowed the maximum amount (Institute for Higher Education Policy, 2006, Table 6). Many professional, graduate and other independent students also borrow up to their limits, even though these are much higher. Significant increases in limits (for

Table 6.3. **Limits on Stafford loans**

Year of enrolment	Dependent ($)	Independent ($)
First	2 625	6 625
Second	3 500	77 500
Third and fourth	5 500	10 500
Undergraduate lifetime limit	23 000	46 000
Graduate or professional per year		18 500
Graduate or professional lifetime limit		138 500

example, to $3 500 for first year undergraduates) are scheduled to come into effect in July 2007, and further increases have been proposed in the 2008 budget (the annual limit for third and fourth year undergraduates would rise to $7 500). However, these limits still fall well short of the cost of attendance.

For subsidised loans, the limits can be justified by budgetary considerations. However, for unsubsidised loans the rationale for the limits is unclear. Extra lending at current rates would appear to benefit students at little, if any, cost to the government. It would reduce financial barriers and enable more potential students to go to college.

There are many possible objections to raising the loan limits. For example, it is often argued that expanding student loans would lead to higher college costs. One would "move up the supply curve". This "problem" applies to any measure that increases demand for education.

A more serious concern is that default rates and hence fiscal costs might be expected to rise with debt levels. This issue was important when unsubsidised loans were introduced in 1993 – the 1990 cohort had an initial default rate of 22%. However subsequent reforms have greatly reduced the problem of defaults – that of the 2004 cohort being only 5% (much of which will probably be recovered). Although concerns about defaults justify some selectivity in borrowing, small adjustments to the interest rate would seem a more efficient solution than the current limits.

An expansion of student loans is often opposed on the grounds that debt burdens are already excessive. Surveys find that 59% of adults and 63% of parents of college students believe that "students today graduate with too much debt" (The Project on Student Debt, 2006). This assessment may be paternalistic, reflecting a view that students borrow irresponsibly. Otherwise, it is difficult to understand, given that default rates are low. It is true that debt burdens of over $40 000 may seem daunting – but these need to be considered relative to capacity to pay. Borrowing to pay for college generates the earning power that makes loans affordable. In 2003, the median bachelor's degree holder earned about $19 000 a year more than the median high school graduate (or $14 000 more, after taxes). This difference is sufficient to repay the average cost of attendance (measured as foregone earnings plus average tuition costs at a public 4-year university, or $87 000 in sum), with interest, by age 33. By age 64, that premium could repay $177 000 in debt at a 5% real interest rate and still have money left over.[9] Compared to these earnings differentials, current debt burdens (Figure 6.6) seem comfortable.

Problems with loans and the rationale for income-contingent repayments

Even though students can afford to (and seemingly want to) repay larger loans than at present, simply making these available would not solve the problem of access to college.

Figure 6.6. **Distribution of student debt levels**
Graduates of 4-year institutions; 2003-2004

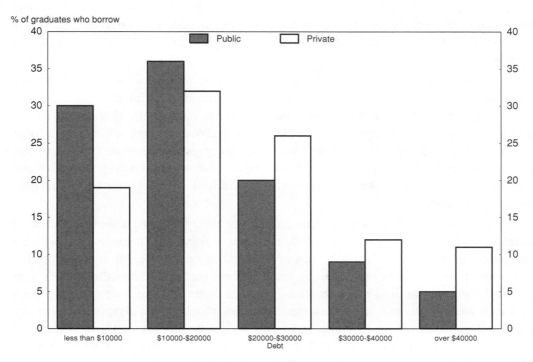

Source: College Board, *Trends in Student Aid*, 2006b, Figure 4b.

StatLink 🔗 *http://dx.doi.org/10.1787/010635754660*

Many students will not take out loans because they are not confident of being able to make the repayments. Although tertiary education is highly profitable for the typical student, many students will not be confident of doing as well as the average. In 2005, the median 35-44 year-old bachelor's degree holder earned $54 800. But 28% of this group earned less than $40 000, while 5% earned less than $20 000 (College Board, *Education Pays*, 2006c). These variations are difficult to predict in advance. Observable characteristics[10] of 1972 high school students going on to college only explain one-quarter of the variation in their subsequent 1986 income (Krueger and Bowen, 1993, p. 196). So it is rational for risk-averse students to avoid fixed mortgage-type repayments. If future income could be insured, that need not be a problem. But because of informational problems, ("moral hazard" and "adverse selection") insurance is unavailable. Or in slightly different terms, human capital is one of the few forms of long-term investment for which equity finance is unavailable. A closely related problem is the overly pessimistic expectations of some students. Many potential students (particularly those from low-income backgrounds where role models are rare) appear to be unaware of the financial benefits of higher education.

It is not clear how important the problems of risk aversion and pessimistic expectations are in economic terms. Researchers have had difficulty finding convincing evidence of their effects. Nevertheless, both policy makers and voters, in the United States as elsewhere, appear convinced that these problems are serious. In particular, they underpin the preference for heavily subsidised forms of financial support (direct subsidies or Pell grants) over loans with fixed repayments. Reform of higher education finance needs to take these assessments into account. It turns out that it is possible to do so at little fiscal cost.

A possible solution to these problems is to make loan repayments vary with income. Successful students pay back more than unsuccessful ones. So, should a student fail to find a well-paying job after graduation, he or she need not fear being stuck with high loan repayments. Essentially, the lender bears much of the risk. Similarly, students with pessimistic expectations need not be afraid of debt – their loan repayments will also be expected to be low.

Economists have long argued that income-contingent loans represent an efficient and equitable means of financing higher education.[11] Countries that have introduced them include Sweden in 1988, Australia in 1989, New Zealand in 1991, South Africa in 1991, Chile in 1994, and the United Kingdom in 1997. In the United States, income contingent loans were introduced as part of the Direct Stafford loan programme in 1993. This allows borrowers to make repayments equal to 20% of the difference between the poverty rate and income, up to a ceiling. Annex 6.A1 provides details of how income contingent loans have been implemented.

Experience in countries with income-contingent loans has often been favourable. For example, the loan programmes in Australia and New Zealand have been credited with the expansion of enrolments of 50% and 90% in those countries (including roughly proportionate increases in enrolment by lower-income students). Several countries have extended their programmes to substantially increase their role. And their spread to other countries seems to be continuing. However, the record also includes disappointments and reversals. Sweden abandoned its programme in 2001.[12] Australia stopped lending for living expenses in 2003.[13] And, in the United States, only 11% of borrowers with direct or consolidated loans have chosen income-contingent repayments (Table 6.4).

Table 6.4. **Percentage of borrowers choosing different repayment options, 2000**

	Direct loans	Consolidated loans
Standard (default)	72	43
Income contingent	7	26
Extended	6	12
Graduated	15	19

Source: US Department of Education and the US General Accounting Office (2001, Appendix IV).

The unpopularity of income-contingent loans in the United States is an important puzzle. Whether, and how, policy should promote these loans depends on the reasons for their unpopularity. Unfortunately, those reasons are not entirely clear. One possible explanation is that the US programme is poorly designed. This has been argued by Bruce Chapman (2006), one of the architects of the Australian programme. Some of the issues he raises are discussed in Annex 6.A1. Another possibility is that problems of risk-aversion and pessimism may be unimportant and that income-contingency is something that borrowers simply do not want. However, the strong political support for grants and subsidies suggests that these are problems that the loan system needs to address. In other countries, income-contingent repayments are commonly described as popular. That assessment is largely political, but also based on limited market data.[14]

A more important factor behind the unpopularity of income-contingent repayments in the United States may be inertia. As research in a variety of different settings has shown, individuals tend to remain with the default option when given choices, particularly for complicated financial decisions (see Beshears *et al.*, 2006).[15] This may explain the choices shown in Table 6.4, where 72% of borrowers in the direct loan programme stick with the default or standard repayment option – which makes equal monthly payments over 10 years. Only 7% choose income-contingent repayments. However, when borrowers are given more time and the opportunity to reflect on their repayments, the popularity of the income contingent option rises. When loans are consolidated (bundled together), 26% choose this option.

Still, even with consolidated loans, the default remains substantially more popular. That is puzzling, but not necessarily a reliable guide to borrower preferences. For complicated decisions, borrowers economise on information costs by choosing the most popular option. This leads to standardisation of financial products and makes it possible for markets to be locked into an undesirable equilibrium.

Reinforcing the importance of inertia, many students are uninformed of their options. In one survey of law students two-thirds of respondents had not heard of income-contingent repayments (Schrag, 2001, cited in Chapman, 2006). These responses are consistent with discussions with financial aid advisors. However, they are puzzling given the ready availability of information. A related problem is the misleading advice that students are given about loan repayment. It is common for interest payments to be summed at a zero nominal discount rate and hence for borrowers to be told that deferring payments "increases" them – even when the present value (or even the real value) of interest payments declines.[16] This mistake is not confined to student loans but is standard financial "advice" in the United States. Obviously, better information and advice would be helpful, although whether this would make much difference is unclear.

More broadly, it may be that income-contingent repayments are too complicated to understand and compare with alternatives. Accordingly, there is a good case for making income-contingent repayments the default. For complicated decisions, individuals will often be better off if the default is the "best" option, even if that is not the simplest or most-familiar alternative. If marginal students are as risk-averse and uninformed as the advocates of subsidies and Pell grants contend, then the income-contingent option would be much better for them.

A further step would be to make income-contingent repayments the only option, as in other countries and as proposed by Gary Becker (2006). This would reduce adverse selection (discussed below) and simplify decision making. Economists who believe individuals frequently err in the face of complicated financial decisions argue that it would make borrowers better off. However, that argument is speculative (albeit plausible) as it applies to student loans. In the absence of evidence that adverse selection or borrower mistakes are serious problems, providing choices, as in the United States, seems preferable.

The economics literature emphasises two potential problems with income contingent loans. "Moral hazard" means that graduates may work less hard or avoid employment in highly paid jobs due to higher effective marginal tax rates. "Adverse selection" means that students who tend to choose income contingent repayments will be those with poor prospects, while those doing professional courses, for example, will try to finance their studies in other ways. These problems also afflict other forms of government support. For example, means-tested grants and the taxes required to finance general subsidies also have undesirable incentive effects. Adverse selection means that the loan scheme may not be able to run at a profit – though, as long as there is some repayment, the cost would still be less than grants or subsidies. These concerns are important to the details of policy implementation, but they do not seem to have been sufficient to prevent the extension and spread of income contingent loans in other countries. A possible exception is Sweden's abandonment of income-contingent loans in 2001, which was partly out of concern for moral hazard effects. But that was in a context of tax rates far in excess of those in the United States. Otherwise, evidence on the importance of these problems is limited. Making income contingency the default would broaden the pool of borrowers and thereby presumably lessen adverse selection. However, increasing loan limits could give rise to new problems. This is an argument for proceeding cautiously, with regular review of programme parameters.

Other issues relating to student loans

The House of Representatives has recently passed legislation reducing interest rates on subsidised Stafford loans. In opinion polls, 88% of Americans support this. However, this proposal seems to be unnecessary and costly, with the subsidy not being well directed from the perspective of improving access. Since most dependent Stafford loan holders already borrow up to the limit, the important constraint is not the net return but the availability of finance. Indeed, increasing subsidies makes it more difficult to raise lending limits.

The interest rate on Stafford loans is fixed in legislation at 6.8%. Accordingly, subsidy levels will change, in unintended ways, with changes in market interest rates. This seems to be a simple design flaw that needs to be rectified; for example, by tying the rate to the long term bond rate. In the meantime, variations in subsidy levels may provide useful information.

A bigger issue is the co-existence of the direct and guaranteed loan systems. One might hope that this dual system could be rationalised. A joint Department of Education and General Accounting Office study (2001) discussed how this might be done, including for income-contingent repayments. However, the appropriate role of government *versus* private lenders is not clear. It depends, for example, on the importance of adverse selection and moral hazard, which are not known. There are arguments for maintaining the dual system until more is known. That said, the current subsidies to private lenders seem clearly excessive. Although precise estimates are controversial, substantial rent-seeking (marketing, lobbying, etc.) and pressures to bend the law suggest that private lenders are receiving more than they need. The House of Representatives and the Administration have both proposed reductions in these subsidies, which is to be commended.

Pell grants

Instead of raising loan limits, as suggested above, perhaps the most widely supported proposal for dealing with financial barriers is to increase Pell grants. These are given to low-income families to pay for their educational expenditures. In 2005-06, the Federal and State governments provided $19 billion and $7 billion respectively in grants. Most of the Federal grants were through the Pell Grant programme. This provided $13 billion per year to 5.3 million students, at an average payment of $2 400.[17] As noted earlier, the Spellings Commission called for an increase in Pell Grants by about two-thirds. This proposal has been warmly received by the Administration, Congress and the higher education community. However, how it might be financed has not yet been explained.

The objective of Pell grants is to facilitate access to higher education for children from lower income families. As previously discussed, this objective seems appropriate from both an efficiency and equity perspective. However, whether grants are effective in addressing this objective is doubtful. Hansen (1983), Kane (1994), Manski (1992-93), and Kitmitto (2004) found that Pell grants had little or no impact on attendance, though Seftor and Turner (2002) found that they increased attendance for students between 22 and 35 years of age.[18] These seemingly weak effects contrast with strong evidence of responsiveness to tuition costs noted previously. There are many possible reasons that may help to reconcile these findings, including the inadequate level of grants, their complexity, their gradually phased-in implementation and the tendency of institutions to offset Pell grants by reducing their own needs-based aid. Proposals to overcome some of these obstacles are discussed below.

For a student from a family with annual income below $15 000, the Pell grant programme provides a grant of $4 050. The Administration's 2008 Budget proposes raising this to $5 400 over the next five years. For better-off students, the grant amount is reduced according to income and assets. However, as noted above, living expenses are much more than this, as is tuition at most 4-year institutions. So, by itself, Pell grants do not make going to college affordable. Students still need to borrow, work, or rely on their families. When, as is often the case, these options are limited, students may choose not to go to college.

The inadequacy of Pell grants may suggest that they should be raised. The main difficulty however, and indeed the main problem with grants in general, is their fiscal cost. Grants are financed by higher taxes, which are bad for the economy and politically unpopular. Hence although Congressional representatives are attracted in principle to increasing grants, the amounts being proposed will still not make college affordable.

The distributional implications of grants are also problematic. Grants represent a transfer to students who are expected to have high lifetime incomes. Even though dependent students come from poorer backgrounds they, as individuals, are better-off than most. Independent students (the majority of Pell grant recipients) need not come from poor families, though they have had one year of low reported income and assets.

Pell grants also distort price signals and impair efficiency. Some of these effects are straight-forward. For example, the means-testing of income provides a disincentive to work. Other effects are more subtle. For example, the marginal "tax rate" on assets is 5.6%. This applies each year a child is in college. So a family with two children undertaking four-year degrees might lose nearly 50% of their accumulated savings. Some assets (529 saving accounts) have borne marginal tax rates of 100% and higher.[19] Offsetting this, housing equity (like retirement savings accounts) is not counted within assets – so this tax is easy (though not costless) to evade by paying down a mortgage prior to college, then refinancing after graduation to recreate the original portfolio. On average, Dick and Edlin (1997) estimate that means-testing raises marginal tax rates on income between 2% and 16% and marginal tax rates on savings between 8% and 26%.

Simplifying the means-test

A commonly suggested explanation for the apparent ineffectiveness of Pell grants is their complexity. The main form for applying for aid, the FAFSA, is considerably longer than the federal income tax form, the complexity of which is already at the top of tax reform agendas. It asks many more questions, in intrusive detail, and requires that records be created and kept that would otherwise not be needed. Partly as a result, many eligible students do not even apply. King (2004) estimates that 850 000 students who would have been eligible for Pell grants in 2000 did not complete the necessary forms. Recognising these problems, the Administration and Congress have made simplifying the application process a priority. Several steps in this direction are noted in Box 6.1, and the College Made EZ Act, currently under consideration by Congress. These involve a number of worthwhile administrative changes, including streamlining the application process and greater sharing of information with the IRS. However, it seems desirable to go further.

Many of the questions on the FAFSA cover means-test criteria that are of little importance. Applicants are asked about IRA rollovers (an asset management tool of benefit only to the very wealthy), welfare benefits (that are a function of other items on the form) and rare forms of income like foreign income and living stipends for clergy. Worse, because the form is complicated, many students (for example, 90% of those eligible for an "automatic zero") answer questions that have no effect on their eligibility. Dynarski and Scott-Clayton (2006) estimate that deleting 80% of the financial questions on the FAFSA would change the Pell grant by less than $500 for 88% of dependent undergraduates and lower expenditure by 0.2%.

A further worthwhile simplification would be to abolish the assets test. As a general principle, taxing saving involves serious distortions, as the recent Tax Panel emphasised. Furthermore, the administrative burden of the assets test is relatively large – requiring records that would not be kept for tax purposes. However, this would be more costly, raising expenditure by 8%. Together with the deleting of unimportant questions noted above, Dynarski and Scott-Clayton estimate that removing the assets test would change Pell grants by less than $500 for 86% of their sample.

A closely related problem has been a lack of transparency. Many families do not know and are not able to calculate their likely eligibility for aid. Unlike a tax form, the FAFSA does not indicate a bottom line – how much aid the student might expect. Rather, the form is mailed away for processing and the student is notified several months before college enrolment. This notice is too short for families to increase their savings or to apply to a different range of colleges.

To clarify aid eligibility (and reduce application time), an internet-based tool for calculating eligibility became available on 1 April 2007. A more radical solution, suggested by Dynarski and Scott-Clayton, would be to simplify the means test sufficiently that information on Pell grant eligibility could be put on a postcard. That alternative could be somewhat costly. And the details are debatable though they probably have substantial efficiency and simplification advantages.

The appropriate role of grants

Loans have similar objectives to grants but avoid many of their problems. In particular, because they are repaid (in part or full), they have less cost to the budget and the taxpayer. Or, equivalently, for a given fiscal cost, loans can put substantially more cash in the hands of students than can grants. Loans involve less redistribution from the general taxpayer to well-off college graduates. Loans involve less distortion of prices. And for unsubsidised loans, no complicated means-testing is necessary. Grants have some advantages over loans with fixed repayments, which are unattractive to risk-averse or pessimistic students, but that does not extend to income-contingent loans.

Were a good system of loans in place, with high limits and income-contingent repayments, then grants would no longer be needed to overcome financial barriers.

However, because of other market failures, a role for grants would remain, though narrower than at present.

Perhaps the most common argument for preferring grants over loans is to deal with those potential students who would not ordinarily consider attending college. It is argued that cash grants focus their attention in a way that more complicated loans do not. However, this argument only justifies grants for the first year of college. After that, information would be both salient and available. Furthermore, it seems to support payments to a more narrowly defined group: students from poor communities without role models. Even then, provision of information, possibly through extra financial aid councillors, would seem a more directly targeted approach.

Means-tested grants can also be justified by externalities (the benefits to others that recipients provide), like the provision of role models in their communities and diversity at college. However, these arguments only apply to students because they are unusual – so would not justify widespread subsidies. Furthermore, diversity benefits to other students are already addressed by grants (tuition discounts) from colleges. In economics language, this internalises the externality. That is, those who benefit from the diversity (other students) pay for it, which seems appropriate. Finally, means-tested grants can also be justified by society's desire to encourage income mobility.

The above arguments for means-tested grants apply to students from low-income families but not necessarily to "independent" students. Independent students are either married, aged over 24, veterans, graduate or professional students, or have children. They need not come from a disadvantaged background. In 2004-05, they accounted for 57% of Pell grant recipients. The rationale for assisting these students rests on capital market failure, which is more efficiently and equitably addressed through loans rather than grants. Furthermore, arguments for grants based on externalities and information also suggest that high school and/or neighbourhood characteristics may be more relevant than individual or family characteristics. Directing grants accordingly would have the added advantage of simplifying the application process.

Overall, were a good system of loans in place, then the costly increases in Pell grants that have recently been proposed would seem to be unnecessary. As noted in Box 6.1, a review of the federal financial aid system is being commissioned. As part of that, the role of the grants should be reconsidered with a view to focussing on informational problems and externalities. That would presumably involve fewer payments. In particular, grants beyond the first year of college and to independents could be reduced.

Tax relief

Federal and state governments also finance higher education through a series of tax breaks for students and their families. Table 6.5 shows federal tax expenditures on education for 2006. Unfortunately, estimates that distinguish tertiary education from primary and secondary education are not available. Not included in the table is the deductibility of state and local taxes used, *inter alia*, to fund education. Although arguably the largest federal tax expenditure on education, issues relating to state and local spending are discussed in the following section. The Lifetime Learning Tax Credit and the HOPE tax credit provide tax credits of up to $2 000 per year per person for the costs of higher education. Alternatively, individuals can deduct from their taxable income up to $4 000 per year in higher education expenses. The other main concession aimed at promoting access

Table 6.5. **Estimates of federal income tax expenditures on education, 2006**

In millions of dollars

HOPE tax credit	3 650
Lifetime Learning tax credit	2 340
Deduction for higher education expenses	1 840
Deductibility of student-loan interest	800
Subtotal (tuition incentives):	**8 630**
Deductibility of charitable contributions (education)	3 680
Parental personal exemption for students age 19 or over	2 500
Exclusion of scholarship and fellowship income	1 450
Exclusion of interest on bonds for private non-profit educational facilities	1 160
Exclusion of employer-provided educational assistance	590
State prepaid tuition plans	540
Exclusion of interest on student-loan bonds	300
Special deduction for teacher expenses	150
Credit for holders of zone academy bonds	130
Education Individual Retirement Accounts	90
Exclusion of interest in savings bonds redeemed to finance educational expenses	20
Discharge of student loan indebtedness	20
Total	**19 260**

Source: 2007 budget. Analytical Perspectives, p. 228.

to higher education is the deductibility of interest paid on student loans. These four "tuition incentives" add up to about $9 billion per year in foregone government revenue, about 1% of total Federal tax expenditures. In 2002, 16 million tax filers claimed one of these preferences. There are also several smaller measures and others that might be considered as addressing other objectives. The parental personal exemption for students aged over 18 (worth $2.5 billion) is sometimes considered as promoting access to education, though others consider it a horizontal equity measure. Total federal tax expenditures on education (not including deductibility of state and local taxes) add up to $19 billion.

The deductibility of student interest payments differs from the other tuition incentives in that it affects loan repayments, rather than current expenses. One feature of this deduction is that it phases out above an Adjusted Gross Income of $50 000 (for singles, $100 000 for couples). This more than halves real interest payments for those on lower post-graduation incomes[20] which gives all student loans an element of income-contingency. The student loan deduction probably does not boost access much – being received well after graduation. However, it does affect perceived interest costs. Its desirability needs to be considered in conjunction with the parameters of income contingent loan repayments and the overall level of subsidy for student loans. The other tuition incentives, which happen to be much larger, are harder to justify.

One problem with the tax concessions is that they mainly benefit middle income earners. Because low income families have low marginal and average tax rates, they benefit little from deductions or non-refundable credits. And the formula for calculating the credits reduces their value as Pell grants increase. Accordingly, about 60% of the value of the three tuition-related preferences flows to families with incomes of more than $40 000 (Figure 6.7). This is not where the main barriers to access are. Only 11% of the value

Figure 6.7. **Distribution of tax preferences by income, 2002**

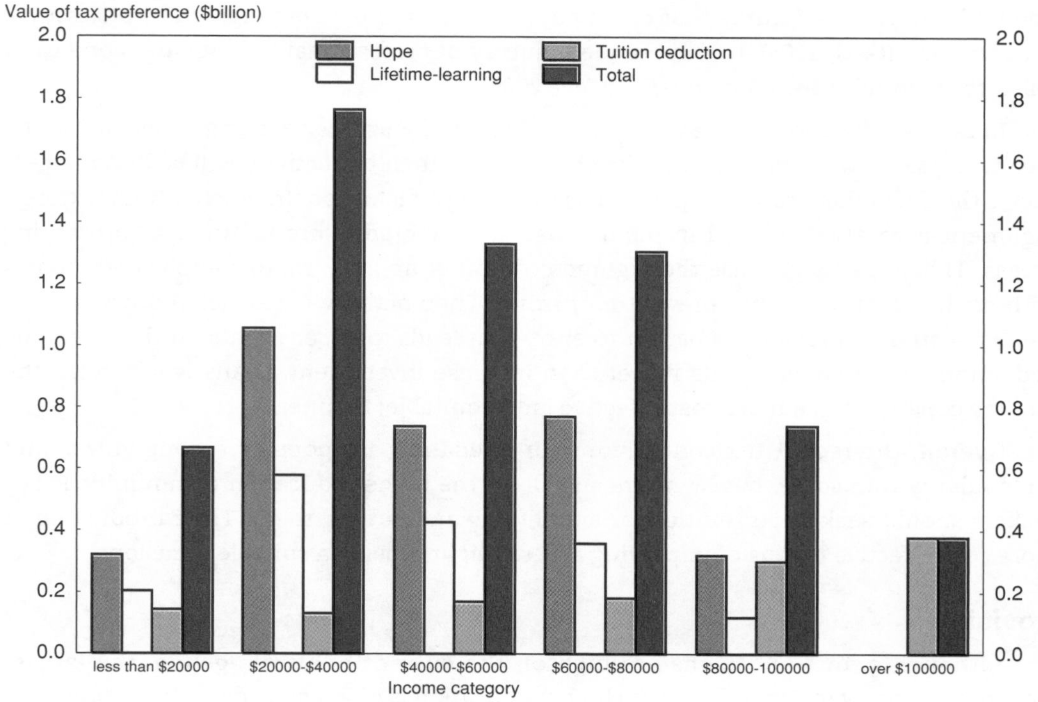

Value of tax preference ($billion)

Legend: Hope, Lifetime-learning, Tuition deduction, Total

Income category: less than $20000, $20000-$40000, $40000-$60000, $60000-$80000, $80000-100000, over $100000

Source: GAO, 2005, Table 6.

StatLink ⫘⫘ http://dx.doi.org/10.1787/010636184017

of the tax preferences went to families with incomes below $20 000. In contrast, 9% of the value of Pell grants to dependent students went to families with incomes above $40 000, while 48% went to families with incomes below $20 000. (GAO, 2005, Table 4). Apart from the obvious equity problems, the credits are not a cost-effective instrument for promoting access.

Another problem is timing. For tuition-related expenses, families do not receive the benefits of the concessions till the year following their outlay. This clearly reduces their effectiveness as a means of relaxing credit constraints.

The interaction with the financial aid system is cumbersome. The US government has one programme (grants) that carefully targets assistance at lower income families. And another (tax concessions) that targets it at middle-income families. Where one programme leaves off, the other kicks in. (See, for example, Table 1 in Kane, 1997). Each programme incurs significant costs to prevent benefits flowing to certain recipients – but then another programme delivers benefits to those recipients. Having two programmes duplicates administration, forms, and bureaucracy.

And it adds complexity, which is perhaps the clearest problem with the tax concessions. The provisions are complicated, require extensive record keeping and interact in non-obvious ways. As one example, they each define qualified education expenses differently. Tax analysts say they require an unusually large investment of knowledge and skill (GAO, 2005, p. 20). Accordingly, many eligible tax payers do not claim them. A GAO Survey found that 27% of eligible tax filers did not claim either the tuition deduction or a tax credit. In doing so, they paid an average $169 more than required, with 10% paying $500 more than required. A further 21% did not claim as much as much as they could. About 50% of the tax returns that could have claimed more were prepared by *professional* tax preparers (GAO, 2005). In a subsequent survey of professional tax preparers one third failed to claim full education benefits (GAO, 2006).

In theory, education can be viewed as an expense incurred in earning an income. If the income is taxed, with no deduction for the expense, then the activity will be discouraged. Hence the deductions can be supported as removing a distortion. In practice, this textbook argument is rarely advanced in public: instead, the credits are justified as promoting access. This is partly because the argument does not apply in more complicated models with credit constraints that prevent borrowing. Then activity is restricted anyway, with credit constraints providing a barrier to entry that leads to super-profits. In that case, the deductions boost super-profits rather than increase investment. Loans would relax the binding constraint in a more cost-effective (and equitable) manner.

Overall, the recent tax concessions for education are popular among voters and unpopular within some, but by no means all, in the higher education community. Policy makers should seek opportunities for simplifying and cutting them. The introduction of more cost-effective means of improving access might provide a suitable occasion.

State provision

Although grants and loans are high on the current political agenda, the largest government intervention in financing higher education is direct subsidies. Direct provision of higher education through locally and state-supported colleges and universities amounted to $160 billion per year in 2001-02. This represented 9% of total state and local government spending and 1.5% of GDP. (NCES *Digest* 2006, Tables 28, 29 and 30). These institutions offer substantially subsidised tuition for in-state students and somewhat less subsidised tuition for out-of-state students. In 1996-97 the average educational expenditure on public four-year institutions was $13 118 per full-time equivalent student.[21] In contrast, the average published tuition fee at these institutions was $2 975. So students without discounts were, on average, paying 23% of the direct costs of their education. Students with grants, of course, paid less.

Over the last two decades, there has been an increasing squeeze on the budgets of public colleges and universities. Government spending per student has increased, but apparently not by enough to match the growing demand. The shortfall has been partly made up by large increases in tuition charges, as shown in Figure 6.8. This increasing reliance on private financing is an international development. In the OECD, the share of tertiary expenditures financed privately has risen from 19% in 1995 to 24% in 2003.

Despite higher tuition, expenditures at public institutions have not kept up with those in the private sector. Since 1980, expenditures per student at *public* four-year institutions have grown about 2% per annum faster than the consumer price index (CPI). Although a good price index for education is not available, it seems that real expenditures were approximately flat in level terms and declining as a share of real income. That is despite a high income-elasticity of demand for higher education. In contrast, expenditures per student at *private* four-year institutions have grown an average 5% a year faster than the CPI. Hence, while private institutions have been increasing staff-student ratios, public institutions have been reducing them. Similarly, private faculty salaries have been

Figure 6.8. **Share of revenue of public tertiary institutions**[1]

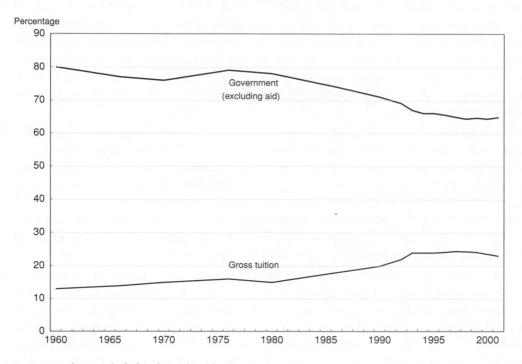

1. Revenue does not include sales and services.
Source: Mcpherson and Shapiro (2006, p. 1408); NCES (*Digest of Education Statistics, 2005*; Table 329).
StatLink ⬛ http://dx.doi.org/10.1787/010716123126

outstripping those in the public institutions. Reflecting this, available measures suggest that the quality of education at public institutions has been deteriorating relative to that at private institutions (Kane, 2006, p. 1375).

The squeeze on public funding seems to reflect growing pressure on state government budgets (in particular from Medicaid) interacting with a finite willingness of many taxpayers to fund investments that benefit those who are better off. These distributional concerns are clearest in states pursuing "high tuition-high aid" strategies, such as Michigan and Virginia, where tuition has risen sharply while public funds have been redirected toward student financial aid. International experience and the prospect of large increases in Medicaid expenditure both suggest that the pressure on public expenditures will continue. So consideration of alternative methods of financing will probably increase in importance.

The desirability of the decline in the share of public support is controversial. Direct provision of higher education by state governments is usually supported on grounds of "improving access" or "removing financial barriers". However the spending is not directed towards students in difficulty. More targeted assistance, such as grants or loans, could achieve greater access at lower cost. Of course, reducing subsidies, in the absence of improvements to loans or grants, impairs access.

General subsidies are also supported on grounds of externalities. That is, there are benefits to society in addition to the private benefits enjoyed by the individual graduate. Examples include taxes, innovation and culture. However, this argument does not convincingly support subsidies at a state level. On the margin, 70% of students educated by public institutions leave the state after graduation (Bound *et al.* 2004)[22] So the taxpayers who finance these graduates' education recoup little of the return. Nevertheless, the argument has more force at a federal level. In particular, a sizeable body of research suggests that encouraging higher education is good for economic growth (see Section 2.3 of Chapman, 2006). However, it provides little guidance as to how large an effort is warranted, and even less on the appropriate means of subsidy (that is, whether through direct provision, grants or loans).

Costs need to be weighed against these benefits. Many observers believe the subsidies are inequitable, because they benefit students who disproportionately come from well-off families. In 1994, 61% of children from high-income families enrolled in a public post-secondary institution, in contrast to 34% of children from low-income families (Akerhielm *et al.*, 1998, Table 4). Furthermore, these students subsequently go on to well-paid jobs, as noted earlier. However, judgments on equity depend on how the subsidy is financed. Although state government revenue tends to come from taxpayers who, on average, earn less than graduates, it is less clear whence marginal revenue comes.

Inefficiencies arise from distorted price signals. For example, there is less pressure on public universities to control costs or to provide a service of value than would be the case were they subject to stronger market forces. In particular, subsidies of within-state tuition restrict interstate competition. Students have less incentive to seek or expect value for money. And the continued squeeze on finances is likely to continue impairing quality. Arguably, providing subsidies to individuals rather than institutions would address many of these inefficiencies. (Payments to individuals, which include Pell grants and subsidised loans, are often referred to as vouchers).

Balancing these arguments is difficult. Conventional analysis would suggest that subsidies should be a federal rather than state responsibility; that they should be paid to individuals rather than institutions; and, possibly, that they could take the form of debt-forgiveness rather than cash grants. However, the economic literature provides little guidance on the central question of the level of subsidy. From an international perspective, Figure 6.1 implies that the public sector bears a smaller share of the costs of financing higher education in the United States than in many other OECD countries, even when allowance is made for the limitations of the data.

Public debate on these questions is hampered by the dominating issue of access. Were a good system of loans in place, then direct government subsidies would no longer be justified to overcome financial barriers. Some government subsidy would still be warranted for reasons of externalities. There may well be more efficient and equitable means of delivering that subsidy than the current system of state government provision. How such a change might be coordinated is unclear. Public opinion will (appropriately) resist reductions in state subsidies while barriers to access remain important.

Box 6.2. **Recommendations on financing higher education**

Income-contingent student loans represent the most efficient and equitable means of overcoming financial barriers to education. Although current loan programmes permit income-contingent repayments, few borrowers choose this option, partly because of poor information and advice.

- Greatly raise limits on Stafford loans, especially for unsubsidised direct loans, so that they cover the full cost of study.

- The default repayment plan should be income-contingent.

- Borrowers who are worried about their future income should be advised to make income-contingent repayments.

Were a good system of loans in place, then the costly increases in Pell grants that have recently been proposed would be unnecessary.

- The role of the grants should be reconsidered with a view to focussing on informational problems and externalities. That would probably involve fewer payments. In particular, grants beyond the first year of college and to independent students could be reduced. Grants should target high school or neighbourhood characteristics rather than those of families.

The Administration and Congress plan to simplify the application process for Pell grants, which is to be commended.

- Remove the assets test and unimportant means-testing criteria. Provide early notification of estimated grant eligibility.

Tax concessions for higher education are a regressive, complicated and cost-ineffective means of promoting access. These problems outweigh the theoretical advantages of the concessions.

- Simplify or abolish tax preferences for higher education expenses.

There are many further details of implementation where financial aid could be improved.

- Reconsider private guaranteed loans, with a view to further reducing their subsidy and encouraging income-contingent payments.

- The forgiveness period for income-contingent loans should be reviewed, with consideration being given to varying the repayment period with debt levels.

- The interest rate on Stafford loans should vary with the long-term bond rate, so as to prevent unintended changes in subsidy levels.

Notes

1. This chapter uses the terms higher education, tertiary education, postsecondary education and college interchangeably, though the latter is often distinguished from trade and graduate schools.

2. In 2004, 23.4% of US 20-29 year olds were enrolled in education, compared with an OECD average of 24.7%. Enrollments for other age groups are also at or slightly below the OECD average. (*Education at a Glance, 2006*, Tables A1.3a, c1.2).

3. The public/private split is only approximate, as countries differ in how they classify expenditures. For example, most countries have their public expenditures artificially boosted by valuing student loans at principal, whereas these are (appropriately) valued at their subsidy cost in the United States. And the estimates do not include tax concessions.

4. These estimates exclude research and development and ancillary services like student housing; *Education at a Glance*, Table B1.1c.

5. The cost of tertiary study can be estimated in different ways, depending on the purpose. For example, Table 6.1 does not include loans or work-study aid. And the net price, as calculated, is negative for many students – reflecting that many grants cover living costs as well as tuition. For many purposes, other assumptions would be appropriate. Alternative estimates for the 2003-04 academic year are available in Berkner and Wei (2006). After allowing for inflation, their estimates (specifically "net price after all grants, veterans benefits and estimated tax benefits"as reported in their Figure H) are similar to those in the "Total" column of Table 6.1, though they do not report a price net of grants and tax concessions that one would add to foregone earnings, as discussed in the text.

6. Conceptually, it would be preferable for books and supplies, which typically average about $900, to be classified as a tuition cost, rather than a living expense, but unfortunately that is not the custom.

7. Among 25-34-year-olds, the annual earnings differential between high-school and college graduates widened from $7 100 to $14 600 between 1980 and 1992, in 1990 dollars (Kane, 2006, p. 1392). The differential for older workers widened somewhat more. Summing $7 500 over 40 years at a discount rate of 6% yields a net present value of $112 000. A small fraction of this was offset by the increase in real tuition fees.

8. This sums federal, state and local rates. In many states and localities, taxes are levied on the basis of federal taxable income (that is, net of tuition and other deductions). Other jurisdictions use gross income. The estimate in the text, which is intended as an illustrative approximation, is a rough average, based on conversations with Federal officials.

9. Based on College Board, *Education Pays*, 2004, p. 10, Tables 1 and 3. The calculation ignores taxes, differential workforce participation and earnings after age 64. Allowing for these factors would change the numbers slightly.

10. 108 explanatory variables from the National Longitudinal Study of the High School Class of 1972 measuring demography, family background, achievement test scores, and so on.

11. See, for example, Kane (1999, 2006), Johnstone (2001), Barr (2001), Chapman (2006) and references cited therein.

12. This was partly out of concern for the high effective marginal tax rate, which added to tax rates that were already very high.

13. The Australian loans for living expenses were implemented through an off-budget intermediary, in order to bypass accounting problems, in which loans were valued at principal rather than at subsidy cost. This proved to be overly complicated.

14. As income-contingency is typically the only repayment option within these schemes, preferences can be difficult to gauge. Nevertheless, borrowers typically have some limited choices. For example, most Australian students would get higher returns by liquidating accumulated savings (especially assets with taxable returns) to discharge their loans early, yet 78% of students prefer to take out income-contingent loans (Thorn, 2005).

15. In one case study, changing a company pension plan from an "opt-in" to an "opt-out" raised the enrolment rate from 49% to 86%. (Madrian and Shea, 2001).

16. A typical (though otherwise praiseworthy) example is the Department of Education brochure *Consolidation – A Smart Choice for In-School and Graduating Borrowers* (undated) which advises students that each form of extended payments "results in higher overall costs of borrowing". In particular, the "Income Contingent Repayment is the most expensive option in the long term (though) it is a good way to avoid default".

17. All estimates are from College Board (*Trends in Student Aid*, 2006b). Other large grant programmes in 2005-06 include $ 4 billion to veterans, $24 billion by institutions (essentially tuition discounts), and $9 billion private and employer grants.

18. Kane (2006, p. 1389), GAO (2005, p. 28) and Long (2007) provide overviews of the research.

19. Dynarski (2004). The Administration's 2008 budget proposes exempting 529 acccounts. For the first seven years of their existence, Coverdell savings accounts (a tax vehicle intended to encourage saving for college!) had an effective marginal tax rate of 120%. Although that was fixed in 2004, it indicates the difficulty of implementing sensible means-tests.

20. The real interest rate above the threshold is 4% (6.8% minus 2.8% inflation). Below the threshold, it is 1¾ per cent (6.8 x 0.65 minus 2.8), assuming a marginal (federal plus state and local) income tax rate of 35%.

21. Kane (2006, p. 1372). This excludes scholarship and fellowship spending (a transfer from one group of students to another) and expenditures of auxiliary operations like hospitals and dormitories.

22. This is consistent with the observation that most graduates remain in the state where they studied. For example, Bradburn, Nevill and Cataldi (2006) find that 70% of 1992/93 graduates were still living in the same state where they received their bachelor degree ten years later. Bound *et al*'s

estimate represents the *marginal* effect of changes in the graduation rates on the stock of graduates in a state, which is the relevant measure for capturing externalities. The latter number, in contrast, is an average ratio. Were some states to expand their colleges, Bound *et al.'s* estimate indicates the new graduates would disperse around the nation and the average ratio would decline.

Bibliography

Akerhielm, K., J. Berger, M. Hooker and D. Wise (1998), "Factors Related to College Enrollment", Report to US Department of Education, Office of Under Secretary, Mathtech, Princeton NJ.

Barr, N. (2004), "Higher Education Funding", *Oxford Review of Economic Policy*, Vol. 20, No. 2, Oxford University.

Becker, G. (2006), "Is student Debt Too High?", December 3, *www.becker-posner-blog.com*.

Berkner, L. and C.C. Wei (2006) Student Financing of Undergraduate Education 2003-04, With a Special Analysis of the Net Price of Attendance and Federal Tax Benefits (NCES 2006-186), US Department of Education, Washington DC, National Center for Education Statistics.

Beshears, J., J. Choi, D. Laibson and B. Madrian (2006), "The Importance of Default Options for Retirement Savings Outcomes", NBER Working Paper, 12009.

Bound, J., J. Groen, G. Kezdi and S. Turner (2004), "Trade in University Training: Cross-State Variation in the Production and Stock of College-Educated Labour" Journal of Econometrics 121, July-August, 143-73.

Cameron, S. and J. Heckman (1999), "Can Tuition Policy Combat Rising Wage Inequality?", Chapter 5, in *Financing College Tuition*, M.H. Kosters (Ed), The AEI Press, Washington DC.

Card, D. (2000), "The Causal Effect of Education on Earnings", in *Handbook of Labor Economics*, Vol. 3, O. Ashenfelter and D. Card Eds), New Holland.

Carneiro, P. and J. Heckman. (2002), "The Evidence on Credit Constraints in Post-Secondary Schooling", *The Economic Journal*, No. 112, Royal Economic Society.

CBO (2005), "Subsidy Estimates for Guaranteed and Direct Student Loans", Washington DC. November.

CBO (2007), "The Budget and Economic Outlook: Fiscal Years 2008 to 2017" , Washington DC, January.

Chapman, B. (2006), "Income Contingent Loans for Higher Education: International Reforms" in *Handbook of the Economics of Education*, Vol. 2, E. Hanushek and F. Welch Eds), North-Holland Publication, Netherlands.

College Board (2004), Education Pays: The Benefits of Higher Education for individuals and Society, The College Board, New York NY.

College Board (2006a), *Trends in College Pricing*, The College Board, New York NY.

College Board (2006b), *Trends in Student Aid*, The College Board, New York NY.

College Board (2006c), *Education Pays: Second Update*, The College Board, New York NY.

Commission on the Future of Higher Education (2006), A Test of Leadership: Charting the Future of US Higher Education, US Department of Education, Washington DC.

Dynarski, S. (2002), "The Behavioral and Distributional Implications of Aid for College", AEA *Papers and Proceedings*, Vol. 92, No. 2.

Dynarski, S. (2003), "Loans, Liquidity, and Schooling Decisions", mimeo.

Dynarski, S. (2004), "The Role of Higher Education Financing in Strengthening US Competitiveness in a Global Economy", Testimony before the Committee on Finance United States Senate, 22 July.

Dynarski,S. and J. Scott-Clayton (2006), "The Cost of Complexity in Federal Student Aid: Lessons from Optimal Tax Theory and Behavioral Economics", NBER *Working Paper*, No. 12227, National Bureau of Economic Research. Cambridge MA.

Gruber, J. (2005), *Public Finance and Public Policy*, Worth Publishers, New York.

Hansen, W.L. (1983), "Impact of Student Financial Aid on Access", in J. Froomkin (Ed), *The Crisis in Higher Education*, New York, Academy of Political Science.

Hanushek, E. (1998), "Conclusions and Controversies about the Effectiveness of School Resources", FRBNY *Economic Policy Review*, March.

Hanushek, E. (1999), "Budgets, Priorities, and Investment in Human Capital", The AEI Press, Washington DC.

Hoxby, C. (1999), "Where Should Federal Education Initiatives Be Directed?", Chapter 3 in *Financing College Tuition*, M.H. Kosters (Ed), The AEI Press, Washington DC.

Institute for Higher Education Policy (2006) "The Future of Private Loans: Who Is Borrowing, and Why?", Washington DC, December.

Johnstone, D.B. (2004), "Cost-sharing and Equity in Higher Education: Implications of Income Contingent Loans", mimeo.

Kane, T. (1994), "College Attendance by Blacks since 1970: The Role of College Cost, Family Background and the Returns to Education", *Journal of political Economy*, Vol. 102, No. 5, pp. 878-911.

Kane, T. (1997), "Beyond Tax Relief: Challenges in Financing Higher Education", *National Tax Journal*, Vol. 50, No. 2., pp. 335-49, June.

Kane, T. (1999), The Price of Admission; Rethinking How Americans Pay for College, Brookings Institution Press, Washington DC.

Kane, T. (2002), "A Quasi-Experimental Estimate of the Impact of Financial Aid on College-Going", mimeo.

Kane, T. (2006), "Public Intervention in Post-Secondary Education", in *Handbook of the Economics of Education*, Vol. 2, E. Hanushek and F. Welch (eds.), North-Holland Publication, Netherlands.

King, J. (2004), "Missed Opportunities: Students who Do not Apply for Financial Aid", *ACE Issue Brief*, American Council on Education, October.

Kitmitto, S. (2004), "The Effects of Pell Grants on Enrollment in Higher Education", mimeo.

Krueger, A. and W. Bowen (1993), "Income-Contingent College Loans", *Journal of Economic Perspectives*, Vol. 7, No. 3, Summer, 193-201.

Long, B.T. (2004), "How does the Availability of Loans affect College Access? Learning from the History of Loan Limits", mimeo.

Long, B.T. (2007), "The Contributions of Economics to the Study of College Access and Success", *Teachers College Record*, Vol. 109, No. 10, 2007, pp. 7-8.

Madrian, B.C. and D.F. Shea (2001), "The Power of Suggestion: Inertia in 401(k) Participation and Savings Behaviour", *Quarterly Journal of Economics*, 4 November.

Manski, C.F. (1992-93), "Income and Higher Education", Focus 14 (3), pp. 14-19, University of Wisconsin-Madison, Institute for Research on Poverty.

McPherson, M. and M.O. Shapiro (2006), "US Higher Education Finance", in *Handbook of the Economics of Education*, Vol. 2, E. Hanushek and F. Welch (eds.), North-Holland Publication, Netherlands.

OECD (2006), *Education at a Glance*, OECD, Paris.

OECD (forthcoming), "The Policy Determinants of Investment in Tertiary Education", paper presented for Working Party No. 1.

Project on Student Debt (2006), "Survey: Americans Want Relief from Rising Student Debt", News Release, 4 May.

Seftor, N.S. and S.E. Turner (2002), "Back to School: Federal Student Aid Policy and Adult College Enrolment", *Journal of Human Resources* 37 (2), pp. 336-352.

Schrag, P.G. (2001), "The Federal Income-Contingent Repayment Option for Law Student Loans", Hofstra Law Review 29, 733-862.

Thorn, W. (2005), "The Higher Education Contribution Scheme: Policy Principles and Program Changes, 1988-2005", Paper prepared for OECD Thematic Review of Tertiary Education, 2nd Workshop, Paris.

US Department of Education and the US General Accounting Office (2001), "Alternative Market Mechanisms for the Student Loan Program", Washington DC, GAO-02-84SP.

US Government Accountability Office (2005), "Student Aid and Postsecondary Tax Preferences", GAO-05-684, Report to the Senate Committee on Finance, GAO-05-684, Washington DC, July.

US Government Accountability Office (2006), "Paid Tax Return Preparers: In a Limited Study, Chain Preparers Made Serious Errors", Testimony Before Senate Committee on Finance by Michael Brostek, 4 April, GAO-06-563T, Washington DC.

US Office of Management and Budget (2006), Analytical Perspectives, Budget of the United States Government, Fiscal Year 2006.

Usher, A. (2005), "Global Debt Patterns: An International Comparison of Student Loan Burdens and Repayment Conditions", Educational Policy Institute, Toronto.

ANNEX 6.A1

Implementation of income contingent loans

Table 6.A1.1 indicates how income contingent loans have been implemented in four illustrative countries: Australia, New Zealand, the United Kingdom, and the United States. At the risk of over-simplifying (there are exceptions to most of the following generalisations) programmes in these and other countries typically specify a threshold below which repayments are not required. In the United States, this is the poverty rate: for a single borrower, $9 800 in most states. Repayments are usually set as a fraction of the difference between income (in the United States, adjusted gross income) and this threshold. The student's outstanding liability then increases in accordance with inflation or interest rates.

Table 6.A1.1. **Income-contingent student loan schemes**

	Australia	New Zealand	United Kingdom	United States
Purpose of loan	Tuition fees	Tuition fees and living costs	Tuition fees and living costs	Tuition fees and living costs
Income threshold at which payments start	A$38 000 (US$30 200)	NZ$17 000 (US$12 000)	POUND 15 000 (US$29 500)	$9 800
Threshold as % of average wage	75%	40%	53%	34%
Repayment rate (% of income above threshold)	4% rising to 8% (on total income)	10%	9%	20% (capped)
Interest rate	an initial premium of 25%, then zero real	zero nominal while student, thereafter 7% p.a.	zero real	A 3% fee, then 6.8% p.a.
Debt forgiveness	Death	Death	Age 65	25 years
Memo items:				
Average tuition fee 2003-04:	US$3 800	US$2 500	US$1 800	US$8 700
Graduation rates, 2004				
Tertiary type A	46%	48%	39%	34%
Tertiary type B	n.a.	21%	16%	9%

Notes: Data for US relate to direct unsubsidised Stafford loans originated after June 2006.
Graduation rates are percentage of tertiary graduates to the population at the typical age of graduation. From *Education at a Glance* (2006, Table A3.1). In the United States, type A courses are academically oriented bachelors, master, associate and professional degrees. Type B are vocationally oriented associate degrees. Tuition fees are for national and in-state students; whereas Figure 6.2 includes some foreign student fees (*Education at a Glance*, 2006, Table B5.1).
Other sources: Usher (2005); Thorn (2005); *http://www.ed.gov/offices/OSFAP/DirectLoan/RepayCalc/dlindex2.html.*

Details for the United States given in the table apply to students in the Direct loan program. Guaranteed loans have a somewhat different scheme and the option of changing plans if they wish to make income contingent repayments. The US programme differs from those in other countries in several ways:

- Perhaps most important, repayments in the United States are much higher. The US threshold is lower, and the repayment rate and interest rate are both higher. This reflects higher tuition costs, lower subsidy levels and the coverage of both tuition and living costs.*

- In the United States, income-contingency is one of four possible repayment options whereas in other countries it is typically the only form of delayed payment.
  - Choice poses a potential problem of adverse selection. To mitigate this, repayment rates in the United States system are capped – they cannot exceed a specified limit.

- In the United States, repayments are collected by the lender whereas in other countries this is the responsibility of the tax agency.

- Income includes spouse's income in the United States but only that of the borrower elsewhere.

- In the United States, debts not repaid after 25 years are forgiven. The forgiven debt is taxable income, giving rise to a potentially large tax liability in the final year.

It is not clear that any of the above features help to explain why income-contingency is popular in other countries but not the United States. High repayments, for example, apply also to other forms of student loan in the United States, so this does not explain why borrowers prefer those forms. Nor is it clear that any of the unusual features of the US system represent design flaws or "anomalies".

Chapman (2006) and others suggest that use of the tax agency lowers administrative costs. However, US authorities consider this to be unimportant, given that they have access to IRS data. Administration costs for direct loans (1.45% of originating principal a year according to the CBO, 2005) appear to be substantially higher than those in Australia (2-3% of collections, so presumably a fraction of a per cent relative to original liability; Chapman, 2006, p. 1494). That may reflect the wider choices given to US borrowers.

It is true that, as Chapman notes, measuring income on a family rather than individual basis will give rise to a "marriage penalty". But this feature seems desirable from an insurance perspective. Furthermore, it reduces one of the more serious instances of moral hazard and adverse selection affecting other countries' schemes – their subsidy of borrowers expecting to leave the paid workforce to rear children.

The issue of forgiveness is important but complicated. If the loan scheme simply deferred payments (at a market interest rate) rather than reduced them – as the "income sensitive" option for guaranteed loans approximately does – it would only insure annual cash-flow. Deferring payments at a subsidised rate (as in other countries) or forgiving debt (as in the US income-contingent plan) means that life-time income is also insured. That is a central part of the appeal of income-contingent loans to prospective borrowers and policy makers. However, this debt remission increases fiscal costs, unless the interest rate is increased to compensate. The counterpart is that it provides a convenient mechanism for subsidising the loan, should that be desired. It creates a moral hazard. And it creates an

---

* However, time to repayment is similar. Chapman calculates that typical repayment in Australia (using 2001 parameters) is 9-12 years, which officials suggest is also a typical repayment period in the US.

incentive to borrow excessively – because the marginal dollar borrowed is more likely to be forgiven (or repaid in the distant future, with a low present value). How policy-makers should trade off these concerns will depend on empirical judgements based on scant information.

Nevertheless, a puzzling feature of the US system is that the forgiveness period (25 years) is independent of the level of debt. So borrowers with small loans repay their debt in full, whereas those with large loans may expect a sizeable subsidy. Extending the period of repayment as debt increases would remove these disparities and reduce incentives to excessive borrowing. Even more puzzling is the taxation of forgiven debt. Although forgiveness is intended to make loans attractive, it is often described as having the opposite effect, because of the tax. Liquidity-constrained borrowers may find income-contingent loans more attractive if forgiveness occurred later, even though that increases the present value of their after-tax payments. There are several possible solutions to this problem, including exempting forgiveness from tax, as is done, for example, for teachers in disadvantaged schools. Another option would be to forgive debts at death.

OECD PUBLICATIONS, 2, rue André-Pascal, 75775 PARIS CEDEX 16
PRINTED IN FRANCE
(10 2007 09 1 P)   ISBN 978-92-64-03271-2 – No. 55583   2007